FREEDOM *NOW!*

The Civil-Rights Struggle in America

EDITED BY

ALAN F. WESTIN

Basic Books, Inc., Publishers

NEW YORK

INTRODUCTION

The Unfolding Civil-Rights Struggle in America

In 1963, the Negro's demand for genuine equality and first class citizenship in the American democracy finally broke through to the moral consciousness of the general American public. Not only did 1963 shatter all existing ground-rules as to the "proper place" for Negroes in North and South, but it also saw the beginning of a new era in terms of the techniques by which Negroes and their white allies would press for civil rights. After 1963, it became clear that at every level of American life—in government and politics, in offices and on construction sites, in housing projects and suburban developments, in the churches and the clubrooms, and in the subtle private forums in which community policies are so often arrived at —the issue of entry and fair opportunity for the American Negro had been raised to the top of the agenda. "There is no power like the power of an idea whose time has come," Tom Paine observed at the beginning of the American and French revolutions, and in 1963, the idea whose timeliness swept all other domestic issues before it like a flood was the civil-rights movement.

Freedom Now! explores, hopefully in all its complex facets, the *moral dimension* of the civil-rights struggle. An issue of "public policy" such as the "civil-rights question" must be discussed carefully in terms of constitutional law, legislative choices, private-group responsibility, and political implications, as must issues such as church–state separation, foreign aid, and medical care for the aged. But, after one hundred years of token emancipation, the discussion of civil rights must be reopened in terms of human beings, with all the religious, moral, and democratic imperatives that national policy on human relationships calls forth from Americans when they are acting in their best tradition. These writings are designed to further such a moral dialogue in American society.

A second major purpose of this book is to probe the *processes* of civil-rights struggle. Writing in 1863, at the height of the struggle against slavery, the famous Negro publicist, Frederick Douglass, warned that without "struggle" there "is no progress."

> Those who profess to favor freedom, and yet deprecate agitation, are men who want crops without ploughing up the ground. They want the rain without thunder and lightning. They want the ocean without the awful roar of its many waters. The struggle may be a moral one; or it may be a physical one; or it may be both moral and physical; but it must be a struggle. Power concedes nothing without a demand. It never did and never will. . . . Men may not get all they pay for in this world; but they must certainly pay for all they get.

Exactly a century later, from his jail cell in Birmingham, Dr. Martin Luther King, Jr., echoed Douglass' credo in a reply to a group of clergymen who had called on him to cease "unwise agitation" movements. The American Negro, Dr. King noted, has "not made a single gain in civil rights without determined legal and non-violent pressure."

> History is the long and tragic story of the fact that privileged groups seldom give up their privileges voluntarily. Individuals may see the moral light and voluntarily give up their unjust posture; but as Reinhold Niebuhr has reminded us, groups are more immoral than individuals. We know through painful experience that freedom is never voluntarily given by the oppressor; it must be demanded by the oppressed.

In this volume, both the sources of civil-rights protest and the techniques of "struggle" and "demand" have been treated in detail,

along with some historical incidents showing the long (and honorable) history of civil-rights struggle in America. Such a sense of historical perspective is a vital part of this problem, and not only in
terms of the American experience.

Twenty-three centuries ago, Aristotle observed that the most important cause of revolutions in the state was the struggle over equality, between those enjoying positions of superiority and those seeking entry into the privileged sanctuaries. In the modern era, the test
of any democratic society with a heterogeneous racial population
is its ability to provide civic and political equality without ripping
apart the delicate balances in the society between the public and
the private spheres and without turning the population into embittered and warring camps. This is our challenge in the 1960's,
and only when we conceive of it in these fundamental terms will
we be psychologically ready to cope with it.

Viewed in another way, the civil-rights struggle explored in this
volume offers the United States the first opportunity it has had
since the Civil War to look deeply into the soul of its society and
work at its dark places. James Baldwin put this thought as follows:

> I cannot be fitted into the society as presently constituted,
> even if I, as a Negro, wished to be. To give a dangerous and con-
> crete example: I do not object to the fact that Senator Eastland
> of Mississippi is alive, but I do object to his power—power which
> is given him by the American republic, or, to put it another way,
> by the previously mentioned cult of mediocrity. . . . I, there-
> fore, speaking as a Negro, expect to achieve "equality" by forcing
> Americans to re-examine the reasons that we all, North and South,
> have allowed so much power to accrue to so many dubious insti-
> tutions, and unworthy habits of thought, and so many mediocre
> men.

In this sense, the civil-rights struggle puts under the scrutiny of
every citizen the whole moral pattern of American civic life, not just
the individual's personal conduct. To portray the issues in these
stark and compelling terms, while reflecting also the tensions and
debates within the civil-rights camp, has been the purpose of this
wholly unneutral volume.

February 1964   ALAN F. WESTIN

ACKNOWLEDGMENTS

Several student assistants—Michael Curzan, Stephen M. Nassau, David A. Rice, and Lawrence Horowitz—aided greatly in the selection and processing of materials used in this book. Lawrence Schopp worked diligently on the Bibliography, with the crucial cooperation of the Institute of Human Relations Library of the American Jewish Committee. Miss Ene Sirvet was unfailingly efficient and cheerful in the face of recurring crises of production. I am grateful to Carolyn Lopreato and Taylor Albert for assistance in the reading of proofs. And, as always, Bea helped most.

CONTENTS

PART II

THE NEGRO CIVIL-RIGHTS STRUGGLE
IN HISTORICAL PERSPECTIVE

PART III

SOURCES OF THE CIVIL-RIGHTS PROTEST

DENIAL OF VOTING RIGHTS TO NEGROES

RACIAL DISCRIMINATION IN EMPLOYMENT

SEGREGATION IN PUBLIC EDUCATION: SOUTH AND NORTH

PART IV

THE TECHNIQUES OF THE CIVIL-RIGHTS STRUGGLE

PART V

AREAS OF TENSION WITHIN
THE CIVIL-RIGHTS MOVEMENT

PART I

NEGRO PERSPECTIVES ON CIVIL RIGHTS IN THE 1960's

1 : *Color and American Civilization*

James Baldwin

. . . White Americans find it as difficult as white people elsewhere do to divest themselves of the notion that they are in possession of some intrinsic value that black people need, or want. And this assumption—which, for example, makes the solution to the Negro problem depend on the speed with which Negroes accept and adopt white standards—is revealed in all kinds of striking ways, from Bobby Kennedy's assurance that a Negro can become President in forty years to the unfortunate tone of warm congratulation with which so many liberals address their Negro equals. It is the Negro, of course, who is presumed to have become equal—an achievement that not only proves the comforting fact that perseverance has no color but also overwhelmingly corroborates the white man's sense of his own value. Alas, this value can scarcely be corroborated in any other way; there is certainly little enough in the white man's public or private life that one should desire to imitate. White men, at the bottom of their hearts, know this. Therefore, a vast amount of the energy that goes into what we call the Negro problem is produced by the white man's profound desire not to be judged by those who are not white, not to be seen as he is, and at the same time a

---

Mr. Baldwin, essayist and novelist, is the author of *The Fire Next Time* (1963), *Nobody Knows My Name* (1961), and *Notes of a Native Son* (1957).

vast amount of the white anguish is rooted in the white man's equally profound need to be seen as he is, to be released from the tyranny of his mirror. All of us know, whether or not we are able to admit it, that mirrors can only lie, that death by drowning is all that awaits one there. It is for this reason that love is so desperately sought and so cunningly avoided. Love takes off the masks that we fear we cannot live without and know we cannot live within. I use the word "love" here not merely in the personal sense but as a state of being, or a state of grace—not in the infantile American sense of being made happy but in the tough and universal sense of quest and daring and growth. And I submit, then, that the racial tensions that menace Americans today have little to do with real antipathy—on the contrary, indeed—and are involved only symbolically with color. These tensions are rooted in the very same depths as those from which love springs, or murder. The white man's unadmitted—and apparently, to him, unspeakable—private fears and longings are projected onto the Negro. The only way he can be released from the Negro's tyrannical power over him is to consent, in effect, to become black himself, to become a part of that suffering and dancing country that he now watches wistfully from the heights of his lonely power and, armed with spiritual traveler's checks, visits surreptitiously after dark. How can one respect, let alone adopt, the values of a people who do not, on any level whatever, live the way they say they do, or the way they say they should? I cannot accept the proposition that the four-hundred-year travail of the American Negro should result merely in his attainment of the present level of the American civilization. I am far from convinced that being released from the African witch doctor was worthwhile if I am now—in order to support the moral contradictions and the spiritual aridity of my life—expected to become dependent on the American psychiatrist. It is a bargain I refuse. The only thing white people have that black people need, or should want, is power—and no one holds power forever. White people cannot, in the generality, be taken as models of how to live. Rather, the white man is himself in sore need of new standards, which will release him from his confusion and place him once again in fruitful communion with . . . his own being. And I repeat: The price of the liberation of the white people is the liberation of the blacks —the total liberation, in the cities, in the towns, before the law, and in the mind. Why, for example—especially knowing the family as I do—I should *want* to marry your sister is a great mystery to me. But your sister and I have every right to marry if we wish to, and no one has the right to stop us. If she cannot raise me to her level, perhaps I can raise her to mine.

In short, we, the black and the white, deeply need each other here if we are really to become a nation—if we are really, that is, to achieve our identity, our maturity, as men and women. To create one nation has proved to be a hideously difficult task; there is certainly no need now to create two, one black and one white. But white men with far more political power than that possessed by the Nation of Islam movement have been advocating exactly this, in effect, for generations. If this sentiment is honored when it falls from the lips of Senator Byrd, then there is no reason it should not be honored when it falls from the lips of Malcolm X. And any congressional committee wishing to investigate the latter must also be willing to investigate the former. They are expressing exactly the same sentiments and represent exactly the same danger. There is absolutely no reason to suppose that white people are better equipped to frame the laws by which I am to be governed than I am. It is entirely unacceptable that I should have no voice in the political affairs of my own country, for I am not a ward of America; I am one of the first Americans to arrive on these shores.

This past, the Negro's past, of rope, fire, torture, castration, infanticide, rape; death and humiliation; fear by day and night, fear as deep as the marrow of the bone; doubt that he was worthy of life, since everyone around him denied it; sorrow for his women, for his kinfolk, for his children, who needed his protection, and whom he could not protect; rage, hatred, and murder, hatred for white men so deep that it often turned against him and his own, and made all love, all trust, all joy impossible—this past, this endless struggle to achieve and reveal and confirm a human identity, human authority, yet contains, for all its horror, something very beautiful. I do not mean to be sentimental about suffering—enough is certainly as good as a feast—but people who cannot suffer can never grow up, can never discover who they are. That man who is forced each day to snatch his manhood, his identity, out of the fire of human cruelty that rages to destroy it knows, if he survives his effort, and even if he does not survive it, something about himself and human life that no school on earth—and, indeed, no church —can teach. He achieves his own authority, and that is unshakable. This is because, in order to save his life, he is forced to look beneath appearances, to take nothing for granted, to hear the meaning behind the words. If one is continually surviving the worst that life can bring, one eventually ceases to be controlled by a fear of what life can bring; whatever it brings must be borne. And at this level of experience one's bitterness begins to be palatable, and hatred becomes too heavy a sack to carry. The apprehension of life here so briefly and inadequately sketched has been the experience of generations of Negroes, and it helps to explain how they have endured and how they have been able to produce children of kindergarten age who can walk through mobs to get to school. It demands great force and great cunning continually to assault the mighty and indifferent fortress of white supremacy, as Negroes in this country have done so long. It demands great spiritual resilience not to hate the hater whose foot is on your neck, and an even greater miracle of perception and charity not to teach your child to hate. The Negro boys and girls who are facing mobs today come out of a long line of improbable aristocrats—the only genuine aristocrats this country has produced. I say "this country" because their frame of reference was totally American. They were hewing out of the mountain of white supremacy the stone of their individuality. I have great respect for that unsung army of black men and women who trudged down back lanes and entered back doors, saying "Yes, sir" and "No, Ma'am" in order to acquire a new roof for the schoolhouse, new books, a new chemistry lab, more beds for the dormitories, more dormitories. They did not like saying "Yes, sir" and "No, Ma'am," but the country was in no hurry to educate Negroes, these black men and women knew that the job had to be done, and they put their pride in their pockets in order to do it. It is very hard to believe that they were in any way inferior to the white men and women who opened those back doors. It is very hard to believe that those men and women, raising their children, eating their greens, crying their curses, weeping their tears, singing their songs, making their love, as the sun rose, as the sun set, were in any way inferior to the white men and women who crept over to share these splendors after the sun went down. But we must avoid the European error; we must not suppose that, because the situation, the ways, the perceptions of black people so radically differed from those of whites, they were racially superior. I am proud of these people not because of their color but because of their intelligence and their spiritual force and their beauty. The country should be proud of them, too, but, alas, not many people in this country even know of their existence. And the reason for this ignorance is that a knowledge of the role these people played—and play—in American life would reveal more about America to Americans than Americans wish to know.

The American Negro has the great advantage of having never believed that collection of myths to which white Americans cling: that their ancestors were all freedom-loving heroes, that they were born in the greatest country the world has ever seen, or that Americans are invincible in battle and wise in peace, that Americans have always dealt honorably with Mexicans and Indians and all other neighbors or inferiors, that American men are the world's most direct and virile, that American women are pure. Negroes know far more about white Americans than that; it can almost be said, in fact, that they know about white Americans what parents —or, anyway, mothers—know about their children, and that they very often regard white Americans that way. And perhaps this attitude, held in spite of what they know and have endured, helps to explain why Negroes, on the whole, and until lately, have allowed themselves to feel so little hatred. The tendency has really been, insofar as this was possible, to dismiss white people as the slightly mad victims of their own brainwashing. One watched the lives they led. One could not be fooled about that; one watched the things they did and the excuses that they gave themselves, and if a white man was really in trouble, deep trouble, it was to the Negro's door that he came. And one felt that if one had had that white man's worldly advantages, one would never have become as bewildered and as joyless and as thoughtlessly cruel as he. The Negro came to the white man for a roof or for five dollars or for a letter to the judge; the white man came to the Negro for love. But he was not often able to give what he came seeking. The price was too high; he had too much to lose. And the Negro knew this, too. When one knows this about a man, it is impossible for one to hate him, but unless he becomes a man—becomes equal—it is also impossible for one to love him. Ultimately, one tends to avoid him, for the universal characteristic of children is to assume that they have a monopoly on trouble, and therefore a monopoly on *you*. (Ask any Negro what he knows about the white people with whom he works. And then ask the white people with whom he works what they know about *him*.)

How can the American Negro past be used? It is entirely possible that this dishonored past will rise up soon to smite all of us. There are some wars, for example (if anyone on the globe is still mad enough to go to war), that the American Negro will not support, however many of his people may be coerced—and there is a limit to the number of people any government can put in prison, and a rigid limit indeed to the practicality of such a course. A bill is coming in that I fear America is not prepared to pay. "The problem of the twentieth century," wrote W. E. B. Du Bois around sixty years ago, "is the problem of the color line." A fearful and delicate problem, which compromises, when it does not corrupt, all the American efforts to build a better world—here, there, or anywhere. It is for this reason that everything white Americans think they believe in must now be re-examined. What one would not like to see again is the consolidation of peoples on the basis of their color. But as long as we in the West place on color the value that we do, we make it impossible for the great unwashed to consolidate themselves according to any other principle. Color is not a human or a personal reality; it is a political reality. But this is a distinction so extremely hard to make that the West has not been able to make it yet. And at the center of this dreadful storm, this vast confusion, stand the black people of this nation, who must now share the fate of a nation that has never accepted them, to which they were brought in chains. Well, if this is so, one has no choice but to do all in one's power to change that fate, and at no matter what risk—eviction, imprisonment, torture, death. For the sake of one's children, in order to minimize the bill that *they* must pay, one must be careful not to take refuge in any delusion—and the value placed on the color of the skin is always and everywhere and forever a delusion. I know that what I am asking is impossible. But in our time, as in every time, the impossible is the least that one can demand—and one is, after all, emboldened by the spectacle of human history in general, and American Negro history in particular, for it testifies to nothing less than the perpetual achievement of the impossible.

When I was very young, and was dealing with my buddies in those wine- and urine-stained hallways, something in me wondered, *What will happen to all that beauty?* For black people, though I am aware that some of us, black and white, do not know it yet, are very beautiful. And when I sat at Elijah's table and watched the baby, the women, and the men, and we talked about God's—or Allah's—vengeance, I wondered, when that vengeance was achieved, *What will happen to all that beauty then?* I could also see that the intransigence and ignorance of the white world might make that vengeance inevitable—a vengeance that does not really depend on, and cannot really be executed by, any person or organization, and that cannot be prevented by any police force or army: historical vengeance, a cosmic vengeance, based on the law that we recognize when we say, "Whatever goes up must come down." And here we are, at the center of the arc, trapped in the gaudiest, most valuable, and most improbable water wheel the world has ever seen. Everything now, we must assume, is in our hands; we have no right to assume otherwise. If we—and now I mean the relatively conscious whites and relatively conscious blacks, who must, like lovers, insist on, or create, the consciousness of the others—do not falter in our duty now, we may be able, handful that we are, to end the racial nightmare, and achieve our country, and change the history of the world. If we do not now dare everything, the fulfillment of that prophecy, recreated from the Bible in song by a slave, is upon us: *God gave Noah the rainbow sign, No more water, the fire next time!*

2 : *Letter from Birmingham Jail*

Martin Luther King, Jr.

[In April of 1963, following the street demonstrations by Birmingham Negroes sponsored by Dr. King, eight Alabama clergymen—Protestants, Catholics, and Jews—who had previously spoken out for obedience to court decisions in racial matters and good-faith pursuit of racial accord, issued a public statement directed to Dr. King. This called for an end to the demonstrations, criticized "outsiders" for organizing them, and asked the local Negro community to work peacefully with responsible white officials and private citizens to resolve "racial problems." The statement praised the city administration and police for the "calm manner" in which the demonstrations "had been handled." On April 16, while he was "resting" in jail in "peaceful Birmingham" for refusing to stop peaceful demonstrating, Dr. King replied as follows.]

My Dear Fellow Clergymen,

While confined here in the Birmingham City Jail, I came across your recent statement calling our present activities "unwise and untimely." Seldom, if ever, do I pause to answer criticism of my

Reverend King, founder and president of the Southern Christian Leadership Conference, wrote *Stride toward Freedom: The Montgomery Story* (1958).

work and ideas. . . . But since I feel that you are men of genuine good will and your criticisms are sincerely set forth, I would like to answer your statement in what I hope will be patient and reasonable terms.

. . . I am in Birmingham because injustice is here. Just as the eighth-century prophets left their little villages and carried their "thus saith the Lord" far beyond the boundaries of their home town, and just as the Apostle Paul left his little village of Tarsus and carried the gospel of Jesus Christ to practically every hamlet and city of the Greco-Roman world, I too am compelled to carry the gospel of freedom beyond my particular home town. . . .

Moreover, I am cognizant of the interrelatedness of all communities and states. I cannot sit idly by in Atlanta and not be concerned about what happens in Birmingham. Injustice anywhere is a threat to justice everywhere. We are caught in an inescapable network of mutuality tied in a single garment of destiny. Whatever affects one directly affects all indirectly. Never again can we afford to live with the narrow, provincial "outside agitator" idea. Anyone who lives inside the United States can never be considered an outsider anywhere in this country.

You deplore the demonstrations that are presently taking place in Birmingham. But I am sorry that your statement did not express a similar concern for the conditions that brought the demonstrations into being. I am sure that each of you would want to go beyond the superficial social analyst who looks merely at effects, and does not grapple with underlying causes. I would not hesitate to say that it is unfortunate that so-called demonstrations are taking place in Birmingham at this time, but I would say in more emphatic terms that it is even more unfortunate that the white power structure of this city left the Negro community with no other alternative.

In any nonviolent campaign there are four basic steps: (1) collection of the facts to determine whether injustices are alive; (2) negotiation; (3) self-purification; and (4) direct action. We have gone through all of these steps in Birmingham. There can be no gainsaying of the fact that racial injustice engulfs this community. Birmingham is probably the most thoroughly segregated city in the United States. Its ugly record of police brutality is known in every section of this country. Its unjust treatment of Negroes in the courts is a notorious reality. There have been more unsolved bomb-ings of Negro homes and churches in Birmingham than any city in this nation. These are the hard, brutal, and unbelievable facts. On the basis of these conditions Negro leaders sought to negotiate with the city fathers. But the political leaders consistently refused to en-gage in good-faith negotiation.

Then came the opportunity last September to talk with some of the leaders of the economic community. In these negotiating ses-sions certain promises were made by the merchants—such as the promise to remove the humiliating racial signs from the stores. On the basis of these promises Reverend Shuttlesworth and the leaders of the Alabama Christian Movement for Human Rights agreed to call a moratorium on any type of demonstrations. As the weeks and months unfolded we realized that we were the victims of a broken promise. The signs remained. As in so many experiences of the past, we were confronted with blasted hopes, and the dark shadow of a deep disappointment settled upon us. So we had no alternative except that of preparing for direct action, whereby we would pre-sent our very bodies as a means of laying our case before the con-science of the local and national community. We were not un-mindful of the difficulties involved. So we decided to go through a process of self-purification. We started having workshops on non-violence and repeatedly asked ourselves the questions, "Are you able to accept blows without retaliating?" "Are you able to endure the ordeals of jail?"

We decided to set our direct-action program around the Easter season, realizing that, with the exception of Christmas, this was the largest shopping period of the year. Knowing that a strong eco-nomic withdrawal program would be the by-product of direct action, we felt that this was the best time to bring pressure on the merchants for the needed changes. Then it occurred to us that the March election was ahead, and so we speedily decided to postpone action until after election day. When we discovered that Mr. [Eugene "Bull"] Connor was in the runoff, we decided again to postpone action so that the demonstrations could not be used to cloud the issues. At this time we agreed to begin our nonviolent witness the day after the runoff.

This reveals that we did not move irresponsibly into direct ac-tion. We too wanted to see Mr. Connor defeated; so we went through postponement after postponement to aid in this community need. After this we felt that direct action could be delayed no longer.

You may well ask, "Why direct action? Why sit-ins, marches, etc.? Isn't negotiation a better path?" You are exactly right in your call for negotiation. Indeed, this is the purpose of direct action. Nonviolent direct action seeks to create such a crisis and establish such creative tension that a community that has constantly refused to negotiate is forced to confront the issue. It seeks so to dramatize the issue that it can no longer be ignored.

I just referred to the creation of tension as a part of the work of the nonviolent resister. This may sound rather shocking. But I must confess that I am not afraid of the word tension. I have earnestly worked and preached against violent tension, but there is a type of constructive nonviolent tension that is necessary for growth. Just as Socrates felt that it was necessary to create a tension in the mind so that individuals could rise from the bondage of myths and half-truths to the unfettered realm of creative analysis and objective appraisal, we must see the need of having nonviolent gadflies to create the kind of tension in society that will help men rise from the dark depths of prejudice and racism to the majestic heights of understanding and brotherhood. So the purpose of the direct action is to create a situation so crisis-packed that it will inevitably open the door to negotiation. We, therefore, concur with you in your call for negotiation. Too long has our beloved Southland been bogged down in the tragic attempt to live in monologue rather than dialogue. . . .

My friends, I must say to you that we have not made a single gain in civil rights without determined legal and nonviolent pressure. History is the long and tragic story of the fact that privileged groups seldom give up their privileges voluntarily. Individuals may see the moral light and voluntarily give up their unjust posture; but as Reinhold Niebuhr has reminded us, groups are more immoral than individuals.

We know through painful experience that freedom is never voluntarily given by the oppressor; it must be demanded by the oppressed. . . . For years now I have heard the word "Wait!" It rings in the ear of every Negro with a piercing familiarity. This "wait" has almost always meant "never." . . . We have waited for more than 340 years for our constitutional and God-given rights. The nations of Asia and Africa are moving with jetlike speed toward the goal of political independence, and we still creep at horse-and-buggy pace toward the gaining of a cup of coffee at a lunch counter.

I guess it is easy for those who have never felt the stinging darts of segregation to say wait. But when you have seen vicious mobs lynch your mothers and fathers at will and drown your sisters and brothers at whim; when you have seen hate-filled policemen curse, kick, brutalize, and even kill your black brothers and sisters with impunity; when you see the vast majority of your twenty million Negro brothers smothering in an airtight cage of poverty in the midst of an affluent society; when you suddenly find your tongue twisted and your speech stammering as you seek to explain to your six-year-old daughter why she can't go to the public amusement park that has just been advertised on television, and see tears welling up in her little eyes when she is told that Funtown is closed to colored children, and see the depressing clouds of inferiority begin to form in her little mental sky, and see her begin to distort her little personality by unconsciously developing a bitterness toward white people; when you have to concoct an answer for a five-year-old son asking in agonizing pathos: "Daddy, why do white people treat colored people so mean?"; when you take a cross-country drive and find it necessary to sleep night after night in the uncomfortable corners of your automobile because no motel will accept you; when you are humiliated day in and day out by nagging signs reading "white" men and "colored"; when your first name becomes "nigger" and your middle name becomes "boy" (however old you are) and your last name becomes "John," and when your wife and mother are never given the respected title "Mrs."; when you are harried by day and haunted by night by the fact that you are a Negro, living constantly at tiptoe stance never quite knowing what to expect next, and plagued with inner fears and outer resentments; when you are forever fighting a degenerating sense of "nobodiness" —then you will understand why we find it difficult to wait. There comes a time when the cup of endurance runs over, and men are no longer willing to be plunged into an abyss of injustice where they experience the bleakness of corroding despair. I hope, sirs, you can understand our legitimate and unavoidable impatience.

You express a great deal of anxiety over our willingness to break laws. This is certainly a legitimate concern. Since we so diligently urge people to obey the Supreme Court's decision of 1954 outlawing segregation in the public schools, it is rather strange and paradoxical to find us consciously breaking laws. One may well ask, "How can you advocate breaking some laws and obeying others?" The answer is found in the fact that there are two types of laws: There are *just* laws and there are *unjust* laws. I would be the first to advocate obeying just laws. One has not only a legal but a moral responsibility to obey just laws. Conversely, one has a moral responsibility to disobey unjust laws. I would agree with Saint Augustine that "an unjust law is no law at all." . . .

All segregation statutes are unjust because segregation distorts the soul and damages the personality. . . . An unjust law is a code that a majority inflicts on a minority that is not binding on itself. This is *difference* made legal. On the other hand a just law is a code that a majority compels a minority to follow that it is willing to follow itself. This is *sameness* made legal.

. . . An unjust law is a code inflicted upon a minority which that minority had no part in enacting or creating because they did not have the unhampered right to vote. Who can say the legislature of Alabama which set up the segregation laws was democratically elected? Throughout the state of Alabama all types of conniving methods are used to prevent Negroes from becoming registered voters and there are some counties without a single Negro registered to vote despite the fact that the Negro constitutes a majority of the population. Can any law set up in such a state be considered democratically structured?

These are just a few examples of unjust and just laws. There are some instances when a law is just on its face but unjust in its application. For instance, I was arrested Friday on a charge of parading without a permit. Now there is nothing wrong with an ordinance which requires a permit for a parade, but when the ordinance is used to preserve segregation and to deny citizens the First Amendment privilege of peaceful assembly and peaceful protest, then it becomes unjust.

I hope you can see the distinction I am trying to point out. In no sense do I advocate evading or defying the law as the rabid segregationist would do. This would lead to anarchy. One who breaks an unjust law must do it *openly, lovingly* (not hatefully as the white mothers did in New Orleans when they were seen on television screaming "nigger, nigger, nigger") and with a willingness to accept the penalty. I submit that an individual who breaks a law that conscience tells him is unjust, and willingly accepts the penalty by staying in jail to arouse the conscience of the community over its injustice, is in reality expressing the very highest respect for law.

Of course there is nothing new about this kind of civil disobedience. It was seen sublimely in the refusal of Shadrach, Meshach, and Abednego to obey the laws of Nebuchadnezzar because a higher moral law was involved. It was practiced superbly by the early Christians who were willing to face hungry lions and the excruciating pain of chopping blocks before submitting to certain unjust laws of the Roman Empire. . . .

We can never forget that everything Hitler did in Germany was "legal" and everything the Hungarian freedom fighters did in Hungary was "illegal." It was "illegal" to aid and comfort a Jew in Hitler's Germany. But I am sure that, if I had lived in Germany during that time, I would have aided and comforted my Jewish brothers even though it was illegal. If I lived in a Communist country today where certain principles dear to the Christian faith are suppressed, I believe I would openly advocate disobeying these anti-religious laws.

I must make two honest confessions to you, my Christian and Jewish brothers. First I must confess that over the last few years I have been gravely disappointed with the white moderate. I have almost reached the regrettable conclusion that the Negroes' great stumbling block in the stride toward freedom is not the White Citizens' "Councilor" or the Ku Klux Klanner, but the white moderate who is more devoted to "order" than to justice; who prefers a negative peace which is the absence of tension to a positive peace which is the presence of justice; who constantly says, "I agree with you in the goal you seek, but I can't agree with your methods of direct action"; who paternalistically feels that he can set the timetable for another man's freedom; who lives by the myth of time and who constantly advises the Negro to wait until a "more convenient season." Shallow understanding from people of good will is more frustrating than absolute misunderstanding from people of ill will. Lukewarm acceptance is much more bewildering than outright rejection. . . .

Actually, we who engage in nonviolent direct action are not the creators of tension. We merely bring to the surface the hidden tension that is already alive. We bring it out in the open where it can be seen and dealt with. Like a boil that can never be cured as long as it is covered up but must be opened with all its pus-flowing ugliness to the natural medicines of air and light, injustice must likewise be exposed, with all of the tension its exposing creates, to the light of human conscience and the air of national opinion before it can be cured. . . .

You spoke of our activity in Birmingham as extreme. At first I was rather disappointed that fellow clergymen would see my nonviolent efforts as those of the extremist. I started thinking about the fact that I stand in the middle of two opposing forces in the Negro community. One is a force of complacency made up of Negroes who, as a result of long years of oppression, have been so completely drained of self-respect and a sense of "somebodiness" that they have adjusted to segregation, and of a few Negroes in the middle class who, because of a degree of academic and economic security, and because at points they profit by segregation, have unconsciously become insensitive to the problems of the masses. The other force is one of bitterness and hatred and comes perilously close to advocating violence. It is expressed in the various black-nationalist groups that are springing up over the nation, the largest and best-known being Elijah Muhammad's Muslim movement. This movement is nourished by the contemporary frustration over the continued existence of racial discrimination. It is made up of people who have lost faith in America, who have absolutely repudiated Christianity, and who have concluded that the white man is an incurable "devil."

I have tried to stand between these two forces saying that we need not follow the "do-nothingism" of the complacent or the hatred and despair of the black nationalist. There is the more excellent way of love and nonviolent protest. I'm grateful to God that, through the Negro church, the dimension of nonviolence entered our struggle. If this philosophy had not emerged I am convinced that by now many streets of the South would be flowing with floods of blood. And I am further convinced that if our white brothers dismiss us as "rabble rousers" and "outside agitators"—those of us who are working through the channels of nonviolent direct action —and refuse to support our nonviolent efforts, millions of Negroes, out of frustration and despair, will seek solace and security in black-nationalist ideologies, a development that will lead inevitably to a frightening racial nightmare. . . .

The Negro has many pent-up resentments and latent frustrations. He has to get them out. So let him march sometimes; let him have his prayer pilgrimages to the city hall; understand why he must have sit-ins and freedom rides. If his repressed emotions do not come out in these nonviolent ways, they will come out in ominous expressions of violence. This is not a threat; it is a fact of history. So I have not said to my people, "Get rid of your discontent." But I have tried to say that this normal and healthy discontent can be channeled through the creative outlet of nonviolent direct action. . . .

I had hoped that the white moderate would see this. Maybe I was too optimistic. Maybe I expected too much. I guess I should have realized that few members of a race that has oppressed another race can understand or appreciate the deep groans and passionate yearnings of those that have been oppressed, and still fewer have the vision to see that injustice must be rooted out by strong, persistent, and determined action. I am thankful, however, that some of our white brothers have grasped the meaning of this social revolution and committed themselves to it. They are still all too small in quantity, but they are big in quality. Some like Ralph McGill, Lillian Smith, Harry Golden, and James Dabbs have written about our struggle in eloquent, prophetic, and understanding terms. Others have marched with us down nameless streets of the South. They have languished in filthy, roach-infested jails, suffering the abuse and brutality of angry policemen who see them as "dirty nigger lovers." They, unlike so many of their moderate brothers and sisters, have recognized the urgency of the movement and sensed the need for powerful "action" antidotes to combat the disease of segregation.

Let me rush on to mention my other disappointment. I have been so greatly disappointed with the white Church and its leadership. Of course there are some notable exceptions. I am not un-mindful of the fact that each of you has taken some significant stands on this issue. . . .

I had the strange feeling when I was suddenly catapulted into the leadership of the bus protest in Montgomery several years ago that we would have the support of the white Church. I felt that the white ministers, priests, and rabbis of the South would be some of our strongest allies. Instead, some have been outright opponents, refusing to understand the freedom movement and misrepresenting its leaders; all too many others have been more cautious than courageous and have remained silent behind the anesthetizing security of stained-glass windows. . . .

I have heard numerous religious leaders of the South call upon their worshipers to comply with a desegregation decision because it is the law, but I have longed to hear white ministers say follow this decree because integration is morally right and the Negro is your brother. In the midst of blatant injustices inflicted upon the Negro, I have watched white churches stand on the sideline and merely mouth pious irrelevancies and sanctimonious trivialities. In the midst of a mighty struggle to rid our nation of racial and economic injustice, I have heard so many ministers say, "Those are social issues with which the Gospel has no real concern." . . .

There was a time when the Church was very powerful. It was during that period when the early Christians rejoiced when they were deemed worthy to suffer for what they believed. In those days the Church was not merely a thermometer that recorded the ideas and principles of popular opinion; it was a thermostat that transformed the mores of society. Wherever the early Christians entered a town the power structure got disturbed and immediately sought to convict them for being "disturbers of the peace" and "outside agitators." . . . They brought an end to such ancient evils as infanticide and gladiatorial contest.

Things are different now. The contemporary Church is so often a weak, ineffectual voice with an uncertain sound. It is so often the archsupporter of the *status quo*. . . .

But again I am thankful to God that some noble souls from the ranks of organized religion have broken loose from the paralyzing chains of conformity and joined us as active partners in the struggle for freedom. They have left their secure congregations and walked the streets of Albany, Georgia, with us. They have gone through the highways of the South on torturous rides for freedom. Yes, they have gone to jail with us. Some have been kicked out of their churches and lost the support of their bishops and fellow ministers. But they have gone with the faith that right defeated is stronger than evil triumphant. . . .

I hope the Church as a whole will meet the challenge of this decisive hour. But even if the Church does not come to the aid of justice, I have no despair about the future. I have no fear about the outcome of our struggle in Birmingham, even if our motives are presently misunderstood. We will reach the goal of freedom in Birmingham and all over the nation, because the goal of America is freedom. Abused and scorned though we may be, our destiny is tied up with the destiny of America.

Before the pilgrims landed at Plymouth, we were here. Before the pen of Jefferson etched across the pages of history the majestic words of the Declaration of Independence, we were here. For more than two centuries our foreparents labored in this country without wages; they made cotton "king"; and they built the homes of their masters in the midst of brutal injustice and shameful humiliation —and yet out of a bottomless vitality they continued to thrive and develop. If the inexpressible cruelties of slavery could not stop us, the opposition we now face will surely fail. We will win our freedom because the sacred heritage of our nation and the eternal will of God are embodied in our echoing demands.

I must close now. But before closing I am impelled to mention one other point in your statement that troubled me profoundly. You warmly commended the Birmingham police force for keeping "order" and "preventing violence." I don't believe you would have so warmly commended the police force if you had seen its angry, violent dogs literally biting six unarmed, nonviolent Negroes. I don't believe you would so quickly commend the policemen if you would observe their ugly and inhuman treatment of Negroes here in the city jail; if you would watch them push and curse old Negro women and young Negro girls; if you would see them slap and kick old Negro men and young Negro boys; if you will observe them, as they did on two occasions, refuse to give us food because we wanted to sing our grace together. I'm sorry that I can't join you in your praise for the police department.

It is true that they have been rather disciplined in their public handling of the demonstrators. In this sense they have been rather publicly "nonviolent." But for what purpose? To preserve the evil system of segregation. Over the last few years I have consistently preached that nonviolence demands that the means we use must be as pure as the ends we seek. So I have tried to make it clear that it is wrong to use immoral means to attain moral ends. But now I must affirm that it is just as wrong, or even more so, to use moral means to preserve immoral ends. . . .

I wish you had commended the Negro sit-inners and demonstrators of Birmingham for their sublime courage, their willingness to suffer, and their amazing discipline in the midst of the most inhuman provocation. One day the South will recognize its real heroes. They will be the James Meredith's, courageously and with a majestic sense of purpose, facing jeering and hostile mobs and the agonizing loneliness that characterizes the life of the pioneer. They will be old, oppressed, battered Negro women, symbolized in a seventy-two-year-old woman of Montgomery, Alabama, who rose up with a sense of dignity and with her people decided not to ride the segregated buses, and responded to one who inquired about her tiredness with ungrammatical profundity: "My feets is tired, but my soul is rested." They will be young high-school and college students, young ministers of the gospel and a host of the elders, courageously and nonviolently sitting in at lunch counters and willingly going to jail for conscience sake. One day the South will know that when these disinherited children of God sat down at lunch counters they were in reality standing up for the best in the American dream and the most sacred values in our Judaeo-Christian heritage, and thus carrying our whole nation back to great wells of democracy which were dug deep by the founding fathers in the formulation of the Constitution and the Declaration of Independence. . . .

If I have said anything in this letter that is an overstatement of the truth and is indicative of an unreasonable impatience, I beg you to forgive me. If I have said anything in this letter that is an understatement of the truth and is indicative of my having a patience that makes me patient with anything less than brotherhood, I beg God to forgive me. . . .

Yours for the cause of Peace and Brotherhood,
                                   M. L. KING, JR.

3 : *The Unpredictable Negro*

Louis E. Lomax

This is the era of the unpredictable Negro. We are unpredictable because we have all but lost faith in the basic integrity of the white power structure. Thus it seems neither practical nor wise that we continue to make our plea through the traditional channels and in the expected manner.

Once upon a time—and everybody didn't live happily ever after —the Negro, North and South, could be relied upon to behave in a fairly well-prescribed pattern. Our reaction to injustices seldom got beyond mass meetings; when they did we moved through recognized leadership organizations to make our plea in the solemnity of the courtroom. Unwittingly to be sure—but no less certainly—by limiting our approach to the courtroom we maintained our predictability and made it possible for the white power structure to thwart our efforts consistently. . . .

To ward off federal action, the South has adopted a philosophy of token integration. A few well-screened, well-scrubbed Negroes have been allowed into previously all-white classrooms and the South is well on its way to confirming Mississippi Senator James Eastland's prediction that efforts toward integration would bring on a century of litigation.

Mr. Lomax, a journalist, television writer, and former professor, wrote *The Reluctant African* (1960) and *The Negro Revolt* (1962).

As a reporter who has tramped the integration circuit from Clinton, Tennessee, to Little Rock to Johannesburg, South Africa, I have heard the smothered cackles of segregationists who felt certain their delaying tactics would wear us down and insure a continuing white-dominated democracy. What they have done, instead, is to shatter our faith in the white power structure's will to live up to its own freedom documents.

It is now painfully clear that the Negro's relief from injustice is, and will be, directly proportional to his ability to embarrass and pressure the government during hours of international crisis. This is a chilling conclusion but, after all, the truth is the truth; and a recognition of this truth makes ashes of Attorney General Robert Kennedy's plea that the freedom riders disembark for a while to allow his brother a monolithic backdrop for the forthcoming talks with Western European and Communist heads of state.

Four basic factors provide the explanation for the current racial unrest:

First, the freedom rides (and they are just the beginning of many such moves) are beyond the scope and control of any one organization. Thus, the white press's eternal search for a "Negro leader" who can account for everything that transpires is all but ludicrous. The initial freedom rides were planned by the Congress of Racial Equality (CORE). After money had been raised and the trip arranged, CORE Director James Farmer, himself a former staff member of the National Association for the Advancement of Colored People (NAACP), called on NAACP Executive Secretary Roy Wilkins to apprise him of the trip. Certain aspects of the rides are at variance with basic NAACP policy and Wilkins could do little more than suggest local NAACP people who would possibly give the riders aid and comfort along the way.

When the rides resulted in bloodshed at Montgomery, Dr. Martin Luther King was in Chicago. It was Sunday and Dr. King was scheduled to fly into New York for an appearance on "Open End," a television program, with Wilkins, Dr. Gardner Taylor, Jackie Robinson, and myself. Instead, and I think rightly so, King flew into Montgomery and used his towering influence to contain the Negro population.

In reality, King had nothing to do with the freedom ride; nor, as I have said, did the NAACP. Yet they all combined to offer comfort and bail to the embattled riders. More, as Montgomery was making headlines, additional freedom riders under separate auspices were boarding buses in Atlanta for further assaults against segregation.

This kind of ground-swell action cannot be contained. No one leader—or group of leaders for that matter—can promise anything. They didn't start the rides; they cannot control them.

Secondly, the point of compromise was passed at Montgomery; the issue is defined and we are now in a fight to the finish. The various civil-rights organizations differ on many things, but in this they are one: The assault upon segregation must get stronger, not weaker; more intense, not less frequent. . . .

Thirdly, current events have reduced the civil-rights struggle to a moral issue. The Attorney General's plea that we cease our efforts is like the policeman telling the good man not to shoot the thief for fear that the report might disturb the slumbering community. Would the Administration admonish the Africans of Angola to relax rather than upset the North Atlantic Treaty Organization? Or would it advise the Africans of Kenya not to press for independence because the white settlers are not quite ready to surrender the cherished white highlands?

Finally, I am moved to comment that we Negroes are convinced that we are, on the whole, better Americans than our white brothers. We believe in what our freedom documents say; the white power structure does not. It follows then—at least in our minds it does—that if this country is to be saved, if it is to assume the posture it professes, we must carry the load by insisting that the Republic become what it swears it already is.

Although we file our suit in the name of civil rights, we actually appear as a friend of freedom and human justice. If our plea is heard and acted upon, the West—the United States, really—will take a long step toward correcting its relationships with the nonwhite peoples of the world. Most of these peoples are Western in mind and temperament; their estrangement—they call it "neutralism"—is largely due to our default on the matter of mistreatment and exploitation.

In basic terms, then, this is what the freedom rides are about. The unpredictable Negro is on the loose; he is apt to oppose segregation anywhere, any time, in any manner. And when he does the powerful leadership organizations will forget their bickering and close ranks about him.

We know the Republic is embarrassed by these incidents. But experience has taught us that our relief is coincident with that embarrassment. We deny, however, that we occasion the embarrassment. When we sit in a waiting room, we are taking the Constitution to mean what it says, we understand the Supreme Court to mean what it says. It is the segregationists who are wielding the iron pipes and unleashing the savage dogs. If those who apply the law embarrass the Republic more than those who abort it, and if the law-abiding rather than the lawbreakers must cease and desist, then the American promise is but a cruel joke on humanity and the American dream dissolves to the most God-awful nightmare.

4 : *Outgrowing the Ghetto Mind*

Ebony

There is a joke going the rounds about a telephone conversation between Martin Luther King and John F. Kennedy. Says the President: "Yes, Dr. King. I know, Dr. King. I understand, Dr. King. But Dr. King—it has *always* been known as the White House!"

If this little yarn carries a moral, it also serves a notice. The Negro is not concerned about the color of the White House, of course, but he does want to know if qualified Negroes will be employed the next time it is painted and when will open occupancy come to 1600 Pennsylvania Avenue.

There was a time, a very long time, when the Negro questioned the nonemployment of Negroes on skilled jobs, but did not demand that they be hired. There was a time, a very long time, when he deplored racial ghettos but did not insist upon integrated housing. There was a time, a very very long time, when the Negro conditioned himself to accept racial segregation and discrimination instead of fighting for his equal rights.

Waiting for promised improvements his frustrations increased, his anger mounted. Rebellion was as inevitable as it was surprising to those who thought the Negro incapable of impatience and afraid to defy his oppressors, but the current storm of protests proves that he has outgrown ghetto mentality which lulled him into believing that a black man could not survive in a white man's world if he challenged the racial *status quo*.

Ghetto thinking, the result of years of ghetto living, is the avoidance of action or degrading oneself to be permitted to survive, according to Dr. Bruno Bettelheim. This kind of reasoning, he says, was largely responsible for the extermination of millions of Jews by the Nazis. The eminent University of Chicago psychologist told the American Council for Judaism that although a few thousand Jews in Warsaw did resist, "hundreds of thousands meekly accepted their fate and co-operated with their exterminators." He was astonished at the number who felt it would be possible to live with Hitler, though they had to submit to degradation to do so.

The counterpart of the Jewish ghetto mentality is what Dr. Martin Luther King, Jr., calls the complacency of Negroes who, "as a result of long years of oppression, have been so completely drained of self-respect and a sense of 'somebodiness' that they have adjusted to segregation."

Not unlike those Jews who actively helped their exterminators, are the Uncle Tom's who collaborate with white racists by playing the roles of apologist and informer. Many middle- and upper-class Negroes have also aided white supremacists by disassociating themselves from The Problem.

Such duplicity and complacency, coupled with the old custom of adjusting to a position of inferiority rather than insisting upon his constitutional rights, would have led the Negro to his Buchenwald, had he not learned the prudence—and the power—of positive resistance.

Undoubtedly the meek shall one day inherit the earth, but it could be a long wait until the demise of the strong and the reading of a will that could leave the meek more weak than wealthy. The Old Negro may be willing to wait for equality in his Father's kingdom, but hopes of a milk-and-honey hereafter do not assuage the hunger pangs of his sons and daughters now.

In this one-hundredth year of *de jure* freedom, today's Negro is not too impressed with how far he has come from bondage. He is, however, depressed by how far he has yet to go before obtaining first-class citizenship. "In two decades," says Dr. Leo K. Bishop, "the Jews and the Roman Catholics have moved into the open society of the United States, and," adds the Jewish leader, "Negroes will make it too."

The big question is, when? Just as the old separate-but-equal

Supreme Court decision of 1896 spelled never, so could the gradualism of its 1954 decision take forever. And forever is a very long
time.

In Montgomery, Alabama, not-so-meek Negroes turned the
deathwatch on eternity into a walking boycott that ended segregated buses. Eight years later in Birmingham, the walk became a
triumphant march that left no doubt that inaction had been re-
placed by positive resistance and the pace toward victory quickened.
Birmingham also marked the passing of the initiative in the Negro's
fight for civil rights, from white hands to black.

The "head of black steam," as columnist Eric Sevareid calls it,
had begun to build. The Negro, at last, had come into his own.
When Congressman Adam Clayton Powell declared that Negro
organizations should be headed by Negroes, he provoked more than
the usual storm of protests that accompany most of his pronouncements, but in a matter of weeks, spokesmen of both races were
agreed that the time had come for the white liberal to assume a
secondary role.

"There is abundant evidence that from this point forward the
burden of the struggle will be carried by the Negroes themselves,"
says writer Max Freedman.

The fear which once made the Negro submissive has passed on
to his intimidators, who, not understanding the change from meekness to militancy, refuse to acknowledge its existence. In losing his
fear, the Negro has gained new faith in himself and a unity of purpose heretofore unknown. For the first time, upper-class Negroes,
those who are as socially and economically secure as nonwhites can
be in a segregated society, have been brought together in a common
cause.

Entertainers who make their livelihood performing before white
audiences, are leading Negro demonstrations in the South or holding vast benefits in the North for organizations fighting racial
bigotry. The executive secretary of the conservative NAACP has
been bailed out of a Mississippi jail, and some of the most comely
colored coeds in the Southland are doing their homework in paddy
wagons. Even the shrill voices of elementary-school children sing
out from barbed-wire stockades as they lend their numbers to the
crusade for freedom.

The voices of essayist James Baldwin and sociologist Kenneth

Clark and black supremist Malcolm X and actor Sammy Davis and author Louis Lomax and gospel singer Mahalia Jackson and comic Dick Gregory and actress Lena Horne—to name a few—are joined in a common plea for equality. Long divorced from the ghetto complex, these, like countless other Negro celebrities and intellectuals, have found a new identity with the unsung and uneducated Negro. They have also found a new pride in their race as well as a working formula for gaining the equality all Negroes seek.

With the shedding of the ghetto mentality and upper-class complacency, the Negro is through with wearing the mask of ambivalence; he is done with survivor's double talk, for he is beginning to think like a man and act like a man and what is most important, to be treated as one. His progress, however, is paltry compared with that of over 200 million of his African cousins who evolved from colonialism to independence in ten dramatic years. He still lags far behind the Roman Catholic and the Jew in acceptance into the open society of the United States. But thanks to his own determined efforts, he is moving faster toward his goal now than ever before. When he reaches it, he will rid democracy of a blot white Americans were either unable or unwilling to erase.

In the meantime, there is still that matter of employment outside of the White House and tenancy within.

5 : *The Management of the Civil-Rights Struggle*

**Kenneth Clark, Roy Wilkins,
Whitney Young, Jr., James Farmer,
Martin Luther King, Jr.,
and James Forman**

CLARK: . . . The men who've come here today to sit down and talk are the leaders of the Negro community who have assumed the risk of transforming American ideals into reality. These men, sometimes labeled the "Big Five," are the captains of five of the most vigorous organizations, different in their history, their methods, and their means, but united in their purpose. They lead the battle for Freedom Now.

Roy Wilkins is Executive Secretary of the oldest and biggest Negro organization, the National Association for the Advancement of Colored People. Its campaign against segregation has historically centered on legal and legislative proceedings. But at

---

Identifying biographies appear in Kenneth Clark's introduction of the participants. Mr. Clark is Professor of Psychology at The City College of New York and a leading Negro intellectual.

its convention in Chicago [in 1963] . . . , thousands of delegates and their leaders insisted upon more militant direct action.

Whitney Young, Jr., is the Executive Director of the National Urban League. With chapters in sixty-five cities, and the largest budget and professional staff of all Negro organizations, the Urban League seeks civil-rights progress by racial co-operation and important social-service programs.

James Farmer is National Director of CORE (The Congress of Racial Equality). CORE, which pioneered the sit-in techniques in the early forties and more recently the freedom rides, is active in the North as well as in the South.

The Reverend Martin Luther King, Jr., the symbol of active nonviolence, is the founder and President of the Southern Christian Leadership Conference. Dr. King, who received national and international prominence after the 1956 Montgomery bus boycott, co-ordinated the . . . demonstrations in Birmingham [in 1963].

James Forman is the Executive Secretary of the Student Nonviolent Co-ordinating Committee. Formed in 1960, at a Raleigh meeting of the Southern Negro College Students, it has provided vigorous, youthful leadership in segregation protest, and has spearheaded the voter-registration drives. . . .

Now, we have said that these are interracial organizations, but you five gentlemen are Negroes. You are assuming the leadership, and you are asking white liberals and white friends to go along with the Negro speaking for himself, rather than speaking through white surrogates.

YOUNG: I would like to make this point, because I think there is a misconception that any white people who happen to serve on our boards or committees are, therefore, automatically there to exercise control and restraint. This is not the experience of the Urban League. There are many white people who serve on our boards, who are asking for more militancy.

I speak for the National Urban League at *their* insistence— not at *my* demanding—because they feel that a Negro is best able to express the hopes and the longings of his people. . . .

CLARK: But this certainly is not the picture that Mr. Powell gave in his recent criticism of the NAACP, and certainly not the persistent picture that Malcolm X and the black nationalists give.

WILKINS: Well, can't we skip both of these gentlemen as being ill-informed on this matter, because as far as the NAACP is concerned, this has been a partnership from the very beginning; and for the past . . . well, I've been there for the past thirty-two years . . . for the past twenty-five years, the Negroes have furnished the bulk of the money to carry the NAACP fight. It's utterly ridiculous to talk about white people controlling the organization.

FARMER: I think, Kenneth, that we ought to make clear that there is a desire on the part of the Negroes for self-expression through leadership of civil-rights organizations. This is important because Negroes have been denied that self-expression for so many years. But this does not mean in any sense of the word, as far as I am concerned, that white persons who are sincere cannot participate and co-operate.

KING: And I think that it is very important to have this participation. I think it would be very dangerous, and even tragic, if the struggle in the United States for civil rights degenerated to a racial struggle of blacks against whites, so to speak.

It is a tension between justice and injustice, and we enlist consciences in the struggle. We appreciate the participation in this movement of white persons of good will, and we have many of them, fortunately. I think the number is growing every day, and this helps to keep the struggle on the level that it should be. . . .

WILKINS: . . . In your student movement, don't you have white students who've been beaten up just like Negro students?

FORMAN: Oh, certainly. Same thing. I'd like to amplify, however, . . . something that Jim said. . . . I think that in the last ten, twelve years, the increased militancy [of Negro youth] has been because they have seen Negroes do things. In a sense, part of the fight that we have had, it seems to me, is to counterbrainwash (if I may use that term) the people and make them feel that they have an identity themselves; that they can do something for themselves. . . .

CLARK: . . . [How about] the President's [proposed] civil-rights legislation [of 1963]? Is this enough?

WILKINS: . . . [Well,] no President has recommended a bill of this scope before, and regardless of how we who suffer may feel its limitations, I think we ought to work with that.

But it's dangerous, as Jim Farmer has said, to pick out priorities and . . . the opposition will start concentrating on your target. They will say, "Well, what do you think is the number one," and this is what we have to avoid.

CLARK: . . . Why do you think President Kennedy did this?

WILKINS: He did it because a crisis was created that demanded the attention of the nation on the highest level, just like . . . well, a dust bowl. It's something beyond the state and beyond the region, and demands federal action. A great disaster like Texas City demands national action. A great flood demands national action. . . . I think there is no doubt that . . . what Martin Luther King and his associates did in Birmingham made the nation realize that at last the crisis had arrived.

CLARK: Well, now, you mentioned so clearly and objectively the important role of Martin Luther King in dramatizing the urgency and insistence of the Negro. The way you said that, it doesn't seem to me to be consistent with the rather persistent rumors that there is rivalry among you. . . .

WILKINS: Well, now, you don't see any of us chained together at this table, do you? We came here voluntarily. The truth of the matter is that we have been meeting off and on over the past few years.

I remember Jim Forman down in Atlanta—in a couple of meetings we had down there. We met Martin Luther King all over the United States. Jim Farmer has, along with Whitney Young, sat in on twelve or fourteen weeks of assessment of the civil-rights picture and a projection of the future. We've just come from a meeting—making some more plans for the March on Washington [in August]—all of us together. . . . Anybody who bets on a Negro split is going to lose a bundle.

KING: Well, I quite agree with that, Roy. I think we are more united than ever before. . . .

This does not mean that there will have to be absolute uniformity. I don't think this is desirable. There must be a diversified attack. . . .

YOUNG: Well, I might inject a note here that might suggest some difference as far as the Urban League and the direct-action groups that are here represented. . . .

The Urban League, in the case of legislation for example, recognizes that most of this legislation will affect largely the South, but have little meaning as far as the North is concerned. Most of these problems are already resolved.

So we are *extremely* concerned that the slogan "freedom" or "equal opportunity" will not become a cruel hoax or an *empty* kind of thing, because of other forces at work. . . .

FORMAN: . . . I'd like to go back to something you brought up, . . . Kenneth, and that is what is the *cause* for this legislation. I would agree with Roy in terms of this crisis. The fact of the matter is that the legislation should have been introduced a long time ago, but it has not been, so it is necessary, it seems to me, . . . to keep a considerable amount of pressure on. . . .

In other words, segregation may be like a piece of old iron— you put it in the fire to heat it up. People outside of Mississippi have to become conscious of what is going on there. For instance, there are forty-five people in jail right now, whose trials were held today, for simply being at a voter-registration meeting. Someone threw a smoke bomb in the church, and they marched down to the . . . deputy sheriff . . . and they were arrested for disturbing the peace. These are old ladies, some of them seventy-five years old. Yet they want to stay in jail. Now there is no recourse. They're in the federal courts and we don't know how this is going to come out. . . .

CLARK: By all means. . . . But each organization conceives the pressure in a different way. Am I right? For example, your concept of pressure isn't exactly the same as the Urban League's.

FORMAN: Except that we *subscribe* to that, but we just don't have time to *do* that. We are so busy with everything else. . . .

WILKINS: You see, the people in the North don't realize . . . the people who have the vote don't realize how much they could do by writing a letter. A congressman said to me, "I have eight letters on civil rights," . . . *eight* from his district . . . *eight* . . . and *five* of those were from white people. Now you don't have to write a polemic. You can just write a postcard saying, "Please vote for the civil-rights bill." . . .

WILKINS: . . . One of the heartening things about this aroused conscience that Martin spoke about a moment ago, is the unprecedented activity of the organized religious faiths.

I think we're going places on this. But I'd like to put in a little sour note here. . . . I get some mail that I can't read on television, that I can't exhibit, and the postmaster delivers. . . . The people say that, "Negroes ought to go back to Africa," and, "You're only apes anyway." "You think we're going to give you the civil-rights bill. You're crazy." And, "We'll run you in the Mississippi River first," and a whole lot of uncomplimentary things.

YOUNG: I'm really more concerned about this so-called "gentle people" who will say, "I'm with you. I am for you. But what about property values," you know, "and the man's right to run his business?" "What about the standards of the school being lowered?" So, for these reasons he would say, "Well, maybe you shouldn't have all of this right now." These are the people that I am concerned about.

FARMER: . . . I agree with you completely. While I share Roy's concern about the extreme bigots, I'm far more concerned about the good, the decent people, who don't throw a bomb as they do in Birmingham or other places in the South, but they quietly pack their bags and move away. And this, it seems to me, is more damaging to our cause, and more dangerous to the total cause of integration.

FORMAN: I guess I'm more concerned about . . . the public officials, you see, who inflict all of this brutality. The millennium is not going to come, primarily because we have no laws to deal with police brutality in the South, which, I think, is a fundamental issue.

CLARK: Well, Jim, I suppose you are very conscious of this because your membership is on the firing line . . . are daily the victims of police. . . .

FORMAN: Dr. King just came from Danville. Over a month ago we saw thirty-five people with holes in their heads as big as this ash tray, inflicted by the *police*, and nothing has been done about it! The government, it seems to me, *ought* to do something about it.

CLARK: What specifically would you suggest for dealing with this?

FORMAN: Well, I would suggest that the government go in and file some suits. When the constitutional rights of a person are denied, the government ought to file a suit in behalf of that person. . . . I mean, there's a whole ring of murderers down there in Greenwood, and we must not forget that the man who killed

Medgar Evers came from Greenwood—the same place where Jimmy Travers almost was killed, you know, when he was shot in the back of the neck. . . .

CLARK: Would it do any good for the President to call a conference of the chiefs of police of these areas in the South?

FORMAN: Well, suggest it to him. I don't know whether he's going to do that or not, but I think that Al Lingo who puts the cattle-shucks on people in Alabama and the police chief of Danville and these other places, ought to sit down and face to face with the President, he should ask [them], "Why are you doing these things?"

WILKINS: Well, I wish I could agree with that, but you know the Attorney General made a trip to Alabama recently, and . . . sat face to face [with Governor George Wallace] and they exchanged insults, one politely, Robert Kennedy; and throughout, both of them were courteous, according to the press, but they were cool and distant. Nobody's mind was changed. And I don't think anybody's mind *would* be changed.

I think the only way to change the mind of a policeman like that is to sue him and convict him, and to convince him that the Constitution has some control over that billy club he has in his hand. . . .

FARMER: Yes, I think we have an additional weapon, and that is the ballot . . . the vote . . . and that is why all of us here are pushing a voter-registration drive. If Negroes are registered in large numbers down there in Greenwood, then the police, of course, will take a different point of view; and in Danville also, because they will know then that they have to be responsible and responsive not only to white voters, but to Negro voters as well.

CLARK: Well, I get the feeling that there are many things which have to be done—voting, pressing for desegregation in public accommodations, keeping the police from themselves being instruments of brutality. Who is—or how do we intend to co-ordinate all of these many things which must be done on the broad civil-rights front?

WILKINS: . . . We cannot promise you . . . that there will be a co-ordinated, organized, structural, formalized attack on these matters and that each will be apportioned a part of this task. But we will say this: like Martin said, there is more unity than there ever has been before, there's more division of work, and there's more co-ordination and backing up of each other than there has been before. Maybe in 1975, or some other time, there will come an over-all organization, but no other group has managed that, and why should we? . . .

KING: Well, aren't we saying, gentlemen, that a program has not yet been worked out to grapple with the magnitude of this problem in the United States, both North and South? Isn't there a need now, because of the urgency and the seriousness of the situation, to develop a sort of crash program to lift the standards of the Negro and to get rid of the underlying conditions that produce so many social evils and develop so many social problems?

I think this is what we face at this time, and I know it leads to the whole question of discrimination in reverse, and all of that. But I think we've got to face the fact in this country, that because of the legacy of slavery and segregation, and the seeds of injustice planted in the past, we have this harvest of confusion now, and we're going to continue to have it until we get to the root of the problem.

WILKINS: . . . The announcement of the Real Estate Brokers Association some time ago advising their members not to pay any attention to fair-housing laws, that property rights still came first; and when you think of the billions of dollars in this country tied up in real estate, there isn't much that the President of the United States could do by going to look at some slums. Let's be fair! The real *power* and *obstacle* there is the property-rights structure in this country, which isn't concerned with how many kids are bitten by rats or how many people live in slums. . . .

YOUNG: Most of you recall that we did announce [in 1963]—our board adopted—this domestic Marshall Plan, and this was consciously given this name because, if you recall, this country has spent some twelve billion dollars on rehabilitation of Europe— war-torn Europe. In a four-year period we have spent millions on refugees from Cuba and from Hungary. We spent all kinds of money giving free education to veterans after the war, and making it possible for them to buy homes.

I think the time has come for us to honestly face up to the fact that this tremendous gap, due to historical deprivation that the Negro has suffered, will not be closed quickly enough unless we consciously and deliberately establish programs that call not just for equal schools, but *better* schools and *better* teachers, and provisions for housing, and conscious recruiting at the level of employment. This has to be done in order to get rid of what I see too much of, and that is the feeling of despair and hopelessness.

CLARK: You're asking, therefore, not only for a comprehensive program, but you're also asking for extra-special help, compensatory. . . .

YOUNG: Well, you can call it what you want—indemnification, reparation. . . .

WILKINS: I'm going to disassociate myself from the word "indemnification." But I do feel that just as you find a backward child or children, you have remedial classes for the child to bring him up to the norm. You must do something extra special for that child; at least we concede that it's the society's duty to do that. You must do something extra special for the Negro, having stood on his neck for 250 or 300 years.

FARMER: I'd like to make a point. I think that Negroes have had special treatment in this country for 350 years . . . special treatment of a negative sort. Now, what Whitney and the rest of us are asking for is special treatment of a positive sort to wipe out that gap. . . .

WILKINS: We're not asking them to skip over white people or to deny white people their chance. But we're saying that just giving the Negro an equal break is not enough.

FORMAN: No, because you see, the distance from which we have to come is so great. You know, if you talk about a sixth-grade education, is the government going to see that the families in Mississippi get more than two dollars and a quarter a day so that the child will not have to come out of school to help raise money to feed the other children? You see, this is the problem, so I think you ought to begin with just universal suffrage. . . .

CLARK: If you gentlemen are correct that [the nation] cannot survive without instituting justice, is it possible that this society will choose not to survive rather than to . . .

YOUNG: Not consciously. And I seem to sense an increasing amount of people are beginning to see integration as an opportunity and not just a problem. . . .

CLARK: Are these only articulate people, though? Are these only the people to whom you talk? What about the masses of American whites: could it be that they are so conditioned to hate Negroes that they would rather see the society go under than to provide for . . .

FORMAN: Some politicians might articulate this. . . .

WILKINS: No, the average white person in this country doesn't want to see his country go under rather than give a fair deal to the Negro. He believes in a fair deal, but he also wants to protect himself and his job, and I don't blame him.

CLARK: Gentlemen, I have read a number of writers on this, and the most eloquent of the writers seems to me to be Mr. Baldwin. And if I read underneath his lines, there seems to be a deep sense that maybe the American white man is not prepared for survival and justice; but as I listen to you gentlemen talk, you do seem much more optimistic than Mr. Baldwin.

FARMER: Kenneth, I would not go so far as to say that the American white man is prepared not to survive in order to avoid giving Negroes equal rights, but I will say that I would not be prepared at the moment to put our cause to a general referendum in this country. I don't think we'd win it.

CLARK: I think I could almost predict what the figure would be: two to one against you.

FARMER: I'm sure it would be.

KING: Well, isn't it true that we're grappling with a problem that constantly emerges in history? You have a few people who are crusaders in the right direction. You always have a few people who are crusaders in the wrong direction. And the vast majority are out there in the middle somewhere, with a great deal of apathy and complacency. And I think we have this in our country today—the vast majority of people are not active integrationists or active segregationists. They are passive adherents to the *status quo*.

CLARK: But they have enjoyed the society in which racism is dominant.

KING: I agree, and I think the job here is for the creative minority to work on this large group, because I think these people are pliable to the legitimate and just demands of the Negro. And I do not choose to follow the path of despair because I think that there is a way out, even though we do have to face the problems that have developed and the conditioning that had developed as a result of this problem existing a long time.

But I do think there is a way out, and I think that, with the creative minority standing up with determination to solve this problem, we can solve it.

WILKINS: Whenever the American people have been faced with a crisis, they've come through. Now, they may have come through in ragged and bloody fashion, but they've come through. I'm convinced that they'll come through this one even though it involves very deep-seated emotions. I think they're going to solve it. . . .

6 : *Freedom Now— but What Then?*

Loren Miller

Within the foreseeable future, eighteen million Negroes will burst the bonds of almost two centuries of isolation and surge into the main stream of American life. Talents and energies now siphoned off into an all-consuming struggle against racial restrictions will be freed for application to man's fundamental problems. Moreover, the coming of that good day will end the enormous expenditures of human and economic resources long frittered away in the futile effort to preserve the segregation system. They, too, will become available for useful social purposes. However, it would be a mistake to assume that these profound changes will automatically usher in a society that will make full and effective use of these new potentials for social progress. We know better. Once before, almost a hundred years ago, a similar promise lighted up the American scene and was snuffed out after a decade of uncertain flickering.

In retrospect, it is apparent that one of the contributing factors to the failure of Reconstruction to sustain a hastily improvised political democracy in the South was lack of foresight and absence of planning for what lay beyond Emancipation. There were no guidelines for those who undertook the task of constructing a new social

Mr. Miller, a lawyer and newspaper publisher in Los Angeles, is a national vice-president of the NAACP.

order to replace the old, which was swept away when two-and-a-half-million former slaves and a half-million disadvantaged free Negroes were incorporated into the American body politic. Everybody hoped for the best; nobody planned for it.

Abolitionists had glued their eyes on the destruction of slavery as an end in itself and, immersed as they were in the doctrine of the natural rights of man, they pitched their hopes for the best on a vague belief that individual merit would triumph in a society of free and freed men. Slaveholders had caught no vision because they could not admit the possibility that their peculiar institution could ever pass away; confronted with the reality, they were more than content to replace the old stratified order with another. Bedazzled by the glitter of white supremacy, poor whites were blind to the opportunity to make common cause with Negroes for an assault on common problems.

The Republican party stumbled into civil war with no design for Emancipation and consequently no blueprint for the problems inherent in victory. In an effort to supply Republican deficiency, Charles Sumner and Thaddeus Stevens prodded their party into enactment of the Fourteenth and Fifteenth Amendments, but it fell under corporate leadership which quickly swapped the shaky democracy that had been created for the privilege of pursuing its own selfish ends. A new social order based on total exclusion of the Negro from political affairs, and his pursuant isolation, grew Topsy-like out of confusion. The history of race relations since that time has been the story of efforts to conserve and implement the Negro's isolation by the myriad devices of the segregation system and the complementary struggle of the Negro to batter down the walls of his Jim Crow prison.

The walls are tumbling down now and it is disturbing to find that we are ill-prepared for the new Reconstruction. . . . Today's unpreparedness, akin to that of a hundred years ago, stems from the fact that intensive preoccupation with immediate and galling racial problems has minimized, almost precluded, consideration of what lies beyond victory. Attainment of civil rights, like Emancipation, has become almost an end in itself.

Like their Abolitionist forebears, civil-rights proponents, traditionally led by the NAACP which now shares leadership with Martin Luther King, CORE, and the student movements, have been

singleminded in outlook: Destruction of the Jim Crow system is
their one aim. Segregationist heirs of the slaveholders cannot, or
will not, admit that their order is done for; they content themselves
with yelling "never" at the top of their voices. Liberals gave their
hearts to gradualism a decade ago and implicitly decided then that
their notion of the future was the incorporation of the Negro in
an evolving society on a pragmatic, step-by-step basis. The Democratic party which, by a strange and ironic reversal of roles, has
fumbled its way into whatever there is of party leadership of the
liberation movement, cannot blueprint an integrated commonwealth because its composition compels it to deny that it envisages
such a development. Lying at the back of everybody's mind has
been the tacit assumption that there was plenty of time to plan
for the future. Nobody had foreseen the explosion of the past few
years.

Birmingham brought the revolution to sudden climax. Why, nobody knows. Maybe it was the dogs, maybe singing school children
trooping into Bull Connor's paddy wagons, or maybe the completely symbolic picture of the white cop with his foot on a Negro
woman's neck. Anyhow, in the expressive Negro idiom, we have run
fresh out of time. The future is upon us. And with victory in sight
and inevitable, we are confronted with the searching question of
where we go from here. In essence, the inquiry is whether civil-
rights victory is an end in itself or only a beginning, a means to an
end. At the moment, Negroes, whose answer is all-important and
perhaps decisive, seem to regard it as an end. The slogans under
which they march are limited in scope. The Freedom Now concept
contemplates putting the submerged Southern Negro or the
trapped Northern ghetto-dweller on a parity with his culturally deprived and disadvantaged white prototype. Fair-housing and fair-
employment laws are designed to give the Negro equal access to
existent supplies of housing and jobs, but fall short of coming to
grips with the fact that vast reforms are necessary to provide an
adequate supply of housing, and to stay the ravages of automation
in those very categories in which Negroes must seek employment.
The examples could be extended. This appraisal does not disparage
Negro demands; they are valid and necessary tactical weapons in
the struggle for equality. But as Whitney Young, National Urban
League director, points out: "There are forces at work such as auto-

mation, urbanization and a host of others that, on the surface, are indifferent to race, which unless identified and remedial steps taken will find the masses of Negroes five years from today with a mouthful of rights living in hovels with empty stomachs."

White Americans also tend to regard attainment of civil rights as an end in itself when they talk about denials of such rights as being harmful to our international image, or by what they say about equalitarian housing and employment legislation, or even when they argue, as [the late] President Kennedy did . . . , that Negroes should be secure in their constitutional privileges because it is morally right that they should enjoy them. Again, these views are valid as far as they go, but they neglect the fact that when the prisoner is freed, the jailer is given his liberty. Both may put their newly found freedom to good use by tackling the problem that made one of them prisoner and the other jailer in the first place. A quick glance will demonstrate how the denial of civil rights has affected, and still affects, the national welfare.

There are no ifs in history and we can never know who would have been elected to the Presidency, to state legislatures, or to Congress in the past three-quarters of a century *if* the Negro had not been deprived of the ballot. We do know that isolation of Negroes bred the one-party system of the South and that, in turn, it isolated that section from the rest of the nation to the detriment of poor whites. Coincidentally, the one-party system aggrandized Southern congressional power and gave Southerners their present life-and-death control over federal legislation. President Kennedy . . . complained that he [was] immobilized by Southern control of the House Rules Committee. Critical urban problems, federal aid to education, and housing issues, to pick a few examples, go unattended by Congress because their resolution will not fit a formula acceptable to the white South. We also know that labor organizations, agrarian-reform movements, trade and professional organizations, even service clubs, and the whole vast array of voluntary groups which play such a vital role in public affairs, have had to tailor their programs to suit the irrational demands of the segregation system.

The nub of the matter is that the existence of an unassimilated, and by definition unassimilable, racial group has had, and still has, telling consequences for the nation. Americans have lived with this fragmentation so long, and it seems so natural to them, that they assume its permanence and reckon that if they extend full civil rights to the Negro component and stop right there they will have settled the issue. On this reckoning rests the widely held assumption that civil rights is an end in itself.

Of course, attainment of civil rights and the wiping out of all racial disabilities would produce immense satisfaction among Negroes and, by the same token, would exert a considerable influence on national life. The Negro bloc would at once become a powerful pressure group, demanding and getting concessions on all sides. Negroes would attend better schools. The Negro relief recipient would get his fair share of the dole. The Negro market for gray-flannel suits would be enhanced. Jobs would be shared and in time the Negro unemployment rate would be lowered to that of the national average. An elite would be created within the Negro pressure group to seek its own ends, sometimes at the expense of other Negroes. Something of that kind has already happened in the comparatively free Northern cities, with not a few middle-class Negroes staking out vested interests in the ghettos and retiring from the civil-rights fight with the feeling that all is well. In any event, the Negro racial bloc is going to persist for a long time to come and will inevitably function as a pressure center. The temptation to preserve and enhance that function will be great, with the conservatives of the middle class pulling in that direction; they are experts in the art of pressure and can be expected to hold fast to a familiar tactic. The gaping wounds of racial conflict can be healed within that context and Negroes have been forced to think in terms of race so long that it will be hard for them to lift their sights.

If, however, civil-rights victory is regarded as only a beginning and a means, and the end envisaged is that of reforms that will cure the social, economic, and political malfunctioning in our society that results in poverty, old-age insecurity, disemployment, lack of educational opportunity, and other social plagues, the long-term yield to Negroes will be enlarged—provided, of course, that those ends can be attained. Freedom Now will be a more desirable prize if the model's freedom approaches completeness. Fair-housing and fair-employment laws will become more meaningful if housing is in complete supply and within common economic reach, and if there is job security for all. In short, the enrichment of American life promises added rewards to all who are permitted to share in it. The

Negro's quest for civil rights has always been two-pronged: the human desire to be treated as a man and the economic drive to get his fair share of what the nation has had to offer.

There is a ferment at work within the Negro community, North as well as South, which pretty well precludes the possibility that Negroes will stop short with civil-rights victory. The new militants who are emergent in terms of leadership are in revolt against the old in the Negro community as well as the old in white society. They are equalitarian in outlook and philosophy and where they now, correctly, see race as the prime inhibiting factor, they will learn soon enough that their civil-rights victory will not be complete without lowering of other barriers that produce inequities and inequalities. And as in the case of Alexander, the young always yearn for new worlds to conquer.

Perception on the part of Negroes that attainment of civil rights must be regarded as a means rather than an end will not solve the problem that confronts the nation. Whites must grasp and apply that lesson as well, but they must do it with their eyes wide open to the fact that Negroes have had their bellies full of paternalism and will have no more of it and that the Negro take-over of the civil-rights movement, no matter what shape it assumes, is permanent and will not be relinquished. However, whites must take the initiative in an offer of alliance and must have more to offer than is presently visible. At the moment, the American scene is singularly devoid of movements calculated to quicken the pulse of the bold and imaginative youngsters who triggered the national upheaval against racial discrimination and pulled the props from under the segregation system. Communism is a deservedly dead letter. Barry Goldwater's invitation for a retreat to the 1920's holds no allure and the cautious pragmatism of the New Frontier smacks too much of an application of gradualism to be attractive. The bogged-down labor movement has lost the verve that set Negroes flocking to its standard in the New Deal era. Who then shall sound the certain trumpet? The answer is that nobody knows. What is certain is that civil-rights victory will release a determined band of restless and eager Negro youth whose energies ought to be channeled constructively.

That constructive purpose can best be served by a broad political movement, in the widest sense of that term, comprehensive of pressing domestic and international issues. Whether such a movement can function within the formalism of our present two-party system is not clear. That will have to be determined on a trial-and-error basis. Negro militants who must be enlisted if such a movement is to succeed are understandably chary about political action at the moment. Their success has been won outside of politics and they are cynical about political action in light of the manner in which civil rights has been used as a football by both parties. But time itself will drive home the lesson that problems entailed in incorporating Negroes into our tremendously complicated social and economic structure are political in nature and will propel the new militants into political action. There is no other road to reform in a political democracy.

Obviously, the nation can, and should, use the imagination that conceived the sit-ins, the pray-ins, the wade-ins, and the freedom rides for application to other social purposes. And it needs to conserve and utilize the boldness and courage that led to the confrontations in hostile Southern cities. . . .

We are back where we began. The nation has been given a second chance to solve the problem that Abraham Lincoln proclaimed with Emancipation a hundred years ago: that of constructing a social order to replace an old one swept away when Negroes burst out of isolation and sought admission to the American body politic. We muffed the first chance and consigned Negroes to a new, and in some ways more galling, isolation, and in the process shackled the nation to the hobbled Negro. That first failure has haunted us ever since. Its consequences have become intolerable. We will achieve only half-success this time if we settle back and accept civil-rights victory as an end in itself. Foresight and planning can transmute that victory into a means for construction of a commonwealth as good as imperfect humans can build.

7 : A "Marshall Plan" for the American Negro

 National Urban League

. . . The National Urban League challenges the responsible leadership of our country to undertake a massive "Marshall Plan" approach program of intensified special effort to close the wide economic, social, and educational gap which separates the large majority of Negro citizens from other Americans.

Such special effort, which may appear to be in conflict with the principle of equal treatment for all, is required to overcome the damaging effects of generations of deprivation and denial and to make it possible for the majority of American Negroes to reach the point at which they can compete on a basis of equality in the nation's increasingly complex and fast-moving industrial economy.

The primary justification for such special effort lies in the fact that the nation itself is in jeopardy as long as it has within its body politic a large group of citizens who are socially and economically handicapped, often dependent, poorly educated, and unable to assume the normal responsibilities of citizenship. And with the impact of automation, it appears possible that these conditions will become worse before they improve and that we may well create a permanent class of dependents unable to make a useful contribution to our way of life.

The second reason for such an effort arises from the fact that the intense needs and problems which are evident in so many Negro communities around the country are a direct result of past and present discrimination and exclusion based on race. Thus, as a matter of historic equity, compensatory effort is justified and may well be the only means of overcoming the heavy aftermath of past neglect. As the following indexes suggest, despite progress in certain areas, a large segment of the American Negro population continues to lag seriously behind other Americans in almost every type of measurement which can be used to determine social and economic well-being. And in certain categories the gap is widening rather than closing.

The median annual income for the Negro family today is $3,233 as compared with $5,835 for whites, a gap of 45 per cent. That the trend is in the wrong direction is evidenced by the fact that the gap in 1952 was 43 per cent. Hence, that one element in the gap has widened rather than narrowed in barely more than a decade.

More than 75 per cent of all Negro workers are found in the three lowest occupational categories—service workers, semiskilled and unskilled laborers, and farm workers. Less than 39 per cent of all white workers are in these categories. And these are the very categories which are being most drastically affected by automation.

One of every six Negro dwelling units in the nation is dilapidated, obsolete, or otherwise substandard, as compared to one in 32 white dwellings. In 1961 Negroes occupied 47 per cent of all public housing units in the country.

The lower earning power of Negro men and the more frequent breakup of Negro families make it necessary for more Negro than white women to become breadwinners. One in every four Negro women with preschool children is at work and not at home.

More Negro youth drop out of high school than white youth, and fewer high-school graduates enter college. During the 1960 school year, 21 per cent of the school dropouts were Negroes. Of youth graduating from high school only 7 per cent were Negro youth.

Unemployment rates for Negroes are substantially higher than for whites at all ages: In 1961, 13 per cent of nonwhite men were unemployed as compared with 5.7 per cent of whites. Nationwide, Negro young people constitute only 15 per cent of the total youth population between the ages of sixteen and twenty-one, yet are 50 per cent of the youth population in this age bracket who are both out of school and unemployed.

To correct the problems indicated by these statistics, the co-operative effort of many social agencies, both public and private, in a massive "crash" attack on the problem is required. Such a crash program, sustained for a reasonable period of time, will realize savings of millions of dollars in the cost of welfare services and public hospitalization. Such a program will reverse the widespread social deterioration of urban families and communities and also help us develop the tools and understanding which will prevent the development of such deterioration in the future.

Specifically, what is involved in this kind of special effort which the Urban League now proposes?

(1) Our basic definition of equal opportunity must be broadened and deepened to include recognition of the need for special effort to overcome serious disabilities resulting from historic handicaps.

(2) Our society must recognize and put a higher value than it has ever before placed on the human potential possessed by Negro citizens. And then it must move positively to develop that potential.

(3) The best schools and the best teachers are needed to prepare Negro children and other educationally disadvantaged youth to the point where they will have the desire for excellence in education and will be motivated to achieve and prepare to advance up the economic ladder with full realization of the rewards that will accrue in the process.

(4) Token integration and pilot placement in business and industry, labor, and government, are not enough. A conscious, planned effort must be made to place qualified Negroes in entrance jobs in all types of employment and in positions of responsibility, including lower and upper management positions.

(5) Affirmative action must be taken to destroy the racial ghetto and open housing opportunities of all types on the basis of need and ability to buy or rent.

(6) Public and private agencies in the health and welfare field must offer to the ghettoized segments of the population the best services, with highly competent personnel who understand the reasons for unstable family patterns, the relation between low socioeconomic status and social problems, and what must be done to rehabilitate urban Negro families.

(7) Qualified Negroes should be sought and named to all public and private boards and commissions, and particularly those which shape policy in the areas of employment, housing, education, and health and welfare services, the areas in which the racial differential is greatest and the need for dramatic change is most urgent. To achieve this objective, strong leadership within the Negro community must be developed. This leadership then will be ready to step into the vanguard of the teamwork effort demanded in resolving the smoldering problems involved in civil rights.

(8) Negro citizens themselves, adults as well as young people, must maintain and even accelerate the sense of urgency which now characterizes the drive for first-class citizenship. Every opportunity for the acquisition of education and technical skills must be utilized. Every means of strengthening the social and economic fabric of the Negro community must be employed.

(9) It is vital that government, philanthropic foundations, business, and industry reassess the extent of their financial support to established organizations committed to securing equal opportunity for Negro citizens to share in the fundamental privileges and rights of American democracy. It is imperative that all of these major sources of financial support substantially increase their contributions to the preventive programs carried on by established, responsible Negro leadership organizations.

(10) Constructive efforts on the part of Negro citizens must be exerted to carry their full share of the responsibilities for participation in a meaningful way in every phase of community life.

The kinds of action set forth in the foregoing represent the only way in which significant breakthroughs on a broad scale can be accomplished. This is compensatory consideration in the form of inclusion, selection, and preference.

The consequences of the "Negro revolt," as it has been characterized, are yet to be seen. It, therefore, behooves America's leadership to give serious consideration to a radical new approach by which the democracy we profess to practice is granted without further delay to all citizens.

8 : *Black Muslims and Civil Rights*

Malcolm X

MALCOLM X: . . . I know the time is near when the white man will be finished. The signs are all around us. Ten years ago you couldn't have *paid* a Southern Negro to defy local customs. The British Lion's tail has been snatched off in black Africa. The Indonesians have booted out such would-be imperialists as the Dutch. The French, who felt for a century that Algeria was theirs, have had to run for their lives back to France. Sir, the point I make is that all over the world, the old day of standing in fear and trembling before the almighty white men is *gone!*

QUESTION: You refer to whites as the guilty and the enemy; you predict divine retribution against them; and you preach absolute separation from the white community. Do not these views substantiate that your movement is predicated on race hatred?

MALCOLM X: . . . The Honorable Elijah Muhammad doesn't teach hate. The white man isn't *important* enough for the Honorable Elijah Muhammad and his followers to spend any time hating him. The white man has brainwashed himself into believing that all the black people in the world want to be cuddled up next to him. . . . When we tell him we don't want to be around him, we don't want to be like he is, he's staggered. It makes him

---

Malcolm X, formerly the leading spokesman for the Black Muslims, now heads his own political organization, the Black Nationalists.

re-evaluate his three-hundred-year myth about the black man. What I want to know is how the white man, with the blood of black people dripping off his fingers, can have the audacity to be asking black people do they hate him. That takes a lot of nerve.

QUESTION: How do you reconcile your disavowal of hatred with the announcement you made last year that Allah had brought you "the good news" that one hundred and twenty white Atlantans had just been killed in an air crash en route to America from Paris?

MALCOLM X: Sir, as I see the law of justice, it says as you sow, so shall you reap. . . . We Muslims believe that the white race, which is guilty of having oppressed and exploited and enslaved our people here in America, should and will be the victims of God's divine wrath. All civilized societies in their courts of justice set a sentence of execution against those deemed to be enemies of society, such as murderers and kidnapers. The presence of twenty million black people here in America is proof that Uncle Sam is guilty of kidnaping—because we didn't come here voluntarily on the *Mayflower*. And four hundred years of lynchings condemn Uncle Sam as a murderer. . . .

QUESTION: Many white religious leaders have also gone on record against the Black Muslims. Writing in the official NAACP magazine, a Catholic priest described you as "a fascist-minded hate group," and B'nai B'rith has accused you of being not only anti-Christian but anti-Semitic. Do you consider this true?

MALCOLM X: Insofar as the Christian world is concerned, dictatorships have existed only in areas or countries where you have Roman Catholicism. Catholicism conditions your mind for dictators. Can you think of a single Protestant country that has ever produced a dictator? . . . Where did fascism start? Where's the second-largest Communist party outside of Russia? The answer to both is Italy. Where is the Vatican? . . .

Let me say just a word about the Jew and the black man. The Jew is always anxious to *advise* the black man. But they never advise him how to solve his problem the way the Jews solved their problem. The Jew never went sitting in and crawling in and sliding in and freedom-riding, like he teaches and helps Negroes to do. The Jews stood up, and stood together, and they used their ultimate power, the economic weapon. That's exactly what the Honorable Elijah Muhammad is trying to teach black men to do. The Jews pooled their money and *bought* the hotels that barred them. They bought Atlantic City and Miami Beach and anything else they wanted. Who owns Hollywood? Who runs the garment industry, the largest industry in New York City? But the Jew that's advising the Negro joins the NAACP, CORE, the Urban League, and others. With money donations, the Jew gains control, then he sends the black man doing all this wading in, boring in, even burying in—everything but buying in. Never shows him how to set up factories and hotels. Never advises him how to own what he wants. No, when there's something worth owning, the Jew's got it.

QUESTION: Isn't it true that many Gentiles have also labored with dedication to advance integration and economic improvement for the Negro, as volunteer workers for the NAACP, CORE, and many other interracial agencies?

MALCOLM X: A man who tosses worms in the river isn't necessarily a friend of the fish. All the fish who take him for a friend, who think the worm's got no hook in it, usually end up in the frying pan. All these things dangled before us by the white liberal posing as a friend and benefactor have turned out to be nothing but bait to make us think we're making progress. The Supreme Court decision has never been enforced. Desegregation has never taken place. The promises have never been fulfilled. We have received only tokens, substitutes, trickery, and deceit. . . .

QUESTION: You say that white men are devils by nature. Was Christ a devil?

MALCOLM X: Christ wasn't white. Christ was a black man. . . . Only the poor, brainwashed American Negro has been made to believe that Christ was white, to maneuver him into worshiping the white man. After becoming a Muslim in prison, I read almost everything I could put my hands on in the prison library. I began to think back on everything I had read and especially with the histories. I realized that nearly all of them read by the general public have been made into white histories. I found out that the history-whitening process either had left out great things that black men had done, or some of the great black men had gotten whitened.

QUESTION: Would you list a few of these men?

MALCOLM X: Well, Hannibal, the most successful general that ever lived, was a black man. So was Beethoven; Beethoven's father was one of the blackamoors that hired themselves out in Europe as professional soldiers. Haydn, Beethoven's teacher, was of African descent. Columbus, the discoverer of America, was a half-black man. . . .

Whole black empires, like the Moorish, have been whitened to hide the fact that a great black empire had conquered a white empire even before America was discovered. The Moorish civilization—black Africans—conquered and ruled Spain; they kept the light burning in Southern Europe. The word "Moor" means "black," by the way. Egyptian civilization is a classic example of how the white man stole great African cultures and makes them appear today as white European. . . . The Incas, the Aztecs, the Mayans, all dark-skinned Indian people, had a highly developed culture here in America, in what is now Mexico and northern South America. These people had mastered agriculture at the time when European white people were still living in mud huts and eating weeds. But white children, or black children, or grownups here today in America don't get to read this in the average books they are exposed to. . . .

QUESTION: [Do you regard the white race] as inferior in quality as well as quantity to what you call the "black nation"?

MALCOLM X: Thoughtful white people *know* they are inferior to black people. Even Eastland knows it. Anyone who has studied the genetic phase of biology knows that white is considered recessive and black is considered dominant. When you want strong coffee, you ask for black coffee. If you want it light, you want it weak, integrated with white milk. Just like these Negroes who weaken themselves and their race by this integrating and intermixing with whites. If you want bread with no nutritional value, you ask for white bread. All the good that was in it has been bleached out of it, and it will constipate you. If you want pure flour, you ask for dark flour, whole-wheat flour. If you want pure sugar, you want dark sugar.

QUESTION: If all whites are devilish by nature, as you have alleged, and if black and white are essentially opposite, as you have just stated, do you view all black men—with the exception of their non-Muslim leaders—as fundamentally angelic?

MALCOLM X: No, there is plenty wrong with Negroes. They have no society. They're robots, automatons. No minds of their own. I hate to say that about us, but it's the truth. They are a black body with a white brain. Like the monster Frankenstein. The top part is your bourgeois Negro. He's your integrator. He's not interested in his poor black brothers. He's usually so deep in debt from trying to copy the white man's social habits that he doesn't have time to worry about nothing else. They buy the most expensive clothes and cars and eat the cheapest food. They act more like the white man than the white man does himself. These are the ones that hide their sympathy for Mr. Muhammad's teachings. It conflicts with the sources from which they get their white-man's crumbs. This class to us are the fence-sitters. They have one eye on the white man and the other eye on the Muslims. They'll jump whichever way they see the wind blowing. Then there's the middle class of the Negro masses, the ones not in the ghetto, who realize that life is a struggle, who are conscious of all the injustices being done and of the constant state of insecurity in which they live. They're ready to take some stand against everything that's against them. Now, when this group hears Mr. Muhammad's teachings, they are the ones who come forth faster and identify themselves, and take immediate steps toward trying to bring into existence what Mr. Muhammad advocates. At the bottom of the social heap is the black man in the big-city ghetto. He lives night and day with the rats and cockroaches and drowns himself with alcohol and anesthetizes himself with dope, to try and forget where and what he is. That Negro has given up all hope. He's the hardest one for us to reach, because he's the deepest in the mud. But when you get him, you've got the best kind of Muslim. Because he makes the most drastic change. He's the most fearless. He will stand the longest. He has nothing to lose, even his life, because he didn't have that in the first place. . . .

QUESTION: Do you feel that the Administration's successful stand on the integration of James Meredith into the University of Mississippi has demonstrated that the government—far from being hypocritical—is sympathetic with the Negro's aspirations for equality?

MALCOLM X: What was accomplished? It took 15,000 troops to put

Meredith in the University of Mississippi. Those troops and
$3,000,000—that's what was spent—to get one Negro in. That
$3,000,000 could have been used much more wisely by the fed-
eral government to elevate the living standards of all the Negroes
in Mississippi. . . .

QUESTION: Has *any* American president, in your opinion—Lincoln,
FDR, Truman, Eisenhower, Kennedy—accomplished anything
for the Negro?

MALCOLM X: None of them have ever done anything for Negroes.
All of them have tricked the Negro, and made false promises to
him at election times which they never fulfilled. Lincoln's concern wasn't freedom for the blacks but to save the Union. . . .

QUESTION: Despite the fact that the goal of racial equality is not
yet realized, many sociologists—and many Negro commentators
—agree that no minority group on earth has made as much social, civil, and economic progress as the American Negro in the
past one hundred years. What is your reaction to this view?

MALCOLM X: . . . Every immigrant ethnic group that has come to
this country is now a genuinely first-class citizen group—every
one of them but the black man, who was here when they came.
. . . You talk about the progress of the Negro—I'll tell you,
mister, it's just because the Negro has been in America while
America has gone forward that the Negro appears to have gone
forward. The Negro is like a man on a luxury commuter train
doing ninety miles an hour. He looks out of the window, along
with all the white passengers in their Pullman chairs, and he
thinks *he's* doing ninety, too. Then he gets to the men's room
and looks in the mirror—and he sees he's not really getting anywhere at all. His reflection shows a black man standing there in
the white uniform of a dining-car steward. He may get on the
5:10, all right, but he sure won't be getting off at Westport.

QUESTION: Is there anything then, in your opinion, that could be
done—by either whites or blacks—to expedite the social and economic progress of the Negro in America?

MALCOLM X: . . . The white man must realize that the sins of the
fathers are about to be visited upon the heads of the children
who have continued those sins, only in more sophisticated
ways. . . .
But there *is* something the white man can do to avert this

fate. He must atone—and this can only be done by allowing black men, those who choose, to leave this land of bondage and go to a land of our own. But if he doesn't want a mass movement of our people away from this house of bondage, then he should separate this country. He should give us several states here on American soil, where those of us who wish to can go and set up our own government, our own economic system, our own civilization. Since we have given over three hundred years of our slave labor to the white man's America, helped to build it up for him, it's only right that white America should give us everything *we* need in finance and materials for the next twenty-five years, until our own nation is able to stand on its feet. Then, if the Western Hemisphere is attacked by outside enemies, we would have both the capability and the motivation to join in defending the hemisphere, in which we would then have a sovereign stake. . . .

PART II

THE NEGRO CIVIL-RIGHTS STRUGGLE IN HISTORICAL PERSPECTIVE

9 : *Ending Jim Crow Schools in Boston, 1855*

Louis Ruchames

. . . It is one of the ironies of history that the segregated school system of Massachusetts, whose abolition was so earnestly sought at a later date, was originally founded at the behest of Negroes and their white friends. The public schools, when first created, were regarded as eleemosynary institutions for the education of the poor. With this "stigma" in mind, friends of the Negro advised him not to attend these schools since "men might reproach them with becoming a public charge," and thus find additional reason for prejudice and hatred. In addition, certain philanthropists who were interested in the welfare of the Negro "deemed it wise to provide separate schools for Negroes to bring them into contact with sympathetic persons who knew their peculiar needs."

In the course of time, free public education came to be regarded by all sections of the population as a right, and the odium which had previously attached to it disappeared. Negroes thereupon began to clamor for their share of public education which they had been

At the time this was written, Rabbi Ruchames was Director of the B'nai B'rith Hillel Foundation of Western Massachusetts.

supporting through taxes but from which they derived no benefit. Together with the Abolitionists, they demanded that public funds be appropriated for existing Negro schools and, where necessary, additional schools for Negroes be created. Because of existing prejudice and fear of being mistreated, they did not demand admission into the white schools. The first primary school for Negro children in Boston was established in 1820. Schools for Negroes were also established in other cities and towns of Massachusetts, for example, Salem, Nantucket, and New Bedford.

It soon became evident that the establishment of separate schools for Negroes was an error. For they proved to be nowise nearly as adequate as the others, their facilities and teaching staffs were inferior, and, perhaps most important of all, the division into two separate school systems served both as a symbol of the inferior social and economic status of the Negro and as an additional strand in the web of circumstances which bound the Negro to that status.

Negroes and Abolitionists, realizing their error, began to seek the abolition of separate schools and the integration of Negro children into the white school system. As a result of sustained pressure over a period of years, segregated schools were abandoned in all towns and cities of Massachusetts except Boston by 1846. The Boston School Committee remained intransigent for almost ten more years. During that period, Boston became the scene of one of the most prolonged and intense campaigns for Negro rights in the history of the North—equaled only one hundred years later, in Massachusetts, in the struggle for the enactment of a fair-employment-practice law.

The leader and initiator of the campaign was William C. Nell, Negro writer and historian. Author of *Services of Colored Americans in the Wars of 1776 and 1812*, and *The Colored Patriots of the American Revolution*, and the first Negro to hold a federal position, Nell determined to strive for the elimination of segregation in the Boston school system as early as 1829 when, as a boy, he attended the Belknap Street school for Negro children. . . .

In 1840, William Lloyd Garrison, Wendell Phillips, Francis Jackson, Henry W. Williams, and Nell signed a petition requesting the city government to eliminate segregation and grant equal rights to Negro school children. The request was rejected. This petition was followed, in the ensuing years, by numerous others bearing thousands of signatures of prominent individuals demanding the elimination of segregation. Nell . . . was the instigator of most of the petitions. . . . Mass meetings, articles in Boston's newspapers, and picketing of the Smith school—the Negro school —to persuade parents to express their opposition to segregation by refusing to send their children to classes, supplemented the pressure of the petitions.

The Boston School Committee, faced with this constant agitation, appointed a committee to investigate the problem. On June 15, 1846, Reverend Mr. Crowell presented a report on behalf of a majority of the committee, in which segregation was upheld. At the same time, a minority report, submitted by Edmund Jackson, urged the abolition of segregation. Several days later, on June 22, following the submission of an opinion by the city solicitor upholding the legal power of the school committee to maintain segregation, the school committee decided, by a vote of 59 to 16, that "the continuance of the separate schools for colored children is not only legal and just, but is best adapted to promote the education of that part of our population."

Despite this adverse ruling, the agitation failed to subside and, if anything, increased in intensity. In 1849, the school committee was forced to reconsider its decision. However, following the presentation of majority and minority reports, it again voted to continue its policy of segregation.

During the same year, a suit was brought by Benjamin F. Roberts, the father of Sarah C. Roberts, a Negro schoolgirl five years of age, against the city of Boston. In April, 1847, Sarah Roberts had applied to the primary school nearest her home and was refused admission. She was, at the same time, advised to attend the Belknap Street school for Negro children which was situated at a far greater distance from her home than any of five schools for white children. Her father appealed to various school authorities but received no satisfaction. On February 15, 1848, Sarah attempted direct action by entering, without the required permission, the primary school nearest her home, but was ejected by the teacher. Her father, thereupon, instituted suit against the city of Boston, under a Massachusetts statute which provided that a child unlawfully excluded from public-school instruction could recover damages from the city or town where the exclusion took place. Charles Sumner, who was to gain fame as Abolitionist and Senator from Massachusetts, acted as counsel and was assisted by Robert Morris, a Negro lawyer. The case was finally brought before the Supreme Court of Massachusetts for its decision.

In his brief to the court, Sumner argued that "equality before the law"—a term which he introduced into the English language in this case—was a basic principle of the Constitution of Massachusetts and was being violated by segregation in two ways: "first, by subjecting colored children to inconvenience inconsistent with the requirements of Equality, and secondly, by establishing a system of Caste odious as that of the Hindus—leading to the conclusion that the School Committee have no such power as they have exercised, and that it is the duty of the Court to set aside the unjust by-law.

. . . "The words Caste and Equality are contradictory. They mutually exclude each other. Where Caste is there cannot be equality; where Equality is there cannot be caste." Moreover, "A separate school, though well endowed, would not secure to them that precise Equality which they would enjoy in the Common Schools. The Jews in Rome are confined to a particular district called the Ghetto, and in Frankfort to a district known as the Jewish Quarter. It is possible that their accommodations are as good as they would be able to occupy, if left free to choose throughout Rome and Frankfort; but this compulsory segregation from the mass of citizens is of itself an inequality which we condemn. It is a vestige of ancient intolerance directed against a despised people. It is of the same character with the separate schools in Boston." . . .

However, the Massachusetts Supreme Court was not convinced, although it did praise Sumner's presentation. Its decision, written by Chief Justice C. J. Shaw, was rendered in favor of the school committee. It maintained that the maintenance of segregation by the committee was not an unreasonable act despite the added distance which Negro children were forced to travel to school and it stressed that the committee possessed the power to classify and distribute school children as it thought necessary for the good of the system as a whole. Since the committee had decided "that the good of both classes of schools will be best promoted, by maintaining the separate primary schools for colored and for white children," the decision of the committee must "be deemed conclusive."

As to the alleged tendency of separate schools "to deepen and perpetuate the odious distinction of caste, founded in a deep-rooted prejudice in public opinion, . . . this prejudice, if it exists, is not created by law, and probably cannot be changed by law. Whether this distinction and prejudice, existing in the opinion and feelings of the community, would not be as effectually fostered by compelling colored and white children to associate together in the same schools, may well be doubted." . . .

Despite the judicial defeat, the campaign continued as before with petitions, picketing, and mass meetings. But having failed in their efforts to achieve success through the courts, Negroes and Abolitionists determined to concentrate their attention upon legislative enactment to reach their goal.

Their activities were not without opposition even within the Negro community. On December 24, 1849, Thomas P. Smith delivered an address before an audience of Negroes in which he praised segregation as "of the greatest advantage to the colored people of Boston," and emphasized that its abolition "would be uncalled for, unjust, inexpedient and injurious." He maintained that Negro schools provided an atmosphere in which Negro children were at peace, free from insults and prejudice, and cared for by teachers who understood their problems and had their welfare at heart. It was in the all-Negro school that the Negro could prove his ability and refute "the taunt of inferiority by the production of scholars from exclusively colored schools, who cannot be excelled by scholars from the best white schools of the same rank in the country." . . .

These remarks, however, represented the views of a very small minority and had little effect upon the ensuing course of events. In 1854, the city government of Boston was prevailed upon to reconsider the problem. Although it took no action other than to order an investigation which resulted in a report recommending equal rights for colored children, it did pave the way for action by the state legislature.

The latter body was confronted, in 1855, with numerous petitions, from cities and towns throughout Massachusetts, demanding action. Following an intensive investigation, the legislature's committee on education, in a report delivered on March 17, urged the abolition of separate schools for Negroes, and reported out a bill to that effect. The bill was approved by the legislature, and was signed by the Governor on April 28, 1855.

It provided that "in determining the qualifications of scholars to be admitted into any Public School or any District School in this Commonwealth, no distinction shall be made on account of the race, color, or religious opinions of the applicant or scholar." Any child excluded "on account of his race, color, or religious opinions" from any public or district school in the state could "recover damages therefor in an action of tort" and file "interrogations for discovery" enabling him to get evidence from city and town officials involved. Finally, "every person belonging to the school committee, under whose rules and directions any child shall be excluded from such school, and every teacher of any such school shall, on application by the parent or guardian of any such child, state in writing the grounds and reasons of any such exclusion."

For the colored citizens of Boston the campaign did not end with this legislative victory. Segregation continued for the remainder of the school year, and the nonsegregated system of education was not put into effect until the beginning of the new school year, on September 3. The intervening period provided an excellent opportunity and the necessary time to prepare for and ensure a smooth and orderly transition to the new order of things, and was so utilized.

On August 27, a meeting of a large number of Negroes was held in the vestry of the Southern Baptist Church. The speakers, all of whom had been active in the campaign, were Garrison, Charles W. Slack, a member of the state legislature, William H. Logan, and Nell. Nell distributed a circular, which he had prepared, containing the addresses of all the public schools of Boston and their respective committees, as well as advice to Negro parents. "It is a very encouraging fact," it read, "that many teachers, committees and others, influential and interested, will extend every facility by way of smoothing the path to those children whose diffidence may not readily submit to the novelty of this arrangement. There may be those, too, yet opposed to this change; but the specific for conquering such prejudices are those essentials of good scholarship— Neatness in dress, Punctual attendance at School, Exemplary behavior, and Diligence in study. That the parents will aim to cultivate these traits, and the children be eager to excel in them, that all parties may soon rejoice in Equal School Rights, is the fervent desire of those who have labored for its promotion."

It was revealed at the meeting that the superintendent of schools had arranged to have Negro children accepted at the schools nearest their homes "without certificates except their countenances"; that teachers were given the responsibility of preventing annoyance to Negro children; that the Smith school was to be discontinued entirely, unless there arose a demand for its use; and that the school committee was prepared to carry out the provisions of the law in good faith. . . .

The exultation of the Negro people and children of Boston, at the approach of September 3, was best described by Nell who witnessed a Negro boy passing by the Smith school on September 2. "Raising his hand," observed Nell, "he exultingly exclaimed to his companions, 'Good-bye forever, colored school! Tomorrow we are like other Boston boys.' "

September 3 finally arrived. To make doubly certain that all would go well a delegation of women accompanied Nell to "the various school houses, to residences of teachers and committeemen, to make sure the law was applied." The effectiveness of these preparations, and the others that have been mentioned, was attested to by the Boston *Evening Telegraph* of September 3, in a description of how the colored children were greeted by white students: "The introduction of the colored youth into the schools, we are happy to say, was accomplished with general good feeling on the part of both teachers and white children. . . . The appearance of the colored children in the heretofore by them unfrequented streets leading to the school houses created a 'sensation' among the neighbors, who filled the windows, probably in anticipation of trouble. So far as we can hear, there was none, however, in any part of the city." . . .

10 : *Ride-in's and Sit-in's of the 1870's*

Alan F. Westin

It began one day early in January when a Negro named Robert Fox boarded a streetcar in Louisville, dropped his coin into the fare box, and sat down in the white section of the car. Ordered to move, he refused, and the driver threw him off the car.

Shortly after, Fox filed a charge of assault and battery against the streetcar company in the federal district court, claiming that separate seating policies were illegal and the driver's actions were therefore improper. The district judge instructed the jury that under federal law, common carriers must serve all passengers equally without regard to race. So instructed, the jury found the company rules to be invalid and awarded Fox damages of $15 (plus $72.80 in legal costs).

Immediately there was sharp criticism of the Fox decision from the city and state administrations, both Democratic; the company defied the court's ruling and continued segregated seating. After several meetings with local federal officials and white attorneys co-operating with them, Louisville Negro leaders decided to launch a full-scale "ride-in."

At 7 P.M. on May 12, a young Negro boy boarded a streetcar near the Willard Hotel, walked past the driver, and took a seat among the white passengers. The driver, under new company regulations, did not attempt to throw him off but simply stopped the car, lit a cigar, and refused to proceed until the Negro moved to "his place." While the Governor, the Louisville chief of police, and other prominent citizens looked on from the sidewalks, a large crowd, which included an increasingly noisy mob of jeering white teen-agers, gathered around the streetcar.

Before long there were shouts of "Put him out!" "Hit him!" "Kick him!" "Hang him!" Several white youths climbed into the car and began yelling insults in the face of the Negro rider. He refused to answer—or to move.

The youths dragged him from his seat, pulled him off the car, and began to beat him. Only when the Negro started to defend himself did the police intervene. They arrested him for disturbing the peace and took him off to jail.

This time the trial was held in Louisville city court, not the federal court. The magistrate ruled that streetcar companies were not under any obligation to treat Negroes exactly as they treated whites and that any federal measures purporting to create such obligations would be "clearly invalid" under the Constitutions of Kentucky and the United States. The defendant was fined, and the judge delivered a warning to Louisville Negroes that further ride-ins would be punished.

But the ride-in campaign was not halted that easily. In the days following, streetcar after streetcar was entered by Negroes who took seats in the white section. Now the drivers got off the cars entirely. On several occasions, the Negro riders drove the cars themselves, to the sound of cheers from Negro spectators.

Then violence erupted. Bands of white youths and men began to throw Negro riders off the cars, windows were broken, cars were overturned, and for a time a general race riot threatened. Moderate Kentucky newspapers and many community leaders deplored the fighting; the Republican candidate for governor denounced the streetcar company's segregation policies and blamed the violence on Democratic encouragement of white extremists.

By this time, newspapers around the country were carrying reports of the conflict and many editorials denounced the seating regulations. In Louisville, federal marshals and the United States attorney backed the rights of the Negro riders and stated that federal court action would be taken if necessary. There were even rumors that the President might send troops.

Under these threats, the streetcar company capitulated. Soon, all the city transit companies declared that "it was useless to try to resist or evade the enforcement by the United States authorities of the claim of Negroes to ride in the cars." To "avoid serious collisions," the company would thereafter allow all passengers to sit where they chose. Although a few disturbances took place in the following months, mixed seating became a common practice. Never again would Louisville streetcars be segregated.

The event may have the familiar ring of recent history, but it is not, for it occurred in 1871. The President who considered ordering troops to Louisville was General Grant, not General Eisenhower. The Republican gubernatorial candidate who supported Negro riders, John Marshall Harlan, was not a post-World War II leader of the GOP but a former slaveholder from one of Kentucky's oldest and most famous political families. And the "new" Negroes who waged this ride-in were not members of the Congress of Racial Equality and the National Association for the Advancement of Colored People, but former slaves who were fighting for civil rights in their own time, and with widespread success.

And yet these dramatic sit-in's and ride-in's and walk-in's of the 1870's are almost unknown to the American public today. Contrary to common assumptions, no state in the Union during the 1870's, including those south of the Mason-Dixon line, required separation of whites and Negroes in places of public accommodation. Policies were up to individual owners. In the North and West, many theaters, hotels, restaurants, and public carriers served Negro patrons without hesitation or discrimination. The same was true in the larger cities of the Southern states.

From 1865 through the early 1880's, the general trend in the nation was toward wider acceptance of Negro patronage. Nevertheless, exclusion and segregation continued throughout the 1870's. To settle the issue (thereby reaping the lasting appreciation of Negro voters), congressional Republicans led by Senator Charles Sumner pressed for a federal statute making discrimination in public accommodations a crime. After a series of compromises, Sumner's forces were able to enact the statute on March 1, 1875.

The act declared that "all persons within the jurisdiction of the United States shall be entitled to the full and equal enjoyment of the accommodations . . . of inns, public conveyances on land or water, theaters and other places of public amusement, subject only to the conditions and limitations established by law and applicable alike to citizens of every race or color. . . ." Any person violating the act could be sued in federal district court for a penalty of $500, could be fined $500 to $1,000, or could be imprisoned from thirty days to one year.

Reaction to the law was swift. Two Negro men were admitted to the dress circle of Macauley's Theater in Louisville and sat through the performance without incident. In Washington, Negroes were served for the first time at the bar of the Willard Hotel, and in Chicago, a Negro broke the color line when he was seated at Mc-Vicker's Theater. But in other instances, Negroes were rejected despite "Sumner's law."

Suits challenging refusal were filed en masse throughout the country. Perhaps a hundred were decided in various ways in the federal district courts during the late 1870's and early 1880's. But it was not until late in 1883 that the Supreme Court made its famous civil-rights cases ruling. . . .

On the afternoon of October 15, 1883, Justice Bradley announced that the Court found Sections 1 and 2 of the Civil Rights Act of 1875 to be unconstitutional. . . .

Bradley's opinion had a tightly reasoned simplicity. The Thirteenth Amendment forbade slavery and involuntary servitude, he noted, but protection against the restoration of bondage could not be stretched to cover federal regulation of "social" discriminations such as those dealt with in the 1875 statute. As for the Fourteenth Amendment, that was addressed only to deprivations of rights by the states; it did not encompass private acts of discrimination.

Thus there was no source of constitutional authority for "Sumner's law"; it had to be regarded as an unwarranted invasion of an area under state jurisdiction. Even as a matter of policy, Bradley argued, the intention of the war amendments to aid the newly freed Negro must have some limits. At some point, the Negro must cease to be "the special favorite of the law" and take on the "rank of a mere citizen."

At the Atlanta Opera House on the evening of the Court's decision, the end man of Haverly's Minstrels interrupted the performance to announce the ruling. The entire orchestra and dress-circle audiences rose and cheered. Negroes sitting in the balcony kept their seats, "stunned," according to one newspaper account. A short time earlier, a Negro denied entrance to the dress circle had filed charges against the Opera House management under the 1875 act. Now his case—their case—was dead.

Of all the nine Justices, only John Marshall Harlan, the Kentuckian and former slaveholder, announced that he dissented from the ruling. . . . He began by noting that the pre-Civil War Supreme Court had upheld congressional laws forbidding individuals to interfere with recovery of fugitive slaves. To strike down the Act of 1875 meant that "the rights of freedom and American citizenship cannot receive from the Nation that efficient protection which heretofore was unhesitatingly accorded to slavery and the rights of masters."

Harlan argued that the Civil Rights Act of 1875 was constitutional on any one of several grounds. The Thirteenth Amendment had already been held to guarantee "universal civil freedom"; Harlan stated that barring Negroes from facilities licensed by the state and under legal obligation to serve all persons without discrimination restored a major disability of slavery days and violated that civil freedom.

As for the Fourteenth Amendment, its central purpose had been to extend national citizenship to the Negro, reversing the precedent upheld in the Dred Scott decision; its final section gave Congress power to pass appropriate legislation to enforce that affirmative grant as well as to enforce the section barring any state action which might deny liberty or equality. Now, the Supreme Court was deciding what legislation was appropriate and necessary for those purposes, although that decision properly belonged to Congress.

Even under the "state action" clause of the Fourteenth Amendment, Harlan continued, the 1875 act was constitutional; it was well established that "railroad corporations, keepers of inns and managers of places of public accommodation are agents or instrumentalities of the state."

In his peroration, Harlan replied to Bradley's comment that Negroes had been made "a special favorite of the law." The war amendments had been passed not to "favor" the Negro, he declared, but to include him as "part of the people for whose welfare and happiness government is ordained.

"Today, it is the colored race which is denied, by corporations and individuals wielding public authority, rights fundamental in their freedom and citizenship. At some future time, it may be that some other race will fall under the ban of race discrimination. If the constitutional amendments be enforced, according to the intent with which, as I conceive, they were adopted, there cannot be in this republic, any class of human beings in practical subjection to another class. . . ."

The civil-rights cases ruling did two things. First, it destroyed the delicate balance of federal guarantee, Negro protest, and private enlightenment which was producing a steadily widening area of peacefully integrated public facilities in the North and South during the 1870's and early 1880's. Second, it had an immediate and profound effect on national and state politics as they related to the Negro.

By denying Congress power to protect the Negro's rights to equal treatment, the Supreme Court wiped the issue of civil rights from the Republican party's agenda of national responsibility. At the same time, those Southern political leaders who saw anti-Negro politics as the most promising avenue to power could now rally the "poor whites" to the banner of segregation.

If the Supreme Court had stopped there, the situation of Negroes would have been bad but not impossible. Even in the South, there was no immediate imposition of segregation in public facilities.

During the late 1880's, Negroes could be found sharing places with whites in many Southern restaurants, streetcars, and theaters. But increasingly, Democratic and Populist politicians found the Negro an irresistible target.

As Solicitor General Phillips had warned the Supreme Court, what had been tolerated as the "fact" of discrimination was now being translated into "doctrine." Between 1887 and 1891, eight Southern states passed laws requiring railroads to separate all white and Negro passengers. The Supreme Court upheld these laws in the 1896 case of *Plessy* v. *Ferguson.*

Then in the Berea College case of 1906, it upheld laws forbidding private schools to educate Negro and white children together. Both decisions aroused Harlan's bitter dissent. In the next fifteen or twenty years, the chalk line of Jim Crow was drawn across virtually every area of public contact in the South.

Today, as this line is slowly and painfully being erased, we may do well to reflect on what might have been in the South if the Civil Rights Act of 1875 had been upheld, in whole or in part. Perhaps everything would have been the same. Perhaps forces at work between 1883 and 1940 were too powerful for a Supreme Court to hold in check. Perhaps "Sumner's law" was greatly premature.

Yet it is difficult to believe that total, state-enforced segregation was inevitable in the South after the 1880's. If in these decades the Supreme Court had taken the same *laissez-faire* attitude toward race relations as it took toward economic affairs, voluntary integration would have survived as a countertradition to Jim Crow and might have made the transition of the 1950's less painful than it was.

At the very least, one cannot help thinking that Harlan was a better sociologist than his colleagues and a better Southerner than the "irreconcilables." American constitutional history has a richer ring to it because of the protest that John Marshall Harlan finally put down on paper . . . in 1883.

11 : *The March on Washington Movement during World War II*

A. Philip Randolph

Though I have found no Negroes who want to see the United Nations lose this war, I have found many who, before the war ends, want to see the stuffing knocked out of white supremacy and of empire over subject peoples. American Negroes, involved as we are in the general issues of the conflict, are confronted not with a choice but with the challenge both to win democracy for ourselves at home and to help win the war for democracy the world over.

There is no escape from the horns of this dilemma. There ought not to be escape. For if the war for democracy is not won abroad, the fight for democracy cannot be won at home. If this war cannot be won for the white peoples, it will not be won for the darker races.

Conversely, if freedom and equality are not vouchsafed the peo-

A. Philip Randolph is the President, Brotherhood of Sleeping Car Porters, Vice-President, AFL-CIO, and organizer of the 1941–1942 March on Washington movement.

ples of color, the war for democracy will not be won. Unless this double-barreled thesis is accepted and applied, the darker races will never wholeheartedly fight for the victory of the United Nations. That is why those familiar with the thinking of the American Negro have sensed his lack of enthusiasm, whether among the educated or uneducated, rich or poor, professional or nonprofessional, religious or secular, rural or urban, North, South, East, or West.

That is why questions are being raised by Negroes in church, labor union, and fraternal society; in poolroom, barbershop, schoolroom, hospital, hair-dressing parlor; on college campus, railroad, and bus. One can hear such questions asked as these: What have Negroes to fight for? What's the difference between Hitler and that "cracker" Talmadge of Georgia? Why has a man got to be Jim-Crowed to die for democracy? If you haven't got democracy yourself, how can you carry it to somebody else?

What are the reasons for this state of mind? The answer is: discrimination, segregation, Jim Crow. Witness the navy, the army, the air corps; and also government services at Washington. In many parts of the South, Negroes in Uncle Sam's uniform are being put upon, mobbed, sometimes even shot down by civilian and military police, and on occasion lynched. Vested political interests in race prejudice are so deeply entrenched that to them winning the war against Hitler is secondary to preventing Negroes from winning democracy for themselves. This is worth many divisions to Hitler and Hirohito. While labor, business, and farm are subjected to ceilings and floors and not allowed to carry on as usual, these interests trade in the dangerous business of race hate as usual.

When the defense program began and billions of the taxpayers' money were appropriated for guns, ships, tanks, and bombs, Negroes presented themselves for work only to be given the cold shoulder. North as well as South, and despite their qualifications, Negroes were denied skilled employment. Not until their wrath and indignation took the form of a proposed protest march on Washington, scheduled for July 1, 1941, did things begin to move in the form of defense jobs for Negroes. The march was postponed by the timely issuance (June 25, 1941) of the famous Executive Order No. 8802 by President Roosevelt. But this order and the President's Committee on Fair Employment Practice, established thereunder, have as yet only scratched the surface by way of eliminating discriminations on account of race or color in war industry. Both management and labor unions in too many places and in too many ways are still drawing the color line.

It is to meet this situation squarely with direct action that the March on Washington movement launched its present program of protest mass meetings. Twenty thousand were in attendance at Madison Square Garden, June 16; sixteen thousand in the Coliseum in Chicago, June 26; nine thousand in the City Auditorium of St. Louis, August 14. Meetings of such magnitude were unprecedented among Negroes.[1] The vast throngs were drawn from all walks and levels of Negro life—businessmen, teachers, laundry workers, Pullman porters, waiters, and redcaps; preachers, crap shooters, and social workers; jitterbugs and Ph.D.'s. They came and sat in silence, thinking, applauding only when they considered the truth was told, when they felt strongly that something was going to be done about it.

The March on Washington movement is essentially a movement of the people. It is all Negro and pro-Negro, but not for that reason antiwhite or anti-Semitic, or anti-Catholic, or antiforeign, or antilabor. Its major weapon is the nonviolent demonstration of Negro mass power. Negro leadership has united back of its drive for jobs and justice. "Whether Negroes should march on Washington, and if so, when?" will be the focus of a forthcoming national conference. For the plan of a protest march has not been abandoned. Its purpose would be to demonstrate that American Negroes are in deadly earnest, and all out for their full rights. No power on earth can cause them today to abandon their fight to wipe out every vestige of second-class citizenship and the dual standards that plague them.

A community is democratic only when the humblest and weakest person can enjoy the highest civil, economic, and social rights that the biggest and most powerful possess. To trample on these rights of both Negroes and poor whites is such a commonplace in the South that it takes readily to antisocial, antilabor, anti-Semitic, and anti-Catholic propaganda. It was because of laxness in enforcing the

---

[1] In view of charges made that they were subsidized by Nazi funds, it may not be amiss to point out that of the $8,000 expenses of the Madison Square meeting every dime was contributed by Negroes themselves, except for tickets bought by some liberal white organizations.

Weimar constitution in republican Germany that Nazism made headway. Oppression of the Negroes in the United States, like suppression of the Jews in Germany, may open the way for a fascist dictatorship.

By fighting for their rights now, American Negroes are helping to make America a moral and spiritual arsenal of democracy. Their fight against the poll tax, against lynch law, segregation, and Jim Crow, their fight for economic, political, and social equality, thus becomes part of the global war for freedom.

12 : *A Chronology of the New Civil-Rights Protest, 1960-1963*

Claude Sitton

The changing mood of the Negro people and the urgency of their drive for equality emerged . . . [in 1963 in] a protest movement only three and a half years old. . . .

Time and again the Negro's hopes were raised by piecemeal steps toward equality: the Emancipation Proclamation, the social changes growing out of two world wars, and the Supreme Court decision in 1954 against public-school segregation. But these resulted largely from action by whites.

Now, his leaders' statements, his own militant behavior, and the new light in which others see him show that he is no longer an interested bystander in the civil-rights struggle.

. . . The Negro believes that he is as much a master of his destiny as any American.

This significant change began to emerge [in the early part of

Mr. Sitton is chief Southern correspondent for *The New York Times*.

1960] in Greensboro, North Carolina, a Piedmont city of 119,574 persons whose industrial growth and two-party politics make it a symbol of the changing South.

For Negroes, the year 1960 had opened on a somber note. A federal grand jury at Biloxi, Mississippi, refused to indict suspects in the slaying of Mack Charles Parker, a Negro who had been dragged from a jail cell in Poplarville, Mississippi, and lynched while awaiting trial on a charge of raping a white woman.

Tuskegee Institute, in its annual report on race relations, asserted that aside from action by federal courts and agencies the nation had done little in 1959 to improve the Negroes' lot.

There had been earlier indications, principally in the Montgomery, Alabama, bus boycott in 1955–56 that Negroes might find the unity necessary for a broadside assault on segregation and discrimination. But nothing approaching it developed until four youths from North Carolina Agricultural and Technical College walked into the F. W. Woolworth store on Greensboro's North Elm Street at 4:45 P.M., February 1, 1960, and sat down at the "white" lunch counter.

There had been other sit-in's but this one marked the beginning of a series that swept the South and later evolved into a widespread civil-rights movement. This generated the crisis now facing the entire nation.

The sit-in's were at first dismissed as just another college fad. But as their frequency increased, whites appeared baffled. Mayor William G. Enloe of Raleigh, North Carolina, issued a statement at the time that reflected the false hope with which some comforted themselves.

"It is regrettable that some of our young Negro students would risk endangering Raleigh's friendly and co-operative race relations by seeking to change a long-standing custom in a manner that is all but destined to fail," he said.

White Southerners appealed to Negro leaders to halt the demonstrations. Instead, these leaders expressed support for the students, who had become almost overnight the cutting edge of the drive for equality. Signs of dissatisfaction over the slow pace of desegregation in schools and other public facilities became increasingly evident throughout the Negro community.

Informal organizations sprang up at colleges and universities outside the South to support the demonstrators. Even a few white Southern students joined Negroes at lunch counters in Durham, North Carolina, Nashville, and Atlanta.

Far more than the Supreme Court school decision, the sit-in's convinced white leaders in the South that the end of segregation was inevitable. A surprising number of them outside the hard-core segregationist states sought to find a compromise. Although many of them were motivated by economic considerations stemming from Negro boycotts and the loss of white business that resulted from the threat of disorder, a number of communities nevertheless removed racial barriers for the first time without legal compulsion.

Seven months after the sit-in's had begun, the Southern Regional Council reported that a survey had found that at least 70,000 Negroes and whites had actively participated in the protests. The campaign had spread to all of the Southern and border states, as well as into Nevada, Illinois, and Ohio—twenty in all. An estimated total of 3,600 students and their supporters had been arrested.

But these, perhaps, were the least important results of the demonstrations. Profound changes began to become apparent with the civil-rights movement, its leaders, and its organizations. These changes included the formation of a new group.

This took place in April, 1960, when representatives of student groups in the South and North met at Shaw University in Raleigh on Easter week end and formed the Student Nonviolent Co-ordinating Committee. Members of Snick, as it is popularly known, soon became and remain today the shock troops of the civil-rights struggle in the South.

The Congress of Racial Equality, which had pioneered the sit-in's, followed its founding in Chicago in 1941, guided and advised many of the demonstrations in 1960 and thus gained a foothold in the South.

The Reverend Dr. Martin Luther King, Jr., who had gained prominence as a leader of the Montgomery bus boycott, stepped up the activity of his Southern Christian Leadership Conference. He founded the organization, chiefly a coalition of local groups led by Negro ministers, in 1957.

The National Association for the Advancement of Colored People, oldest and largest of the civil-rights organizations, began to place increasing emphasis on sit-in's and other forms of direct action against racial barriers. The stimulus came from criticism that its leaders had relied too heavily on legal action.

One success followed another as the movement picked up strength and intensity. Additional impetus came from the Kennedy Administration's inauguration of a much stronger civil-rights policy. Negroes continued to find a sympathetic hearing in the federal courts, especially above the district-court level.

The sit-in's at lunch counters lost momentum but Negroes turned to other forms of protest in attacking segregation in restaurants, churches, parks, playgrounds, and beaches. They also began to press for equal job opportunity, now their chief goal throughout much of the nation.

The freedom riders met a riotous reception in Anniston, Birmingham, and Montgomery, Alabama, in May, 1961. This phase of the movement was short-lived and involved no more than a thousand persons. But it brought a ruling from the Interstate Commerce Commission prohibiting segregation on buses and in bus terminals and it spurred Justice Department action against all segregation in public transportation.

White Southerners reacted to the rising pressure by making token adjustments, sometimes violently but far more frequently with peaceful, though grudging, acceptance of the inevitable. However, Negroes met increasing resistance as the tide of social change rolled into the deep South.

In Albany, Georgia, local Negroes assisted by Dr. King and other sympathizers from both the South and North encountered a pattern of sophisticated resistance to change as yet unmatched in any other community. There was little or no violence during the campaign's initial stages in 1961, or in 1962 when it was renewed. The police under Chief Laurie Pritchett simply arrested virtually every person who persisted in protesting in the streets.

By far the most serious federal-state controversy since the Civil War developed over federal court orders directing the University of Mississippi to accept James H. Meredith [in 1962]. When he finally entered the university after repeated acts of defiance by Governor Ross R. Barnett and Lieutenant Governor Paul B. Johnson, a riot erupted in which two men died and 375 were wounded. President Kennedy was forced to dispatch troops to assist deputy federal marshals in restoring order.

[The year 1963] brought what some already are calling the turning point of the fight for equality. It began with a spirited drive by Negroes of the Mississippi Delta for voter registration, high-lighted by the demonstrations and arrests in Greenwood.

But it was the conflict between Negroes and resisting white segregationists in Birmingham, with its police dogs and fire hoses, that caught the attention of the nation and touched off demonstrations in the South and North.

Out of Birmingham, one observer has said, came a realization that "the alternatives may not be those of the Civil War—indivisible union or irreparable separation—but they are no less stark and serious: total equality or total repression." . . .

PART III

SOURCES OF THE
CIVIL-RIGHTS
PROTEST

DENIAL OF VOTING RIGHTS TO NEGROES

13 : *Bullets and Ballots in Greenwood, Mississippi*

Claude Sitton

The night of February 28 [1963] was mild with a hint of early spring as the black sedan rolled westward along U.S. Route 82 across the Mississippi Delta. One of its three Negro occupants recalled later that as a string of traffic faded to the rear near Itta Bena, a car that had trailed them from Greenwood pulled alongside. Two white men sat in front, one in back.

Bursts of gunfire rang out. Thirteen .45-caliber bullets stitched a ragged seam of finger-sized holes along the sedan's left side and one copper-jacketed slug burned into the driver's shoulder to within an inch of his spine.

The wounded man, James Travis of Jackson, Mississippi, recovered. He has since returned here to his voter-registration work as a

Mr. Sitton is chief Southern correspondent for *The New York Times*.

field secretary for the Student Nonviolent Co-ordinating Committee.

Five days after the shooting Sheriff John Ed Cothron of Leflore County arrested three Greenwood whites, who were charged with felonious assault. Two are well-known citizens—William H. Greenlee, a petroleum-products wholesaler, and Wesley Kersey, service manager for an industrial company. The third is a juvenile.

This shooting incident, the first of several, set off a string of events that has turned Leflore County into a major battleground in the Southern civil-rights struggle.

Mr. Travis' companions in the car were Robert P. Moses, a field secretary of the student committee and director of the Council of Federated Organizations, and Randolph Blackwell, field director of the Voter Education Project.

The council, known as COFO, is a coalition of Negro organizations that began a concerted voter-registration drive in the Delta last summer. The voter-education project, established last year by the Southern Regional Council, has provided funds for COFO's work.

The attack on the three men set off an angry flurry of activity in the project's headquarters at 5 Forsyth Street in Atlanta. Wiley A. Branton, director of the project, announced a saturation campaign to register Leflore's Negroes, who make up about 64 per cent of the county's population of 47,142.

"The State of Mississippi," he asserted, "has repeatedly thrown down a gauntlet at the feet of would-be Negro voters, not only by the discriminatory practices of the registrar, but also by the economic pressures, threats, coercions, physical violence and death to Negroes seeking the right to vote," he said.

"The time has come for us to pick up the gauntlet. Leflore County has elected itself as the testing ground for democracy and we are accordingly meeting the challenge there."

Leflore County lies on the eastern bulge of the Delta, a football-shaped expanse of fertile fields, pasture lands, and swampy stands of hardwood. This alluvial plain, bounded roughly by the rolling loops of the Mississippi and Yazoo rivers, stretches flat as a table for two hundred miles between Memphis and Vicksburg. . . .

In recent years, increasingly efficient machines and chemicals have revolutionized agriculture here. But mechanization has slashed the need for labor by more than half. Many Negroes have moved away but many still remain.

Greenwood is the state headquarters for the Citizens' Council, a militantly segregationist organization founded in 1954 in adjoining Sunflower County. The John Birch Society followed the council to Greenwood. Many whites consider the voter-registration campaign a Communist plot. Mayor Charles E. Sampson, a loyal member of the Citizens' Council, echoed their sentiments last week when he said that "the only purpose of these agitators is to follow the Communist line of fomenting racial violence."

There are a number of whites who disagree with this attitude and who contend that some compromise must be made with the demands of the Negroes. But they are afraid to speak out publicly.

The Student Nonviolent Co-ordinating Committee began a registration campaign last August in Leflore County. This committee, which grew out of the 1960 sit-in demonstrations against lunchcounter segregation, has headquarters in Atlanta.

Two young Delta Negroes were designated as field secretaries for the project—Willie B. Peacock of Charleston, Mississippi, and Samuel T. Block of Cleveland, Mississippi. A tall, gaunt youth of twenty-five, Mr. Block became the chief target of white animosity in the campaign's early stages. He initially called attention to himself by asserting that he had been beaten by whites at a local automobile-parts business. This drew the first in a long string of denials from whites, who said that they had seen no bruises on him.

The Leflore voter drive met little success last year, according to Mr. Moses. The twenty-eight-year-old Negro, who holds a Master's degree in philosophy, left his job as a mathematics teacher at the Horace Mann School in New York in July, 1961, to come to Mississippi as a field secretary for the student committee.

His explanation for the poor showing is the same one repeated privately by white officials: under present state voting regulations, few if any Negroes can pass the test. Most whites of voting age were registered [before] the more stringent regulations went into effect.

Mrs. Martha T. Lamb, Leflore County Circuit Court Clerk and Registrar, said she did not know how many Negroes were registered because records were not kept by race. She and six other Mississippi registrars are defendants in a broad-scale legal attack on the voting laws that is now before a federal court.

The Justice Department, which brought the suit, states in its complaint that there are 10,274 whites and 13,567 Negroes of voting age in Leflore County. Approximately 95.5 per cent of the whites and 1.9 per cent of the Negroes are registered.

The suit contends that white political supremacy is maintained by regulations that include the following:

Registrants must be able to read, write, and interpret any section of the Mississippi Constitution to the registrar's satisfaction.

Registrants must be of good moral character, as determined by the registrar.

Names of applicants and their addresses must be published for two consecutive weeks in a newspaper of general circulation in the county.

"It applies equally to all, white and black alike," said a member of the County Board of Supervisors with a grin in defending publication of the names.

Despite their dismal prospects, Negroes began applying for registration in increasing numbers in February. The key factor in the increased applications for registration, according to Mr. Moses and a number of white observers, was the growing hunger among the field hands and the refusal of the county to relieve it by distributing surplus food provided by the federal government. Until last fall, Leflore gave the food to public-welfare recipients all year long. It expanded the program during the winter months to include all needy persons.

The county spent only $38,000 of its $2,095,874 budget for the 1961–62 fiscal year to store and distribute the food to 27,000 persons, about 90 per cent of whom were Negroes.

But the Board of Supervisors voted to drop the program for non-welfare recipients last fall. They explained recently that it had cost more than the county could afford and was not needed because of a bumper crop.

Four Justice Department lawyers who toured the county earlier this month reported that they had found widespread evidence of malnutrition. Among the cases they described was that of a mother who could offer her children only a breakfast of fried hoecake and syrup made from water and sugar. Another family had had no breakfast at ten o'clock and said their dinner the night before had been pinto beans and black-eyed peas. Other families said they had one big meal a week—chicken for Sunday morning breakfast.

A thirty-four-year-old widow with nine children, ages one to thirteen, had only one bed and a bottomless chair in her shanty home. She said the plantation manager had given her three dollars a week "furnish money" to be repaid from her earnings and those of her children. She was asked what she did after the cotton chopping and picking seasons.

"Ain't nothing to do but just wait on the calendar," she replied.

A night visit by two newsmen to a plantation cabin found a fifty-seven-year-old Negro hand, his wife, and eleven of their thirteen children crowded before an old television set in one of four rooms.

The crisp stage setting of the *Mikado*, which they were watching, contrasted with the few pieces of sagging furniture, the split and peeling paper on the walls, the pine floor studded with patches of ancient linoleum, and a two-eyed wood stove resting on an automobile wheel rim.

The man, a carpenter and mechanic's helper in the plantation's repair shop, said he made 40 cents an hour or about $20 a week. He receives $10 after payments on a Christmas loan and medical bills are deducted.

The family had just finished a supper of cornbread and fried potatoes. There was no milk for the children.

He was asked what he would choose if granted one wish.

"Rights," he replied. "Freedom, free to speak, free to have a voice, to speak, not be condemned or nothing like that. You know we don't have no voice out here."

As a result of the Justice Department's investigation, the Department of Agriculture told the county that the federal government would pay the cost of distributing the surplus food. If the county still refused, the department said, the government would step in and do the job.

The Board of Supervisors agreed reluctantly to resume the program, with the government paying the cost. And . . . hundreds of Negroes flocked to a warehouse here to receive the food.

Hunger and the urging of the voter-registration workers brought more and more Negroes to the county courthouse on the Yazoo's south bank to register. Committee officials obtained a three-room office in a ramshackle building on McLaurin Street and the harassment resumed.

The campaign workers reported another violent episode the night of March 6. Mr. Block said a station wagon had pulled alongside a car in which he and three others were sitting. A shotgun roared once.

The charge of buckshot was fired at such close range that it failed to disperse as it smashed one front window of the car and then the other before gouging into the wall of a home, the Negroes said.

[A city official,] in a statement, suggested that the incident was a hoax.

"Either by good luck or prearrangement, none of the occupants of the car was injured by the gunfire," he said.

No explanation was offered for the fact that three occupants had been cut by flying glass.

The next night, Mr. Moses reported, a sedan carrying four whites drew up in front of a Negro theater. One pulled out a pistol and fired toward a group waiting on the sidewalk. No one was hit.

Last week brought more violence and the federal intervention that the city had sought to avoid. Night riders fired two blasts of buckshot into a voter worker's home Monday.

"Again, through good fortune or advanced planning, no one was hurt," Mayor Sampson and the City Commissioners said in a statement.

The next morning, about one hundred Negroes marched to the city hall to protest the incident and to demand protection. At the Mayor's orders, the police dispersed them with a German shepherd dog. The dog attacked two voter-registration workers.

In all, nine of the workers, including the top leaders, were arrested. Eight of them were later given the maximum penalty for disorderly conduct—four months in prison and a $200 fine.

The Reverend D. L. Tucker, a minister active in the drive, was bitten Wednesday by the police dog as officers scattered a group of Negroes marching homeward after having applied for registration. He was scrambling to get away from the dog when bitten. . . .

Meanwhile, the Justice Department had filed a request for a federal court order against city and county officials before District

Judge Claude F. Clayton, Jr. It sought to force them to take the following actions:

Release the eight registration workers from prison.

Refrain from further interference with the campaign.

Permit Negroes to exercise their constitutional rights to assemble for peaceable protests and to protect them from whites who might molest them.

The action marked the first time in the civil-rights struggle that the department had interceded to preserve the right of peaceful protest.

However, the department and the city agreed yesterday that Justice Department attorneys would delay their attempt to obtain the injunctions and the city would stay execution of the sentences against the eight registration workers.

The department reportedly was concerned over the threat of violence in Greenwood and the possibility that mass demonstrations might lead to a riot.

There is considerable evidence that an explosion has been averted here so far only because leaders of the Citizens' Council have restrained the more emotional whites. The council's members here include the city's business and professional leaders.

The department's action disappointed sponsors of the voter-registration drive. Campaign leaders issued a statement yesterday pledging continued attempts by prospective voter applicants to walk in groups to the courthouse.

However, a temporary truce in the crisis was reached today between voter-campaign leaders and city officials. The latter agreed that while racial tensions made it necessary they would provide bus transportation between the drive's headquarters and the courthouse.

After tensions subside, according to Police Commissioner B. A. Hammond, the city will permit groups of no more than twenty or so to walk to the courthouse together so long as there is no threat of disorder.

Despite the violence, harassment, and intimidation, the campaign has picked up momentum. Hundreds of persons packed the mass meetings in the city's Negro churches to cheer top leaders in the civil-rights movement.

If local whites could hear the statements being made they might question the accuracy of the Commonwealth's recent observation that "nothing will be changed after democracy has been tested here."

"The white folks are scared," asserted the Reverend James Bevel at one such session. "That's why they turned the dogs loose."

Leflore County's whites have blamed the voter-registration workers, the Kennedy Administration, and the "Communists," in about that order, for the racial crisis.

"It's outsiders that's causing it," said Mayor Sampson recently. "We give them everything. We're building them a new swimming pool. We work very close with the nigger civic league. They're very satisfied."

However, some whites conceded readily in private that it would take more than a new swimming pool to resolve the controversy. Sooner or later, they said, the county will be forced to administer "reasonable" voting tests and to place all qualified persons on the rolls.

14 : *The Pattern of Southern Disen-franchisement of Negroes*

Burke Marshall

For ninety-four years our Constitution has forbidden the states and their officials to deny any of our citizens the right to vote on account of their race. The broader right to vote freely in national elections is a privilege of United States citizenship that federal law has long protected from arbitrary infringement—state or private.

Despite these long-standing guarantees, the United States Commission on Civil Rights has found that racial denials of the right to vote occur in sections of eight states. In five of those states Negroes constitute more than a quarter of the adult population, but very few of these Negroes are registered to vote. For example, in Mississippi only 5 per cent are registered; in Alabama only 14 per cent are registered; in South Carolina, 16 per cent are registered; in Georgia, 26 per cent are registered; and in Louisiana, 29 per cent are registered. Registration among adult whites invariably exceeds 50

Mr. Marshall is Assistant Attorney General in charge of the Civil Rights Division of the United States Department of Justice.

per cent. In eleven counties where Negroes are in the majority none are registered. In ninety-seven counties fewer than 5 per cent of the adult Negroes are on the rolls. Indeed, in most counties with sizable Negro populations the Negro voter totals are significantly below the state-wide percentage of eligible Negroes registered and neither figure approaches the white voter percentage.

In our experience Negro nonvoting results almost exclusively from racial discrimination by state officials and fear among Negroes engendered by the attitudes and actions of white persons—including some officeholders.

After more than eighty years of civil-rights desuetude, Congress adopted a voting statute in 1957—the Civil Rights Act of 1957. Together, the act's four principal sections authorize the Attorney General to institute civil suits in the federal district courts (regardless of whether the persons aggrieved have exhausted other remedies) to prevent and redress racial and other arbitrary interferences with the right to vote.

In 1960 Congress amended the Civil Rights Act in two important ways: (1) The district courts are now authorized to appoint voting referees after finding a pattern of discrimination. The voting referees are to assist the court in receiving and passing upon applications for registration from Negroes in the affected county, if, after court judgment, local officials deny registration to Negroes. (2) The state may be joined as a party defendant in a proceeding involving Section 1971(a) rights, or the state alone may be sued if, prior to the institution of the action, the offending state or local officials have resigned and no successors have been appointed.

Title 3 of the 1960 Act requires that all records and papers relating to registration, the payment of poll taxes, or other acts requisite to voting in federal elections be retained and preserved for a specified period and that they be made available to the Attorney General for inspection and copying. . . .

ILLEGAL SUPPRESSION OF NEGRO VOTING

Four cases have been against defendants who attempted to squelch Negro interest in registration by intimidation, threats, and coercion.

A case which arose in Walthall County, Mississippi, illustrates intimidation by the misuse of local criminal processes. The defendants are the registrar of voters, the sheriff, city attorney, and the district attorney of Walthall County. The government's affidavit in support of its motion for a temporary restraining order recites that John Hardy, a Negro who was conducting a registration school in Walthall County, accompanied two local Negro applicants to the registrar's office. They had barely arrived when the registrar ordered Hardy from the office and struck him on the head with a gun as he complied. The sheriff arrested Hardy a few hours later, charged him with disturbing the peace, put him in jail where he was interviewed for several hours by the district attorney with a tape recorder, and required him to post bond before being released and to appear in the justice-of-the-peace court for trial.

The court of appeals has enjoined the state's prosecution of Hardy pending a hearing in the federal district court on our contention that the treatment of Hardy is an illegal intimidation of Walthall County's Negro would-be voters.

Three cases involving economic coercion arose in Haywood and Fayette counties, Tennessee. They seek to enjoin more than 150 defendants, including landowners, banks, and business associations, from intimidating and coercing Negro citizens for the purpose of interfering with their right to register to vote in federal elections.

Despite their numerical preponderance in both counties, no Negroes were registered in Haywood in 1959 and very few were on the rolls in Fayette. The department's complaints charge that when registration by Negroes began in 1959 the defendants undertook to circulate lists of the names of Negroes who were active in the registration movement for the purpose of inducing the white community to engage in a variety of economic reprisals against them, including loss of employment, denial of loans and other credit. The complaint also charged that when this form of intimidation was not successful, the defendants began a series of mass evictions of share croppers who had registered to vote. Consent judgments favorable to the government have just been entered in the Beaty, Barcroft, and Atkeison cases. Significantly, about 3,000 and 2,000 Negroes are now registered in Fayette and Haywood counties, respectively.

The fifth case involved intimidation of Francis Joseph Atlas, a Negro farmer from a Louisiana parish in which no Negroes are registered although they outnumber the white persons. Francis Joseph Atlas, a Negro cotton farmer who had raised twelve children and given college educations to all but the youngest two (they were in high school), tried several times to register to vote. He was told when he took his cotton to be ginned that his cotton wouldn't gin. When he asked why, the ginner replied, "Civil rights." Mr. Atlas had been subpoenaed to testify about his efforts to register and when this was known all of the cotton ginners in the community decided that they would not gin any more of Mr. Atlas' cotton.

The soybean processors refused to process his beans. Merchants from whom Atlas had bought farm supplies refused to trade with him. For example, the one feed-store clerk in the store told Atlas that he had orders not to handle sales to Atlas and that he would have to see the manager. Atlas went to the manager and the manager said, "Yes, I gave those orders. I have enough customers without you. I don't need your business. I would appreciate it if you don't come back."

The Department of Justice complaint asked the court to issue an order requiring the cotton ginners and other merchants in Atlas' community to open the channels of trade to him on the same basis as they were open to other citizens. Under pressure from the court Atlas' cotton was ginned and he is still farming in his community. He is still not registered, but the government has also brought suit to prevent the local registrars from denying Negroes their franchise and this suit has already been submitted to the district court on the merits.

DISCRIMINATORY DISQUALIFICATION OF NEGRO APPLICANTS

Where Negroes are unafraid and undeterred by discriminatory rejection of their leaders who attempt to register, they apply in significant numbers. Often there are threshold problems; e.g., registrars secrete themselves in unlikely places in the courthouse and, when ferreted out, they resign their offices which go unfilled for long periods.

However, most of the rejections of qualified Negroes are effected by the manipulation of the lengthy and intricate registration procedures and standards that are employed in five of the problem states. Many of these "tests" were originally designed to facilitate the arbitrary exclusion of Negro applicants and their present use to that end is widespread.

1. *Identification Device*

Negroes have been prevented from applying for registration by the requirement that they produce one or more registered voters to "vouch" for them, that is, to identify them. Louisiana law authorizes this procedure where the registrar "has good reason to believe that [the applicant] is not the same person" whom he represents himself to be. The Alabama application form contains a similar requirement. Where few or no Negroes are registered, they are, in effect, dependent upon white voters to vouch for them. Three cases filed by the Department of Justice attack this requirement as applied.

The first case arose in Bullock County, Alabama, where only five of the 4,450 Negroes of voting age were registered in 1960. The county board of registrars had a rule that applicants for registration must be "vouched" for by a registered voter and that a voucher could identify only two applicants in a calendar year. The only Negro applicant during 1960 was a minister who was rejected twice. One of the Negro registrants vouched for him on both attempts. Later the voucher accompanied his son, a teacher, to the registration office. The teacher was not permitted to apply because his father had exhausted his "vouches" for 1960. The district court invalidated the limitation rule as patently unconstitutional.

The second case arose in East Carroll Parish, Louisiana. No Negroes have been registered there since 1922 although they are the adult majority. The suit charges that Negroes have been effectively denied the opportunity to apply by the requirement that they must produce two registered voters to identify them. White persons have had no difficulty with the identification requirement because, among other reasons, they are permitted to be identified by their previous registration. The case was decided favorably to the government; as of mid-July the procedures of the 1960 statute were being invoked to determine the qualifications of Negro applicants.

The third case arose in Madison Parish, Louisiana, where no Negro has been registered since 1900. The facts alleged are essentially those of the East Carroll case. No trial date has been set.

The discriminatory use of Louisiana's identification requirement was held unconstitutional in 1952 when the registrar of voters of Bossier Parish was enjoined from engaging in this practice. This illustrates one of the recurrent problems faced by the Department of Justice: one injunction against a practice does not necessarily end that practice in other counties. The result is a time-consuming multiplicity of suits.

2. Devices Involving Literacy and Understanding

Negroes who overcome the threshold problems and make application to register may be rejected on one or several grounds even though they possess the same qualifications as white persons who are registered in the county. This results from the discretion vested in registrars to administer ostensibly neutral literacy and understanding tests. In some states, including Georgia and Alabama, applicants for registration are required to be able to read and write any paragraph (or article) of the Constitution of the United States (or of the state). In Alabama applicants are also required to fill out a lengthy application and questionnaire without assistance.

In Louisiana and Mississippi applicants for registration are required to understand (or read) and give a reasonable interpretation of any section of the Constitution of the state (or of the United States). These states also require each applicant to fill out a form without assistance.

(a) The Read and Write Test. The Georgia and Alabama reading and writing requirements have been involved in two cases brought by the Department of Justice under Section 1971(a).

One case arose in Terrell County, Georgia, where only fifty-three of 4,057 Negroes over eighteen were registered in 1958. Negro schoolteachers had been denied registration on account of their failure to pass the oral reading test. One of the teachers mispronounced the word "equity." A Negro applicant with one year of college was rejected on the ground that he could not write legibly. In fact, by dictating unreasonably fast, the registrar made it impossible for the applicant to transcribe the passage accurately. The court found that Negroes were required to read and write more lengthy and difficult constitutional provisions, that the procedures resulted in easier tests for white applicants, and that a higher literacy level was required of Negroes.

The Alabama case arose in Macon County where Negro applicants, including many with college degrees, had been denied registration on the ground that they had made "errors" in filling out their applications. White applicants, including at least one illiterate and others with little or no education, were assisted in filling out their applications and were registered.

Negro applicants were repeatedly required to copy lengthy portions of the Constitution, ostensibly to demonstrate their literacy. For example, Mrs. Marie Williams, who had had three years of college and who applied unsuccessfully five times, was required on each try to copy Article II of the United States Constitution (about 1,000 words). She wrote a total of twenty pages. Thus was the literacy test used to discourage and delay Negro registration.

(*b*) The Application Form as a Test. In counties in Alabama, Mississippi, and Louisiana the application forms themselves have been used as a test. These forms appear to be intended to secure routine, superficial information about the applicant and they are unobjectionable when used in this way. But, again and again, well-educated Negroes, who set forth all the substantive data called for, have been denied registration because they made trivial errors on the form. Because the states have not issued prescribed answers, even to the registrars, eminently qualified Negroes are compelled to play a humiliating, futile form game with registrars who set their own standards and who often refuse to apprise unsuccessful applicants as to where they erred.

Conversely, white applicants usually get all the help they need, from each other and from the registrars, to fill out the form. Moreover, white applicants whose forms contain errors for which Negroes are rejected are almost invariably registered if the basic information requested by the form appears on it in some comprehensible way.

Several cases illustrate these practices. In one Alabama action the government showed that, between January 1, 1956, and June 16, 1961, a board of registrars accepted 96.6 per cent of the white applicants while rejecting 75.4 per cent of the applications by Negroes. Seven hundred and ten of the "unqualified" Negroes had twelve or more years of formal education and among them they had filed over 1,200 applications. These Negroes' applications were rejected as improperly executed. It developed that, as applied to white persons, the forms were questionnaires, not tests.

Similarly, documents and testimony in a Mississippi case disclose that white registrants' applications bear "x" marks at an oath line which Negroes, whose applications are unmarked, were rejected for their failure to sign.

Finally, several thousand Negro voters were challenged and removed from the rolls in Louisiana on the ground that they had made errors in filling out their original application cards. White registrants who had made similar or worse errors were not even challenged. The Department of Justice has attacked this practice in four cases under Section 1971(a) and the two cases decided have resulted in the restoration to the voting rolls of more than 1,800 Negroes.

(c) The Interpretation Test. The Louisiana interpretation test has been challenged per se in *United States* v. *Louisiana*. The requirement that applicants for registration must be able to understand and give a reasonable interpretation of any section of the Constitution is attacked on the ground that the history and setting in which this test was adopted and has been enforced, and the uncontrolled discretion which is vested in registrars who administer the test, render it unconstitutional under Section 1971 and under the Fourteenth and Fifteenth Amendments.

The discriminatory administration of the test is challenged in four other suits which have previously been filed by the department under Section 1971. Only one of these cases has been tried and decided. There, Negro schoolteachers, one of whom had a Master's degree from Stanford University, were denied registration on the ground that they did not interpret a provision of the Constitution to the satisfaction of the registrar. The court found that less stringent standards were applied to white applicants, who were invariably registered, than to Negro applicants, none of whom had been registered. On the other hand once the registrar adopted the formality of giving the constitutional interpretation tests to whites, sections such as "there shall be no imprisonment for debt" were used or if the section was harder the white applicant was given an opportunity to copy an answer.

The government's proof on a motion for a preliminary injunction in a Mississippi case shows that all Negro applicants have been subjected to the interpretation test but that none of the white persons took it before January 1961. Moreover, the Negroes are invariably confronted with lengthy, highly legalistic provisions and none have been registered since the mid-fifties.

3. Impeding Poll Tax Payments by Negroes

Five states now require the payment of poll taxes as a prerequisite to voting, although not to registration. By now the tax itself is a negligible, biracial deterrent to voting. However, local officials occasionally manipulate the requirement so as to disfranchise Negroes.

In one Mississippi county white voters pay their poll taxes to "collecting deputies" in either of the county sheriff's widely separated offices. Negroes who proffer their payments to the deputies are invariably told to see the sheriff, who is rarely in either office and never in both.

The Section 1971(a) case, which seeks to equalize the payment procedures, is presently on appeal from the district court's denial of the government's motion for a preliminary injunction.

4. A White Primary

It is generally assumed that white primaries are extinct. In 1959, however, as Negroes began to register in significant numbers in rural Fayette County, Tennessee, local Democratic leaders hit upon a plan to insure continued white control of county offices. For the biennial local primary, election notices were placed in each ballot box to the effect that voter participation was confined to white Democrats. The election officials followed the notices and our Section 1971(a) suit followed the election.

A consent judgment barring discrimination in any process used to select local candidates was entered prior to the 1961 primary in which Negroes voted freely. . . .

RACIAL DISCRIMINATION IN EMPLOYMENT

15 : *Jobs for Negroes—the Unfinished Revolution*

A. Philip Randolph

. . . With the advent of World War I, masses of Negroes migrated North, many of them refugees from technological displacement in Southern agriculture, and Negroes for the first time made an entry into modern industry. The rate of unemployment among the race was reduced and its earning capacity increased. Still, Negroes remained concentrated in domestic service and unskilled occupations throughout the prosperous twenties, and their position was less secure than that of white workers. Although Negroes constituted only 5 per cent of Detroit's male workers in 1926, they composed 16 per cent of the unemployed.

A. Philip Randolph is the President, Brotherhood of Sleeping Car Porters, Vice-President. AFL-CIO. and organizer of the 1941–1942 March on Washington movement.

The Negro's marginal economic position was catastrophically demonstrated during the great depression of the thirties, during which nearly half of the Negroes in skilled occupations were displaced. In 1931, 60 per cent of the Negro workers in Detroit were unemployed, as compared with 32 per cent of the white workers. Unemployment among both races was understandably higher in the industrialized North than in the more agricultural South, but in the North, in 1937, Negro unemployment stood at 39 per cent and white unemployment at 18 per cent. In 1935, more than half of the Negroes in Northern cities were on relief as compared with one-third in Southern cities.

President Franklin D. Roosevelt's New Deal brought many benefits to the pauperized black man, but he remained industrially submerged on the eve of the armaments build-up that immediately preceded World War II. The Negro had been trained in small-scale construction and was handicapped when government-financed construction programs were undertaken in the early thirties. Racial discrimination persisted in hiring, as it did in the administration of the welfare measures of the New Deal, especially in the South. As late as October 1940, after eight years of the New Deal, approximately one-fourth of the Negro work force was unemployed, as against 13 per cent of the white work force. Nor was the problem, then as now, simply education. Only 4 per cent of all Negro college graduates in 1940 had an annual income of $2,500 or more. The comparable figure for whites was 34 per cent.

The launching of the defense program in 1940, however much it may have aided white workers, did not lead to a significant increase in the employment of Negroes by arms producers. Despite the antidiscrimination pronouncements of the New Deal administrators, Negroes continued to be barred from these industries. The Negro relearned a basic lesson: Even from his friends he could expect little unless he backed up his demands with large-scale social pressures.

Thus the March on Washington movement was born. Thousands of Negroes throughout the country, spearheaded by the Brotherhood of Sleeping Car Porters, mobilized for a 100,000-strong convergence on the nation's capital with a demand for equal employment opportunities in the defense industries. Many efforts were made to have the march called off, and on one occasion I was summoned to talk with President Roosevelt at the White House. When it became clear that we would not be cajoled, a reluctant President signed an executive order in June, 1941, reaffirming the government's policy of nondiscrimination and establishing a Fair Employment Practices Commission to investigate violations of this policy in defense industries.

To what degree FEPC was responsible for the rise in Negro employment that followed has been debated. Certainly, where FEPC was successful, it was accompanied by government pressure, training opportunities, and the existence of full employment. Without full employment generally, the effectiveness of fair-employment practices legislation would have been diminished as competition for jobs increased. The New Deal never succeeded in achieving full employment for either race until the initiation of full war production.

Of comparable importance for the Negro workers was the rise of industrial unionism in the late thirties. For the first time since the decline of the Knights of Labor, an active effort was made to bring Negro workers into the unions. Not surprisingly, the leaders of the new movement were those unions in which Negroes had all along been represented, particularly the United Mine Workers, which in 1900 could claim one-third of the total organized Negro labor force. Negroes played an important role in organizing the steelworkers, and in New York City the Negro Labor Committee helped bring Negroes into a wide variety of CIO unions. Only isolated instances of segregated locals in the Southern textile industry marred the CIO's early nondiscrimination policies. By 1940 the CIO had received into membership 210,000 Negroes, who gradually acquired new industrial skills. In 1940, 4.4 per cent of Negro male workers were skilled; four years later the figure had risen to 7.3 per cent. Correspondingly, the figure for the semiskilled rose from 12 per cent to 22.4 per cent. It was during this period that Negroes became predominantly urbanized.

At the same time the Negro made large gains in civil and economic rights, principally because of the militance of industrial unionism, but the fundamental precariousness of his position was demonstrated once again at the end of World War II. With the curtailment of war production, Negroes lost jobs more rapidly than did whites. Negroes not only lacked seniority, but many of them were concentrated in those war industries that were least convertible to peacetime production. The plight of Negro labor was callously aggravated when Congress killed the FEPC in 1946.

In withdrawing its support of the equal-opportunities principle, Congress paved the way for the decline of skilled Negro craftsmen and foremen. Having won the war against racism abroad, with the help of her thirteen million Negroes, the nation apparently no longer felt constrained to continue that war at home. Once again the federal government had abandoned the Negro to economic oppression.

Recent years have seen progress in the Negro's struggle for equal opportunities. In the absence of federal legislation, a score of states and numerous cities have enacted their own fair-employment practices programs. Direct action by Negroes at the 1948 Democratic party convention was largely responsible for President Harry S. Truman's executive order ending segregation in the armed forces. President John F. Kennedy's Committee on Equal Employment Opportunity, established in March 1961, is a considerable improvement over its predecessor, though it still lacks some of the powers of Roosevelt's FEPC. The 1961 Civil Rights Commission report provided documentation that discrimination persists in employment created by federal grants-in-aid and loan programs, as well as in national guard and reserve units. Moreover, the commission has reported: "Efforts of the Federal government to promote nondiscriminatory employment by government contractors and Federal agencies have not generally been effective in overcoming resistance to hiring Negroes in any but the lower categories."

The labor movement itself has made some advances. During the forties, there were still twenty-six AFL affiliates where constitutions barred Negroes from membership—and thus from fruitful employment. Today only the Brotherhood of Locomotive Firemen and Enginemen explicitly excludes Negroes. Twenty-six international unions and seventeen state central bodies have established civil-rights committees. One and a half million Negroes are now members of labor unions, and they have won increasing representation in labor's governing councils, even in the South. The 1961 AFL-CIO civil-rights resolution forthrightly proclaimed:

"The AFL-CIO is in the forefront of the civil rights revolution in our land. It is a foremost force in the drive to eliminate and prevent every form of race discrimination and race injustice in the American community."

No comparable statement has come from any national manufacturing organization.

Still, resolutions are not enough. In apprenticeship training, hiring policies, seniority lists, pay scales, and job assignments, discrimination persists in many locals, especially in the building trades. Negroes continue to be barred from some unions, segregated in others. To combat these evils, hundreds of Negro trade-unionists banded together in 1959 to found the Negro American Labor Council, the most recent of the Negro's efforts to achieve equal employment opportunities. Loyal to the labor movement and recognizing it as the most progressive institution in our society, the NALC has fought vigorously to cleanse the trade-unions of every vestige of Jim Crow. Racism, the NALC insists, is incompatible with labor's needs and aspirations; it is no less an evil than Communism and corruption, and must be met with equal severity.

It is foolish to deny as it is fruitless to proclaim that progress in employment opportunities has been made during the past century. But progress does not controvert the fact that the Negro today faces an economic crisis without precedent. For progress is relative, and we are in a period when rapid forward movement is required merely to stand still.

The crisis confronting the Negro worker today can be summed up in one word: automation. The displacement of men by machines hits the unskilled and semiskilled workers first and hardest, and these are the jobs to which Negroes traditionally have been relegated.

As late as 1955, only 12 per cent of the Negro work force, as compared with 42 per cent of whites, had risen into professional, technical, managerial, and white-collar clerical and sales jobs. Forty-seven per cent of working Negroes were in service and other unskilled nonfarm jobs. Another 15 per cent were in agriculture. At present there is no single skilled craft in which Negroes constitute even 2 per cent of the workers. More ominous than the figures themselves is the fact that the elevation rate of the Negro into more skilled occupations has fallen behind the rate of automation displacement.

Nowhere is the crisis more starkly revealed than in unemployment figures, which point to an almost steady deterioration in the position of the Negro worker. Whereas the unemployment rate during the years 1947–55 did not exceed 8.9 per cent for Negroes and 4.6 per cent for whites, the rate in 1958 was 12.6 per cent and 6.1 per cent respectively. In August, 1962, the Bureau of Labor statistics revealed 11.4 per cent of the Negro work force unemployed as compared with 4.6 per cent of white workers. Labor economists have informed me that in reality the number of Negro unemployed may run twice that percentage. In Detroit, 60 per cent of those workers currently unemployed are Negroes, although Negroes constitute only 20 per cent of the population. Thus, despite all progress, the Negro unemployment rate has remained double that of whites for decades, and at the moment it is two and one-half times that of whites.

The extent to which the Negro unemployment rate is traceable to automation is suggested in the statistics on chronic unemployment, most of which involves victims of technological displacement. At present, among those unemployed for more than fifteen weeks, 23.8 per cent are nonwhite.

In comparing incomes, the ratio is reversed: whites take home twice as much in wages as do Negroes. This, too, has been true for decades. But, as Dr. Whitney Young of the National Urban League has recently reported, the average annual Negro income is now $3,233, 54 per cent of the average white family's income of $5,835, whereas ten years ago the proportion was 57 per cent.

Statistics can be endlessly elaborated, and their meaning is always plain: The relative position of the Negro in the economy has remained astonishingly static over the years, and the future threatens worsening of even that woeful position. The Negro is not the only loser. According to the United States Civil Rights Commission, automation is likely, ultimately, to create more skilled jobs than there will be men to fill them. Yet, as a nation we passively observe the languishing of untapped talent in stagnant pools of unskilled labor continuously drained by automation into the sewers of unemployment.

Meanwhile, we have passed the stage where fair-employment practices on the part of management, unions, and government can, in themselves, suffice. A massive job retraining program is required on a scale infinitely more ambitious than anything now envisioned.

Segregation and discrimination in education, on all levels, must be abolished without delay, so that future generations of Negroes will not inherit the handicaps of the past and present. As a matter of inflexible principle, federal funds must be withheld from all institutions and enterprises, public or private, that practice, condone, or acquiesce in discrimination. There is pressing need for large-scale public-works programs to provide immediate jobs for the millions of unemployed Negroes. . . .

16 : *The Waste of Negro Talent in a Southern State*

Gene Roberts, Jr.

. . . In North Carolina, the lack of job opportunity for Negroes is a sweeping problem. It affects not only the high-school graduate, but the Negro who has earned a college degree, the valedictorian as well as the public-school dropout. During a detailed study of the state's Negro population, the State Welfare Department's consultant on Negro affairs became convinced that the lack of job opportunity is North Carolina's major racial question. "The job to the mass of North Carolina Negroes," said John R. Larkins, "means largely four types of work: common labor, personal service, domestic service and agriculture pursuits. Jobs in which Negroes have a virtual monopoly are in logging camps, fertilizer plants, as laborers in stores, janitors of buildings, elevator operators, woodyard workers, and general common laborers. Female workers are usually domestic servants and laundresses."

Larkins completed his study in 1957, but later statistics have reinforced his conviction. In 1959, the State Employment Security

Mr. Roberts is a political reporter for the Raleigh, North Carolina, *News and Observer.*

Commission succeeded in placing only one Negro in professional and managerial positions for every seventy-four whites. For every sixty-two clerical and sales positions that went to whites, the Negroes received one. Nine skilled jobs and eight semiskilled positions were given white workers for each one that went to Negroes. It was only in service positions and unskilled jobs that the Negro held an employment edge. Seven Negroes were placed in service jobs for every two whites, and in unskilled work five Negroes were hired for every two whites. . . .

State-government employment, like that in private industry, is also largely closed to Negroes. Out of the estimated seven thousand jobs in Raleigh's state administrative headquarters, there are only about two dozen Negroes who hold jobs above the rank of janitor and messenger. There are three secretaries serving one Negro administrator in the Welfare Department, and seven Negro supervisors in the Department of Public Instruction. State Prison headquarters employs three Negroes—a rehabilitation supervisor, a chaplain, and a recreation supervisor. The Probation Commission has three probation officers who are Negroes; and eight Negroes work as investigators with the State Alcoholic Beverage Control Board.

How much does a college degree assist a Negro in getting a job in North Carolina? If the college graduate wants a career in teaching, law, or social work, he may find his degree of some assistance. But if he wants a job in business or industry, his college years may have been spent in vain. "I know of no industries which actively try to hire our students," said Dr. Rufus Perry, president of Johnson C. Smith University for Negroes in Charlotte. At Livingstone College for Negroes in Salisbury, none of the ninety-two students who graduated in 1960 found employment in business or industry. Other North Carolina Negro colleges reported similar job-placement results. In contrast, recruiters for business and industry swarmed onto the campus of the predominantly white University of North Carolina last spring. The University Placement Service said that 393 firms "from throughout the nation" conducted 2,803 campus interviews in the four months preceding the end of the school term. In addition, 357 job openings were listed by letter with the placement service.

Blocked from entering industrial fields, the Negro graduates arm themselves with teaching certificates and flood the state's market for Negro teachers. Out of 1,007 prospective teachers who graduated from North Carolina's eleven Negro colleges in 1961, only 50 per cent of the elementary teachers and 22 per cent of the high-school teachers found teaching positions in the state. Five months after graduation, 12 per cent of the teacher graduates in the elementary field were unable to find work either in or out of the state. Of the graduates trained to teach in high school 10 per cent were still seeking employment. In the white teaching field, the state had difficulty filling all of the vacancies. Less than 1 per cent of the white teacher graduates were in need of jobs at the end of five months. The jobless whites were unable to find employment only because they majored in "overcrowded teaching fields," Department of Public Instruction officials said.

What do the Negroes do when their ambitions are frustrated in North Carolina? Some accept jobs as maids and elevator operators, but many leave the state. William Peace, for example, is twenty-five, a college graduate, and a statistic—one of an estimated 185,000 Negroes who have left North Carolina since 1950.

William had to leave [said his mother, Mrs. W. H. Peace of Raleigh]. He graduated from Shaw University in February in the upper one-fourth of his class. He looked around and looked around for a job, but the only thing he could find was janitorial work. Maybe he could have got a job eventually in the school system, but he didn't think he was meant to be a teacher. So in May, he borrowed his father's car, packed up his clothes and headed for New York. He's got a good job now as a social investigator with the New York Public Welfare Department.

North Carolina Negroes packed their suitcases like William Peace and left the state at the rate of forty-three per day in the decade of the fifties. . . . Included in the migration statistics were too many William Peace's, Dr. Hamilton concluded. "Migration losses are heaviest among Negroes who have had high school and college training," he said. "And without exception, the lowest net migration loss rates among non-white males are found in the no-education category."

. . . In Goldsboro, Barnes Business College for Negroes graduated thirty-five students in 1961. Four months after graduation,

only seven were employed in North Carolina in the work for which
they were trained.

As some North Carolinians see it, the outward flow of Negroes
is more than a simple population loss. It is a financial blow to the
state, as well. McNeill Smith, chairman of the State Civil Rights
Advisory Committee, once said:

> If, instead of employing on a merit basis, we confine Negroes
> and Indians by custom if not by law to menial jobs, then we neg-
> lect and drive away the skilled graduates of the schools we have
> built and keep the remaining ones in oversupply. We pay for this
> waste not only in reduced gross product of our state, but directly
> in welfare and unemployment benefits, charities, and dissipation
> of character. . . . In addition, our industry and commerce are de-
> prived of a substantial market for our goods and services.

Harry Golden, editor of the *Carolina Israelite*, observed that

> [t]he citizens of our state year after year, with loyalty and gen-
> erosity, pay out thousands upon thousands of tax dollars to edu-
> cate the children of our state. They send the children to elemen-
> tary school, junior high, high school; provide dental care, lunches,
> transportation, books, and even college training if it's desired.
> And, after all that trouble and expense, on the day that the boy
> belonging to one segment of our population receives a diploma,
> he also buys a railroad ticket to Philadelphia, Pennsylvania, or
> Flint, Michigan. We have lavished all of that wealth and trained
> him for a specialized job and then refuse to expose him to the
> possibility of getting that job.

Numerically, North Carolina's Negro population has increased
in every decade since 1900. But, because of migration, the proportion of Negroes in the state has dwindled from 33 per cent in 1900
to 25.4 per cent in 1960. "And this proportional decline has occurred in spite of a relatively high birth rate and a decreasing infant
mortality rate among Negroes," said Welfare Consultant Larkins.
Job migration problems are not confined to North Carolina alone,
however. Both problems may well be more acute in other Southern
states. In Mississippi, the Negro migration rate in the fifties exceeded the birth rate. And, when the National Urban League surveyed more than two hundred of the South's leading industrial

plants two years ago, it found a few Negro white-collar workers in North Carolina. Other Southern states had none.

Much of the Negro's employment dilemma seems to have sprung directly from prejudice and discrimination. When the American Friends Service Committee surveyed business firms in Greensboro in 1958, it found that 235 firms were not willing to employ "without discrimination." Another 114 indicated they were willing to employ without discrimination in some of their jobs. Only fifty-three firms said they were willing to hire for all jobs without regard to race, color, or creed. Did the firms with discriminatory hiring policies feel that the passage of time might temper the policies? Forty-three firms said that they might in the future enlarge the number of jobs open to any qualified person, but 174 said they definitely will not employ without discrimination in the future.

Discrimination, however, does not appear to be the only factor contributing to the Negro's job dilemma. Many Negroes lack the training for technical and highly skilled jobs. Most Negro high schools, like many of their white counterparts, offer no vocational courses other than agriculture and elementary industrial arts. But white North Carolinians can take specialized industrial training in the state's network of industrial-education centers. Negroes, for the most part, are not admitted for the industrial-education courses. Again, employment is closed to the Negro in some fields because he doesn't have the necessary experience. Here, he is caught in a vicious circle. He can't get the job without experience and he can't get experience without the job.

Some of the responsibility for the lack of Negro job opportunity may rest with the Negro educators themselves. Because Negroes traditionally have been kept out of certain employment fields, principals and teachers often discourage their students from investing time and money for training that, at best, would be a long-shot gamble at job opportunity. . . .

North Carolina's leadership has sensed the need for more jobs and has launched an extensive industrialization program. The announced objective is to raise the state's low (forty-third in the nation) per capita income. In the fifties, 200,793 new jobs were created in the state by new and expanded industries. An overwhelming majority of the jobs, however, went to whites. "A number of new industries hire some Negroes and a few have given employment exclusively to Negroes," said William R. Henderson, who heads the industrialization program for the State Department of Conservation and Development. "Most of the new industries, however, have an all-white labor force." It seems an almost elementary economic fact that North Carolina and other Southern states cannot succeed in raising per capita income until they have found employment for the Negro population. "Until we find adequate income for all of our people we are not going to enjoy a good per capita income in the state," Henderson said. In the South, in 1959, the median income of nonwhite males was only one-third as much as for white males. In the Northeastern, North Central, and Western states, the gap between white and Negro income was not nearly so wide. Nonwhites in the non-Southern states had a median income three-fourths that of the white population.

Employers who hire on the basis of merit instead of race often find the policy helps, not hurts, their businesses. . . . The Archdale Hosiery & Machine Company of High Point instituted a program in 1954 to train Negro girls as loopers. The firm's secretary-treasurer, G. E. Brewer, described the result:

> The relationships between the colored and the whites in the business proved so satisfactory that we decided in 1959 to put in Negro knitters. We took several young men who had never seen a knitting machine and trained them. In nine weeks after we started this program our production was back up ninety-four per cent. Our experience with them has been excellent. We have found them to be very congenial, eager to learn and anxious to raise their standard of living. It is my belief that if other mills would try it they would find the same satisfactory results.

Is there any likelihood that other firms will follow the lead of Archdale Hosiery? One of the best hopes for further Negro employment breakthroughs is a new federal policy which forbids firms with government contracts to discriminate in their hiring practices. But the potential of the policy, which applies to Southern as well as Northern firms, is far from being realized in North Carolina. . . .

In at least two North Carolina cities, Durham and Raleigh, Negroes have brought pressure to bear on merchants and city officials in attempts to break down employment barriers. Last Easter, Durham Negroes began boycotting a group of retail outlets which hired no Negroes. Within six months, twenty-five supermarkets, downtown clothing and department stores had employed thirty-five Negro sales clerks. In Raleigh, the Citizens Association and the NAACP launched an employment-improvement program with a less successful boycott of food stores and with an appeal to the city council for equal employment opportunity in city government. There are no Negro firemen, secretaries, or administrative workers in city government in Raleigh, a delegation told the council. The city employs no Negro policemen above the rank of patrolman.

One of the state's Negro newspapers, the *Carolina Times* in Durham, has urged Negroes to consider voting Republican in an effort to open employment opportunities in state government. "So long as Negro voters continue to be 'in the bag' for the Democratic Party or any other party in this state, just so long will they be compelled to remain satisfied with the crumbs that are thrown from its political table," the Durham paper said.

No widespread solution to the job dilemma may come, however, until both Negro and white leaders recognize the problem as one that must be solved if the state is to progress. There have been only a few attempts to deal with the dilemma through interracial co-operation. A Negro industrialization drive, in which whites also participated, recently resulted in the establishment of a sewing factory in Clinton. In Rocky Mount, a community development program attracted the Dunlee Corporation, a firm that manufactures plastic baby pants. "We consider it a matter of our own self-interest to help these Negroes qualify for good jobs at steady wages," said Hugh Sawyer, executive secretary of the Rocky Mount Chamber of Commerce. "We at the . . . Chamber know that, regardless of color or sex, a citizen has to make more than the amount of money necessary to satisfy the landlord and the grocery bill in order to be an economic asset to our city."

Any community which solved its Negro job problem could expect more than an economic dividend, according to State Welfare Department Consultant Larkins; the social conditions and physical setting of a community are closely tied to the job problem. "The majority of homes occupied by Negroes are dreary dwellings on neglected streets without pavement, littered by accumulated waste, in the oldest and least desirable residential sections of the city." Why? The lack of economic opportunity had stifled ambition in many Negroes and contributed directly to squalid living conditions. When ambition existed in a Negro family, Larkins learned, its members rarely had the economic means to improve their surroundings. Crime and delinquency can also be traced to the economic problem.

The high rate of crime and delinquency among Negroes is an indication of individual and group maladjustment [Larkins said]. This maladjustment is easily understood in the light of unequal opportunities, economic insecurity and substandard living conditions. In many cases, the head of the household can't earn enough to support the family. So the mother leaves her children at home to care for someone else's children as a domestic. Without someone at home to care for them the children go undisciplined; they play in the streets; their problems go unsolved. I sometimes wonder why we don't have more crime and delinquency than we do.

17 : *Racial Barriers in Union Apprentice Programs*

Herbert Hill

. . . The current status of the Negro wage earner is characterized by drastic change and crisis. Many traditional sources of Negro employment, as on the nation's railroads and in mass-production industries, are rapidly disappearing as a result of automation and other technological changes in the economy. The fact that there is such a great concentration of Negroes in the ranks of the unskilled and semiskilled means that the increasing introduction of advanced methods of production causes the large-scale displacement of Negroes previously employed in unskilled jobs. . . .

For many occupations the only way a worker can be recognized as qualified for employment is to successfully complete apprenticeship training programs. This is true for the printing trades, among machinists and metal workers, in the various crafts in the building and construction trades, and many others. By apprenticeship we mean registered programs that consist of formal on-the-job training and related classroom instruction in the theory, content, and techniques of a great variety of skilled craft occupations and which in-

---

Mr. Hill is Labor Secretary of the NAACP.

volve a minimum of four thousand hours of instruction with a rising scale of wages for each thousand hours of participation. . . .

Recent studies, such as that made by the New York State Commission against Discrimination, as well as by the NAACP, clearly bear out . . . that no significant advances are being made by Negroes in those craft-union apprenticeship training programs which have historically excluded nonwhites. An examination of available data makes evident that less than 1 per cent of the apprentices in the building and construction industry throughout the United States are Negro. In the ten-year period, 1950–60, in the state of New York, the increase of Negro participation in building-trades apprenticeship programs rose only from 1.5 per cent to 2 per cent.

Open access to plumbing and pipe-fitting apprenticeship, controlled by the Plumbers Union, is a very rare experience for young Negroes in the North as well as in the South. Similarly Negro youth are almost completely excluded from apprenticeship programs operated by the Sheet Metal Workers Union, the Lathers and Plasterers Union, the Ornamental and Structural Iron Workers Union, and from other craft unions operating in the construction industry.

Among the most important of the building-trades craft unions is the Carpenters Union, which has severely limited the opportunities of colored craftsmen by organizing segregated Negro locals (in those instances where Negroes are permitted to join) and giving them jurisdiction over areas where there was little or no construction or prospect of construction. In addition, Negro locals are subjected to jurisdictional raids by all-white units, these latter being much better situated in terms of resources and power. This is true both in Southern and Northern areas, where the jurisdiction of the Negro local is usually limited to the Negro ghetto, and therefore, Negro carpenters are barred from employment on the major construction projects. As a consequence, many Negro carpenters have left the trade entirely.

The railroad craft unions as well as the railroad operating brotherhoods remain adamant in their opposition to Negro craftsmen and openly bar apprenticeship opportunities to Negro youth. Almost equally exclusive are the printing-trades unions. In a survey made by the NAACP of the seven major New York City newspapers, we find that, excluding building services and maintenance personnel, less than 1 per cent of those employed on the major newspapers are Negro. Virtually all of the Negroes employed on these newspapers are in the white-collar jurisdiction of the New York Newspaper Guild.

In Fort Wayne, Indiana, not a single Negro participates in the apprenticeship training programs conducted by either the Electricians Union, the Plumbers and Steam Fitters, or the Mason and Plasterers Unions; in Milwaukee, we are unable to find a single Negro in apprenticeship training, and the same holds true for Minneapolis in relation to the building trades, the printing trades, and the metal-crafts industry. In Newark, New Jersey, where there are 3,523 apprentices currently participating in approved apprenticeship training programs, there are exactly two Negroes enrolled; in New Orleans, not a single Negro apprentice is to be found in electrical installation, plumbing, painting, and other building-trades apprenticeship programs; in Philadelphia, less than 4 per cent of the apprenticeable trades are accessible to qualified Negroes; in St. Louis, Missouri, there are no Negro apprentices in the following training programs: electrical, plumbing and steam fitting, carpentry, masonry, cement finishers, lathers, and painters. There is one Negro apprentice at a nonunion, Negro-owned sheet-metal company. It is estimated that there are exactly fourteen Negro apprentices in St. Louis. These are six bakers, one bricklayer, two machinists, one sheet-metal worker, and four meat cutters. In Tulsa, Oklahoma, not a single Negro apprentice; in Springfield, Illinois, not a single Negro enrolled in any registered apprenticeship training program; in Warren, Ohio, there are no Negro apprentices in the building and construction trades crafts; in Washington, D.C., there are no Negro apprentices in such crafts as electrical, plumbing and steam fitting, masonry, lathing, and plastering. There is, however, one Negro in the carpenters' apprenticeship program. These data are indicative of the national pattern.

In most of these programs the role of the labor union is decisive because the trade-union usually determines who is admitted into the training program and, therefore, who is admitted into the union. . . .

A careful analysis of most apprenticeship training programs currently operating in the printing trades, the metal crafts, the construction industry, and in many other skilled craft occupations will clearly indicate the utter lack of a system of objective standard criteria for admission into apprenticeship training. At the present time there is no objective basis for determining admissions. Persons are admitted or not admitted because of nepotism and the caprices of certain union officials acting in collusion with management. The Bureau of Apprenticeship and Training of the United States Department of Labor in certifying apprenticeship programs in effect provides the sanction of the United States government for a variety of antisocial practices, of which racial discrimination is one important aspect.

On the level of the small shop and local union, the tradition of racial discrimination has now become deeply institutionalized. A form of caste psychology impels many workers to regard their own positions as "white men's jobs," to which no Negro should aspire. These workers and, often, their union leaders, regard jobs in their industries as a kind of private privilege, to be accorded and denied by them as they see fit. Often, Negroes are not alone in being barred from such unions, which attempt to maintain an artificial labor shortage. This is especially true of trade-unions in the building and construction industry and printing trades, which have much of the character of the medieval guild. On the local level, the tradition which sustains discrimination is to be found among skilled workers in big industry as well as among craftsmen, and in the North almost as commonly as in the South.

The discriminatory policies and practices of craft unions described here are in direct contravention of twenty-four state statutes which prohibit the barring of employment opportunities on the basis of race or color. They appear also to be in opposition to the intent of executive orders prohibiting discriminatory employment practices in the fulfillment of federal government contracts. But the record will clearly indicate that AFL-CIO federation and the affiliated "old-line" craft unions have refused to tackle this problem seriously and that they have not to any significant degree eliminated the traditional national pattern of Negro exclusion from trade-union controlled apprenticeship training programs in a variety of skilled craft occupations. The repeated protests of Negro workers from all over the country, as well as the detailed reports and requests for action made by the NAACP and other civil-rights organizations to the AFL-CIO, have proved to be a futile exercise. . . .

There have been, admittedly, some small gains. Recently the NAACP secured the admission of a Negro for the first time into the sheet-metal apprenticeship training program in St. Louis, Missouri. . . . Recent action by the New York State Attorney General, acting at the request of the NAACP, made possible the admission of the first Negro into the apprenticeship training program operated by the Plumbers Union in the state of New York. A sustained program of activity by the Oregon Fair Employment Practices Commission and the State Apprenticeship Council resulted in the admission of Negroes for the first time into various apprenticeship programs conducted by unions affiliated with the Oregon AFL-CIO Building Trades and the Metal Trades Councils. These isolated actions, however, are completely inadequate, as they do not eliminate the broad national pattern of Negro exclusion from apprenticeship training programs. . . .

Federal, state, and local governments are significantly involved in the operation of apprenticeship training and particularly in terms of providing the essential subsidies without which most of these programs could not operate. It is equally clear that governmental agencies have not, with very few exceptions, exercised their considerable power to assure that apprenticeship training programs are open to all youths regardless of race, creed, color, or national origin.

It is essential that federal and state agencies, as a matter of basic policy, refuse certification and withhold funds and other forms of subsidy from apprenticeship training programs which refuse to admit Negroes or members of other minority groups; that municipal and county boards of education immediately withdraw all forms of support from discriminatory apprenticeship programs, including the use of vocational-school buildings and other facilities; that management institute fair-employment policies and insure their fulfillment by subordinate employees; and that the great industrial corporations operating with United States government contracts begin to comply with federal executive orders prohibiting bias in employment.

Federal and state apprenticeship agencies have the responsibility of establishing an atmosphere of equality of opportunity in which integration may be achieved by individual apprenticeship units, especially in the matter of recruitment procedures and the establishment of objective standards which will be uniformly applied in accepting or rejecting applicants.

All of the foregoing should take place in the context of full employment and economic growth and should be given the highest priority by the basic institutions of American society with the understanding that there is an urgent need to make possible the complete realization of the abilities and talents of all of our citizens if the United States is to continue to function as a powerful and free nation in a world where industrial power is decisive.

18 : *Corporate Hiring Policies and Negroes*

Newsweek

Rarely in the past had such a major change in climate forced American businessmen to re-examine their policies so closely. . . .

In the Negro view, the soul-searching comes none too soon—and statistics tell the reason. Not only is the jobless rate among colored workers double that for whites, but Negroes are paid meagerly, too; the median income of a Negro male college graduate in 1960 was $5,020—actually $160 less than the earnings of white males with only one to three years of high school.

One of the most vexing facts about such figures is that in most cases they are not the product of a deliberate policy of bias. Industry basically has only one bias—in favor of profits. But over the years business has drifted into bias of another sort, and has been held there by inertia.

Northern-based companies with plants in the South, for instance, have traditionally and easily subscribed to segregated local customs and hiring practices to keep their white workers, local civic officials, and the townfolk happy. Feeling they have a tough enough job wrestling over wages and hours—and viewing it as none of their business anyway—executives have seldom challenged the equally traditional bias of unions.

And on the employment front, rather than go through the extra trouble and expense of training an unskilled Negro, industry has tended to reject him as unqualified—and let it go at that.

Management can, and does, argue that these problems lie mainly outside its sphere of responsibility. But increasingly, Negroes, and the nation as a whole, have been insisting that business assume greater social obligations.

With constant urging from press and pulpit, and with pressure from government, it now seems almost ordained that more Negroes will be hired in better jobs. Some companies will integrate for moral reasons; others will act out of self-interest, for Negroes are both customers and employees; still others will move defensively.

But even those businessmen who have decided to act are still troubled. For lack of experience and for fear of the unknown, they aren't sure exactly how to go about creating equal opportunity. How many Negroes should a company hire? In what capacity? And with just how much fanfare?

"Within the past week," reports Vice President Frank Cassell of Inland Steel (a firm with a good integration record), "I've had a dozen calls from other company personnel men asking how they can integrate their work force."

How, for instance, should a company go about hiring a Negro for a middle-management position? To begin with, morale of the current staff might suffer, since many companies firmly believe in promoting from within. Assuming no trouble there, where to find that middle-management Negro? Beginners can be recruited from college, but finding experienced talent is very often an informal process; a friend of a friend is hired, or someone a corporation executive has recommended to another.

Should a firm try to hire only outstanding Negroes? The risk of failure would be reduced. But as one Negro notes: "We have plenty of good potential around, but we're running out of Jackie Robinson's."

Would it be easier to hire a number of qualified but not outstanding Negroes? Then, if a few don't measure up and are let go, others will remain and the integration process will move along.

Hiring Negro engineers and plant workers is one thing. But companies often pause when the job at stake involves contact with the public, for fear of adverse reaction from customers. "It still takes a policy decision all the way up to the board to hire a single Negro salesman or a writer," complains W. Hampton McKinney of the Chicago Urban League. In Miami recently, one jewelry-store owner hired a Negro woman as a well-paid bookkeeper, but he asked her to wear a maid's uniform so that his customers wouldn't know she had a "white" job.

Even if such immediate problems were overcome, it wouldn't be enough to satisfy most Negro leaders. To make up for years of deprivation, poor schooling, and collapsed incentive, they say, colored workers should be given a leg up. Like all new things, the idea is being approached gingerly by management—and some are actually adopting it. It goes by the name of "compensatory hiring" or "compensatory discrimination." When a white and a Negro apply for the same job, says a Chicago personnel director, "all other things being equal, we'll take the Negro."

Compensatory hiring won't be easy, if only because white workers will protest. And government policy is that companies should hire *qualified* Negroes only, while doing more to search them out, and more to train and educate them.

The pursuit of job equality, of course, didn't start with the racial crisis of 1963. While industry as a whole may be judged backward, scores of companies have pursued the goal for years—with good results and good marks from Negro leaders.

Western Electric, whose integration policy at lower levels has been in effect long enough to have skilled Negroes on pension, sent recruiters to four Negro colleges last year, expects to double the number of campuses visited this year. Lockheed Aircraft Corporation supplies a daily list of job openings to the Urban League office in Los Angeles. For the past two years, Carson Pirie Scott & Co., a Chicago department store, has sought out potential Negro employees from the ranks of the city's high-school dropouts and given them job training. Carson President C. Virgil Martin describes his Double-E (for education and employment) program as "a conscious effort to bring Negroes into the store."

The Golden Gate National Bank of San Francisco may well be the most integrated firm in the country. Ten per cent of the bank's employees are Negroes and 25 per cent belong to other minority groups—Japanese, Chinese, Mexicans, and Jews. When Russian-born Jacob Shemano founded the bank two years ago, he brought in Jefferson A. Beaver, president of a Negro savings and loan association, as a director. Shemano's simple philosophy: "Hire people on the basis of ability."

That kind of philosophy is considerably easier to follow in California than in the South. But at R. J. Reynolds' new $32 million Whitaker Park plant in Winston-Salem, North Carolina, Negroes get a sizable share of the payroll, and in some cases supervise white workers. The tobacco company laid its groundwork carefully, making an effort to hand-pick whites and Negroes who could work together without friction. Chairman Bowman Gray explained that Reynolds would fill jobs without regard to race "because it is the right thing to do."

Integration created no major problems at Western Electric's Southern plants, either. Workers develop a loyalty to their company and their jobs, says Frank Lefebvre, superintendent of personnel administration, and unless they're rabid segregationists, integration doesn't much matter.

But for every Western Electric, Lockheed, or R. J. Reynolds making sincere desegregation efforts, there is another firm—more likely several others—practicing "tokenism." "There are a lot of showcase companies which say 'Look, there's our Negro over there,'" reports Atlanta's Noyes Collinson, an executive of the American Friends Service Committee.

Negro leaders hurl the tokenism charge at all the steel, auto, and textile giants, at the airlines and most banks and utilities, and at the communications industry. In fact, while many individual companies get high ratings (examples: Union Carbide, Pitney-Bowes, North American Aviation, and International Harvester), integration officials say they can't name a single industry which is going all-out to integrate. . . .

[The late] President Kennedy [in 1961] established a Committee on Equal Employment Opportunity with power to cancel the government contracts of companies which refused to end discriminatory practices. Almost overnight, the aero-space industry became a leader in the field of job integration. The committee, actively run by [former] Vice President Johnson, enforces nondiscriminatory orders on government contracts covering 20 million workers in industry, plus the 2.5 million federal employees. Reviewing the results . . . , Johnson [said]: "I believe we can say objectively that . . . more progress toward meaningful employment opportunity has been made in the last two years in this country in this field than in the last twenty years." Commenting on the job Johnson has done, Urban League's Guichard Parris says: "He has made the industrial giants believe he really means business." But Parris adds that the job is nowhere near complete.

Years of frustration and broken promises have taught the Negro community one thing: hope for help, but count on yourself. Much of what the Negro has gained recently has come from direct action and the use of economic muscle.

Many bakeries, breweries, and soft-drink bottlers now employ colored help because Negro customers demanded it and backed up the demand with boycotts. In Philadelphia, where four hundred local ministers developed the selective-boycott strategy, nearly one thousand Negroes now have jobs they were barred from previously. A similar campaign in Atlanta, say desegregation leaders, has increased Negro income $1 million a year because of new and upgraded jobs. In Detroit, Negro leaders threaten a campaign to "turn off the lights in every Negro home for 24 hours—as a beginning" unless Detroit Edison upgrades Negro workers. And on the national level, there is talk of turning the boycott weapon on the auto industry.

Corporations with the best of intentions find it difficult, if not impossible, to recruit Negroes qualified for anything but the most menial jobs. E. T. Mattison, director of industrial relations for the Lockheed plant near Atlanta, says: "The door is open, but to go through it requires qualifications, and not many Negroes are qualified."

The fact is that one million Negro adults are illiterate and 2.3 million Negroes twenty-five and older have failed to complete five years of schooling. Only 42 per cent of the nation's young Negroes now finish high school. . . .

Another reason there aren't enough well-trained Negroes: until recent years, nearly every Negro college man planned to become a teacher, minister, dentist, doctor, or social worker. A Negro engineer, mathematician, or business administrator had little hope of finding a job.

With business now awakening to the challenge, with the government firm, and the Negro firmest of all, progress is in the works. It will not come as quickly as many desire. . . . Nevertheless, observes Hobart Taylor, Jr., the executive director of the Committee on Equal Employment Opportunity: "I think we are reaching the end of another day, the day when the Negro had to be better. I think we're coming to the day in which a man has to be simply as good."

19 : *School Integration
Statistics in the
South—the Crawl-
ing Revolution*

Alan F. Westin

Each year since the Supreme Court's ruling in 1954 that segregation
in public education was unconstitutional, tallies have been made of
how many Negro children were actually attending public schools
alongside whites. By the early 1960's, Negro civil-rights leaders were
convinced—as was almost everyone else—that progress in integrated
education was proceeding at a snail's pace and that unless the
process was drastically speeded up, it might take generations before
most Southern Negro children would sit alongside whites. The 1963
enrollment figures, based upon the spring survey of the impartial
and expert *Southern School News,* showed the following patterns:

First, in the border states—Delaware, Kentucky, Maryland, Missouri, Oklahoma, West Virginia, and the District of Columbia—where segregation was less firmly rooted than in the deep South and where integration had been expected to proceed rapidly, only half of the Negro school children attended schools with whites in 1963. About 48 per cent of the Negro school population still remained in 100 per cent segregated schools. Even more important, the rate of change had fallen off badly in the 1960's. Between 1962 and 1963, the increase of integrated facilities in the border states had been less than 1 per cent, and a projection of the annual increases suggested that it would be the twenty-first century before integration reached the 90 per cent mark. The state-by-state figures were as follows:

SEGREGATION IN EDUCATION

The Seven Border States, June 1963

State	Negro Enrollment	Negroes in Schools with Whites	% of Negroes in Schools with Whites
Delaware	16,992	9,498	55.9
District of Columbia	110,759	87,749	79.2
Kentucky	45,000	24,346	54.1
Maryland	153,215	69,147	45.1
Missouri	90,000	35,000	38.8
Oklahoma	44,800	10,557	23.6
West Virginia	25,250	15,500	61.4
TOTAL	486,016	251,797	51.9

While some 485,000 Negro children attended public schools in the border states, more than 2,800,000 Negroes attended public schools in the eleven-state area known as the "Old South." The pattern of integration here made the border-state record seem to be a study in split-second speed and wholesale compliance with the Constitution. Alabama, Mississippi, and South Carolina had no Negro children attending classes with whites. Arkansas, Georgia, and Louisiana had tiny "token" contingents, with 247, 44, and 107 integrated Negro children in the respective states. The most "integrated" Southern state was Texas, with 7,000 Negroes, out of a Negro school population of more than 300,000, in integrated classes. The over-all figures showed that only 12,868 Negro students out of the 2,840,452 Old South Negro school children, or 0.004 per cent, had been integrated by the close of the 1963 school year. Again, the rate of change was so small—only a few hundred Negro students integrated since the 1962 school year—that any optimism about the pace of progress had to be wholly self-generated. The state-by-state figures for the Old South were as follows:

SEGREGATION IN EDUCATION

The Eleven Southern States, June 1963

State	Negro Enrollment	Negroes in Schools with Whites	% of Negroes in Schools with Whites
Alabama	280,212	0	0.
Arkansas	117,064	247	0.21
Florida	227,291	1,551	0.67
Georgia	325,141	44	0.01
Louisiana	301,720	107	0.03
Mississippi	290,000	0	0.
North Carolina	341,352	879	0.25
South Carolina	265,288	0	0.
Tennessee	159,299	1,810	1.1
Texas	303,980	7,000	2.3
Virginia	229,105	1,230	0.53
TOTAL	2,840,452	12,868	0.004

It was against this backdrop of wholesale noncompliance and "tokenism" in the Old South and a seeming halt to the process of integration in the border states that the Negro community looked at school integration as the 1963 school year came to a close.

20 : *The Techniques of Southern "Tokenism"*

J. Kenneth Morland

A new term—"token integration"—has emerged in the struggle for racial equality in public schools in the South. Although employed in more than one way, the term is generally used to describe deliberate efforts to keep racial integration at a minimum. It differs from "massive resistance," aimed at preventing any integration, for it allows for some breakdown of racial segregation. But token integration has essentially the same goal as massive resistance: it seeks to preserve, in effect, the established pattern of segregation. Thus it differs from gradual desegregation which urges a slow pace in the process of changing the segregated pattern, but which at the same time envisions the elimination of segregation eventually. . . .

A basic method for keeping desegregation in public schools at token levels has been through the adoption of [pupil]-placement laws. The eleven former Confederate states [1] have passed such

Mr. Morland is Professor of Sociology at Randolph-Macon Woman's College, Lynchburg, Virginia.

[1] Alabama, Arkansas, Florida, Georgia, Louisiana, Mississippi, North Carolina, South Carolina, Tennessee, Texas, Virginia (see U.S. Commission on Civil Rights, *Civil Rights USA: Public Schools, Southern States*, 1962, p. 4, footnote 12, for reference to where these plans might be found).

laws, which, in essence, authorize either a state or local board to assign pupils individually to different schools. The criteria for assignment range from a few broadly stated principles, such as "orderly and efficient administration of the school," to as many as twenty or more detailed considerations. Included in the latter may be the availability of teachers and transportation, the pupil's preparation and ability, the moral and health condition of the pupil, and the anticipated effect of the admission on other pupils and on the community itself. None of the plans mention race itself as a criterion of assignment; instead, they allow the operation of racially separate schools to shift to other grounds. . . .

In actual operation pupil-placement laws have been used with the assumption that initial assignments could be by race. Negroes have been assigned to all-Negro schools and whites to all-white schools, even though ostensibly on criteria other than race. The limited amount of integration that has taken place has come through application for transfer from the school of initial assignment through provisions of the placement laws. If an individual wishes to contest his assignment, he is allowed to do so, but he must carry his request through an involved and cumbersome administrative route. Just how elaborate this procedure may be is illustrated by Section 4 of the North Carolina School Placement Law:

Any person aggrieved by the final order of the county or city board of education may at any time within ten (10) days from the date of such order appeal therefrom to the superior court of the county. . . . Upon such appeal, the matter shall be heard *de novo* in the superior court before a jury. . . . The record on appeal to the superior court shall consist of a true copy of the application and decision of the board, duly certified by the secretary of such board. If the decision of the court be that the order of the county or city board of education shall be set aside, then the court shall enter its order so providing and adjudging that such child is entitled to attend the school as claimed by the appellant, or such other school as the court may find such child is entitled to attend, and in such case such child shall be admitted to such school by the county or city board of education concerned. From the judgment of the superior court an appeal may be taken by any interested party or by the board to the Supreme Court in the same manner as other appeals are taken from judgments of such court in civil actions.[2]

. . . The comparatively few Negro children who have successfully protested their assignment and who have been admitted to former all-white schools have constituted the "token" numbers of Negro pupils in school with whites. Because there have been so few, the pattern of racial segregation has, in fact, prevailed where placement laws are the only means for desegregation.

A number of states with pupil-placement laws have included "local option" provisions which allow communities to close schools ordered to desegregate. The arrangement has usually been to leave the decision of continuing or suspending the operation of schools up to the localities themselves, either through vote or through the action of the school board or board of supervisors. In order to make school closing legal, constitutional statutes requiring the state to maintain public schools have been amended. . . .

Another device for avoiding integrated schooling has been the offer of tuition grants to allow pupils to attend private, nonsectarian schools instead of public schools. Six states—Alabama, Arkansas, Georgia, Louisiana, North Carolina, and Virginia—have passed such legislation. . . .

Still another way of keeping integration at low levels has been the grade-a-year or stair-step plan. Nashville was the first city to utilize such a plan. It began desegregation with the first grade in the fall of 1957 and reached the sixth grade in the 1962–63 session. Initial assignment in most plans has been made on geographical proximity, the child being assigned to the school nearest him. But Nashville and most of the other cities adopting such a plan have allowed those children assigned to a school in which they were in a racial minority to transfer to the nearest school in which their race is in a majority. Such a transfer provision has been aptly termed "restrictive," for it applies to certain children and not to others.[3] Whites in predominantly Negro schools may transfer under this provision while Negroes in that school may not; Negroes in predominantly white schools may transfer while whites in that school may not.

[2] *Race Relations Law Reporter*, Vol. 1 (1956), pp. 240–41.
[3] U.S. Commission on Civil Rights, *Civil Rights USA: Public Schools, Southern States*, 1962, p. 14.

The effect of this restrictive transfer arrangement has been to re-segregate the previously all-Negro school. As a rule, white children assigned to all-Negro schools seek and are automatically granted a transfer to the nearest school in which whites are in a majority. Some Negro children assigned to all-white schools ask for a transfer, and those remaining constitute the comparatively few in integrated schools.

Just how effective have been these devices in keeping integration at token levels? The figures on the number of desegregated school districts and the proportion of Negro pupils in schools with whites provide an answer to this question.

When the Supreme Court declared in 1954 that racial segregation in public schools was unconstitutional, seventeen states and the District of Columbia required the separation of races in public education. Since the Supreme Court ruling, the District of Columbia and six of the states—Delaware, Kentucky, Maryland, Missouri, Oklahoma, and West Virginia—have moved more or less steadily toward compliance, and may therefore be called "compliant" states. The other eleven states—Alabama, Arkansas, Florida, Georgia, Louisiana, Mississippi, North and South Carolina, Tennessee, Texas, and Virginia—have passed legislation to prevent or to slow down desegregation. They may be called "resistant" states. In order to gain even a rough impression of the effectiveness of the plans for token integration, it is necessary to separate the extent of school integration in the compliant states from that in the resistant states.

We may look first at the number of school districts that have desegregated since 1954. A school district is regarded as desegregated when a single Negro child enters a school formerly attended only by whites, or when a single white child enters a school attended up to that time only by Negroes. Such desegregation is possible only in biracial school districts, that is, districts in which there are both white and Negro children residing. . . .

Little more than one out of ten of the biracial districts in the eleven resistant states have been desegregated, while slightly more than nine out of ten have been desegregated in the compliant states. Moreover, it should be noted, of the 270 desegregated districts in the resistant states last fall, 176 were in Texas alone.

Because a district is desegregated, it does not follow that all Negroes and whites in the district go to school together, for, as previously noted, a single child in school with children of a different race makes an entire district desegregated. . . . *In the resistant states only 2 per cent of all the Negro children in the desegregated school districts were actually attending school with whites.*[4] *Or, stated another way, 98 per cent of the Negroes in desegregated districts in the resistant states went to segregated, all-Negro schools.*

. . . The caption on the lead article of the December 1962 issue of *Southern School News*—"7.8 per cent of Negro Pupils in Classes with Whites"—is, therefore, exciting until one reads further to see that 95.2 per cent of those Negroes in school with whites are from the compliant states (i.e., 243,150 of the total of 255,367 Negroes in school with whites).

Thus racial integration in public schools is by any standard at token levels in resistant states, where 98 per cent of the Negro pupils in desegregated districts and 99.6 per cent of the Negroes in all school districts are in segregated schools. And thus the segregated pattern continues to prevail in the eleven resistant states. . . .

Token integration plans are under strong attack in the federal courts. Pupil-placement plans, initially accepted as constitutional on their face, are being declared unconstitutional as practiced in some school systems and are being rejected as valid plans for desegregation. School closing is being challenged if other public schools in the state remain open, and tuition grants have been stopped in the one county where public schools are closed. Grade-a-year plans are being speeded up, and restrictive transfer provisions that result in resegregation are being rejected. One by one the devices for keeping integration at token levels are being blunted and eliminated by the courts.

Throughout the complex of court rulings runs a clear and consistent thread, namely that school boards must proceed in *good faith* to develop a single school system, without regard to race, and that they must do this with all deliberate speed. These rulings, therefore, strike at the heart of token integration, which as noted, seeks to maintain a dual system of schools in which the races are,

[4] It is of interest to note that in one school district, Nashville, of the 810 Negroes reported as being in schools with whites, 540 of them were in a school with two non-Negroes, a white and a Chinese-American child. U.S. Commission on Civil Rights, *Civil Rights USA: Public Schools, Southern States*, 1962, pp. 112, 115.

in effect, segregated. Ostensibly the plans for keeping integration at token levels have been devised to try to satisfy the courts. It is quite obvious now that they are not doing so, and that the courts are becoming less and less patient with the bad faith implicit in them. . . .

21 : *Englewood, New Jersey—a Case Study in* De Facto *Segregation*

Paul Hope

Suburban Englewood—quiet, tree-lined, wealthy, and Northern—is becoming, like Birmingham, a symbol of the Negro's stepped-up integration movement. While there hasn't been the violence that has attended the Southern demonstrations, the Englewood movement has been a long and intense one. It has been marked by Negro sit-in's at a predominantly white school, an unsuccessful attempt to boycott downtown stores, a sit-in at the school superintendent's office, picketing of the governor's office in Trenton by Englewood sympathizers, and periodic rallies featuring well-known Negroes.

The . . . demonstrations [in May of 1963] started . . . when some thirty Negro students from a predominantly Negro elementary school began sitting in classes at a predominantly white school. School authorities have refused to register them but have let them sit in rather than provoke possible violence by keeping them out.

Mr. Hope is a reporter for the Washington, D.C., *Washington Evening Star.*

The Negroes are considered interlopers at the white school and largely are being ignored by teachers. Parents have been fined for violating a state law requiring children to attend school. The cases have been appealed. And the sit-in's go on while the Negro parents picket outside and police keep a watchful eye.

The struggle in Englewood is not the same as in Birmingham, but it could have great significance in the Negro's fight for more integration in the North. Here, the Negro is not fighting for minimum legal integration. He already has that and more. Here, he is fighting to break out of a containment brought about by housing patterns, tradition, economics, and resistance from the white community. As one Negro leader put it, they are fighting for "respect, equality, and a full share of community life."

Many of the white leaders think the Negroes want more than equality, that they want favored, special treatment. Some of them think Englewood will begin to slide downhill if the Negro demands are met. And though some whites, perhaps a large number, are in sympathy with the objectives of the Negroes, the white community seems to be nearly unanimous in condemning the tactics being used.

Nor is the Negro community completely united behind the protest demonstrations which have kept the community stirred up for more than a year. The Negro president of the school board, who has been called "Uncle Tom" by leaders of the sit-in movement, said he believes Englewood has been picked and is being "used by somebody as a sort of guinea pig." He didn't identify the somebody.

The sore spot with the Negroes is the Lincoln School, ostensibly desegregated but in fact nearly 99 per cent Negro. The reason for this *de facto* segregation is that elementary schools are set up on a neighborhood basis and the Lincoln School is in the heart of a Negro residential area. The Negro demonstration leaders claim, and their contention is supported by the superintendent of schools, that segregated schools, *de facto* or otherwise, are detrimental to the students attending them.

The Negro leaders have not laid out a plan they want the city to follow but they want something done to correct what they call the racial imbalance in the schools. They look upon Englewood as a testing ground in the fight to break down *de facto* segregation in the North.

"Lincoln School is just the manifestation of the problem in the North," said Paul B. Zuber, a Negro attorney from New York who has been a leader in the direct-action movement. "We're looking for dignity, a new approach, a new respect. Englewood has forced itself to become the symbol of what is wrong with racial relations in the North."

Mr. Zuber was attorney for a group of Negroes who won a court decision forcing New Rochelle, New York, school authorities to allow the transfer of students from a predominantly Negro school. In that case, however, the court found an obvious gerrymandering of school boundaries to maintain maximum segregation, a situation which has not been shown in Englewood.

"This is the battleground of the Northern suburbs," said Vincente Tibbs, the lone Negro on the Englewood City Council. "We have here the subtle (segregation) line. It's in housing, employment, government. There are people here who won't even admit there's a problem."

Englewood, lying just across the Hudson River from New York, has been primarily a commuter town for many decades. Even before the advent of the auto, it developed as the bedroom community for a wealthy class from New York who could commute to their offices by rail and ferry. The first Negroes were mostly domestics employed by the wealthy whites. The Negroes at first lived with white neighbors in what is known as the fourth ward. As the Negro population grew, the whites moved out of the section and the fourth ward became almost entirely Negro. The Negro population has grown rapidly since 1920 and now accounts for 27.3 per cent of the city's 26,000 population. During the decade of the 1950's there was almost no change in the number of white residents, but the Negro figure jumped from 4,172 to 7,000.

Englewood schools were desegregated before the 1954 Supreme Court decision. But since, there have been protests, off and on, from the Negroes about segregation brought about by school-district lines. The school population is about 37 per cent Negro. The city eliminated its predominantly Negro junior high school about six years ago and now has one junior high which is about 40 per cent Negro. It has only one senior high school, which is about 26 per cent Negro.

There are five elementary schools: Lincoln, almost 99 per cent Negro; Liberty, 63 per cent Negro; Roosevelt, about 12 per cent Negro; Quarles, about 5 per cent Negro; and Cleveland, less than 1 per cent Negro. It is at the Cleveland School that the Negroes are sitting in. The sit-in demonstrators are boycotting the Lincoln School, which is several blocks away.

White officials claim there is no intentional segregation in the elementary schools. Mayor Austin N. Volk, an insurance broker in New York, says the Negroes leading the demonstration are asking for "special treatment" not accorded other pupils. Under a 1955 ruling of the New Jersey Department of Education, students are to be assigned by local school boards on a neighborhood basis. They are not allowed to transfer outside their district. Mayor Volk said the Negroes are asking for something the white students are not allowed.

Negro leaders attempt to bolster their case by pointing to tests which show the level of achievement by pupils at Lincoln School to be two years behind that at other city schools. Their claims that pupils at Lincoln are at a disadvantage are upheld by a committee appointed by the state commissioner of education to study the Englewood situation. The committee said in a report last fall that it could find "no supportable evidence that school authorities have maintained segregation by design," but it said committee members had a "strong feeling that the Negro child is at a psychological disadvantage" because of *de facto* segregation.

City Superintendent Mark Shedd and former Superintendent Harry L. Stearnes, who retired last year, also take the position that schools which are almost entirely Negro lead to attitudes among students that affect learning. Dr. Shedd said, however, that he strenuously objects to the tactics being used by the demonstrators. He and the school board issued a statement saying:

"Since orderly channels for hearing grievances exist and time after time have proven effective, the board cannot condone methods and approaches for obtaining changes that circumvent the law, and which attempt to gain their ends by techniques of intimidation and disruption."

Mayor Volk claims the low achievement of pupils at Lincoln School is not the fault of the school but largely of parents "who don't give a damn." He also said there has been an influx of Negroes from Southern areas which has tended to pull down the average achievement level at Lincoln School.

The mayor and city council have put out a fact sheet, declaring that Englewood "is one of the most fully integrated communities in the Nation." The mayor claims the demonstrations are not supported by the Negro community but are the result of "resentment by a small group of people." He said outsiders like Representative Adam Clayton Powell and other national Negro leaders are brought in periodically "to keep up interest in the movement." They note there are Negroes on the school board, the city council, and other boards and commissions and that the fire and police departments, city parks, churches, civic organizations, restaurants, and stores are integrated.

Negro Councilman Tibbs says, however, that this is mostly for show and that the Negroes have very little voice in city government.

John H. Perry, Negro president of the school board, agrees with Mayor Volk that the tactics being used by the sit-in demonstrators are supported by "a minority of the Negro community. All the Negroes want a fuller, better, richer life," said Mr. Perry, who teaches school in New York. But he said he believes in using "regular channels and regular procedures" to achieve the goals. The demonstration leaders say this takes too long and is subject to too many obstructionist tactics by patronizing whites. They say Mr. Perry is a tool of white officials.

Byron Baer, a leader of the recently organized Bergen County Congress of Racial Equality, which is active in the sit-in movement, said Mr. Perry is doing a disservice to his race. Mr. Baer, a thirty-three-year-old white man, was arrested in Mississippi as a freedom rider and said he served forty-five days in the Mississippi penitentiary.

There is some evidence that the leaders of the sit-in movement have not been able to muster as much support as they would like. They recently announced plans to conduct sit-in's at the two other predominantly white schools but failed to carry it out. But there is strong evidence that the demonstrations and the turmoil they have engendered are producing results.

State Commissioner of Education Frederick M. Raubinger handed down a ruling [in May of 1963] in an Orange, New Jersey, case in which he held that a situation similar to that in Englewood should be corrected. Mr. Raubinger said that a 99 per cent Negro school in Orange "constitutes . . . a deprivation of education opportunity for the pupils compelled to attend the school." Most Englewood officials expect a similar ruling to be handed down shortly for that city.

White residents who have organized a Committee to Save Neighborhood Schools may try to upset the commissioner's ruling through appeals to the state board of education or the courts. Mrs. Louis Pugach, a spokesman for the committee, said the group will "fight with all legal means" to keep the neighborhood school system.

One of the solutions proposed by the school board was to set up a single school for fifth and sixth graders. It was expected this would be the first step toward gradually eliminating Lincoln School and distributing the remaining pupils among the other schools. The city council turned down a request for funds to set up the so-called intermediate school. The plan also was soundly rejected in an advisory referendum held last fall.

One of the fears of some white leaders is that a breakdown in the neighborhood school system will mean white families will begin to move to other areas. "This is a situation in which nobody can really win," said August J. Weisner, Jr., vice president and editor of the city's only newspaper, the weekly *Press Journal*. "If the Negroes appear to win, there will be an outmigration of white residents. If the whites appear to win, the demonstrations will continue."

22 : *The Facts of De Facto*

 Time

In 1960 most of the 77,000 citizens of New Rochelle, N.Y., viewed school segregation as a disease confined to the distant likes of Little Rock, Ark. The town's ethnic mix—14 per cent Negro, 30 per cent Jewish, 45 per cent Irish and Italian Catholic—was so faithfully reflected in the high school that the Voice of America once touted it as a shining example of integrated education. Only a year later, New Rochelle became the "Little Rock of the North," convicted in a federal court of gerrymandering to promote segregation. Case in point: Lincoln Elementary School, 94 per cent Negro.

More in hurt than anger, New Rochelle defended Lincoln as a typical "neighborhood school" that, like Topsy, just grew that way. The trial told a different story. Back in 1930, the school board redrew lines to make the Lincoln district match the Negro area. It also allowed whites to transfer out—and they did. By 1949 the school was 100 per cent Negro.

The board tried to bring resident whites back to the school by revoking transfers. Instead, whites switched to private and parochial schools or moved away, making the district more Negro than ever. By 1960 Lincoln's pupils in general were academically behind every other elementary school in town. The board, nobly it thought, got a citywide vote to build a fine new Lincoln on the same spot. Negro parents countered with a federal suit on then-novel grounds: it is just as unconstitutional to compel Negroes to attend a *de facto* segregated school in the North as a *de jure* segregated school in the South.

Federal Judge Irving R. Kaufman did not decide that question (nor has any other federal court so far). He ruled only that gerrymandering had violated equal protection under the 14th Amendment. The outcome jogged white minds all over the North. Given free access to other schools, Lincoln's pupils on the whole did better, except for some who landed in a white school that overwhelmed them. Because two-fifths of Lincoln's pupils chose to remain, New Rochelle is now closing the 65-year-old building, assigning the children to balanced schools, and launching an extensive bus service to help keep the entire city desegregated.

ON THE ATTACK

The experience of New Rochelle is a case history in a development that is spreading across the Northern U.S.: a movement against *de facto* segregation of schools. Victory in New Rochelle spurred the N.A.A.C.P. to a successful attack on *de facto* school segregation last year [1962] in a dozen Northern communities, from Coatesville, Pa., to Eloy, Ariz. This summer [1963] it is "mobilizing direct action" in 70 cities throughout 18 Northern and Western states. School boards are responding, and many a change will have been made by September. All kinds of tools are being tried. Samples:

Open Enrollment. The most widely used method so far, it modifies the neighborhood-school concept enough to let students of mostly Negro schools transfer to mostly white schools that have sufficient room. Open enrollment was pioneered in New York City, is used or will be starting in some form next September [1963] in Baltimore, Detroit, Pittsburgh, Buffalo, San Francisco and many smaller cities. Usually only a fraction of the eligible Negro students take advantage of it.

Rezoning—which is often the same as ungerrymandering. In San Francisco, mostly white Grant School lies near mostly Negro Emerson School in a rectangular area cut by a horizontal attendance line; made vertical, the line would integrate both schools. New

York City's school zoning boss, Assistant Superintendent Francis A. Turner, a Negro, is such a skilled mixmaster that balanced schools are rapidly increasing.

The Princeton Plan, so called for the New Jersey town that devised it. Formerly segregated schools are rematched, so that one school accommodates all children of perhaps three grades, a second school the next three, and so on. This works well in small communities, might do in big cities by clustering each grade group in several nearby schools to avoid long bus trips.

Recombination. An example: A Negro elementary school can be turned into a junior high school serving a wider area, or into a school for gifted or retarded children, while the original pupils are sent to other schools.

School Spotting. New schools are built only in areas of integrated housing. For fast-changing big cities, the latest idea is "educational parks," putting all new schools in one or several central clusters. Last week a New York City board of education member suggested a perfect site: the World's Fair grounds, where after 1965 an education center could accommodate 15 public schools and a teachers' college, enrolling a total of 31,000 students.

FEARS & ILLUSIONS

All these changes stir deep fears and emotions. Negroes, demanding more than token integration, have lately attacked *de facto* segregation by street-marching protests in Los Angeles and Philadelphia, "study-in's" at the white schools of Englewood, N.J., sit-in's at the boards of education of New York and Chicago. Whites envision their neighborhood schools being flooded with poorly prepared Negro pupils or their own children being forced to integrate Negro slum schools. A feeling of "discrimination against the majority" has sparked reactions like that of white parents in Montclair, N.J., who filed a federal suit under the 14th Amendment, claiming that Negro children were allowed free transfers while theirs were not. The long-honored concept of the neighborhood school—a homey place that children can walk to, a living symbol of local pride and progress—seems in danger.

Yet behind the stresses and strains is a consensus, by many school authorities, some courts and most Negroes, that *de facto* segregation must go. The problem is to break the low-income Negro's vicious circle of slum birth to slum school to bad education to low-paid job and parenthood of more slum children. The widely accepted premise is that the circle can and must be broken at the school stage. Equally important is that segregated neighborhood schools refute the original aim of Horace Mann's "common school," strengthening democracy by serving all races, creeds and classes. Integrationists believe that schools can help to heal U.S. race relations by returning to Mann's ideal.

SEGREGATED EQUALS BAD

Nothing in theory prevents the hundreds of predominantly Negro schools in the North from excelling, but in practice a school that becomes 30 per cent to 50 per cent Negro is in for trouble. Whites pull out and it "tips" toward 100 per cent. Gone are the "motivated" bright white children who might have been models for slum kids to copy and compete with. Good teachers become hard to get (although the "spirit of the Peace Corps" is diminishing this problem, according to Cleveland's School Superintendent William B. Levenson). "Once we become concentrated, we become ignored," says a Boston Negro leader. Most of Los Angeles' 53 Negro schools are on double sessions. Chicago's Urban League calculates that in operating expenses Negro schools get only two-thirds as much per pupil as white schools.

The result is unsurprising. In Boston, where special high schools require entrance exams, one Negro boy typically complains: "I never saw that kind of math before I went for the exam." In his recent [1963] civil-rights speech, President Kennedy said: "The Negro baby born in America today has about one-half as much chance of completing a high school as a white baby, born in the same place, on the same day; one-third as much chance of completing college; one-third as much chance of becoming a professional man; twice as much chance of becoming unemployed."

BIG-CITY PROBLEMS

While small Northern cities may attack the situation in the manner of New Rochelle, big cities, with miles of Negro ghettoes, have problems that range up to hopeless. Washington, where even the most civil-righteous New Frontiersmen are prone to send their children to private schools, can hardly give classes a desegregated look when 85 per cent of public school students are Negro. Chicago, Boston and Philadelphia are marking time. A measure of New York's quandary is that some integration crusaders have proposed mass transfer of whites into Harlem schools, although few officials see it as a workable solution.

Nonetheless, the nation's biggest city school system is also the most enterprising. New York is trying to make slum schools so good that Negroes can rise more easily into an integrated society. It devised the famed Higher Horizons program, heavy on culture and counseling, which now involves 64,000 students in 76 schools. At state level, New York's Commissioner of Education James E. Allen Jr. recently requested school boards to report by September [1963] on what steps they intend to take to balance schools with more than 50 per cent Negro enrollment.

"In the minds of Negro pupils and parents," says New Jersey's State Commissioner of Education Frederick M. Raubinger, "a stigma is attached to attending a school whose enrollment is completely or exclusively Negro, and this sense of sting and resulting feeling of inferiority has an undesirable effect on attitudes related to successful training." Raubinger has issued orders to end *de facto* segregation in three New Jersey communities. In the same vein, a former foe of "social engineering via bussing," Dr. John Fischer, president of Columbia's Teachers College, warns that schools must "take positive action to bring Negro children into the mainstream of American cultural activity." And in California, the state supreme court in June came close to outlawing *de facto* segregation. Where it exists, ruled the court, "it is not enough for a school board to refrain from affirmative discriminatory conduct." No exact racial ratio is required, but schools must take "corrective measures."

The ideal integration situation, says Psychiatrist Robert Coles, after studying Southern schools, is apparently a middle-class school with diverse ethnic groups and high teaching standards. In a forthcoming report, sponsored by the Southern Regional Council and the Anti-Defamation League of B'nai B'rith, Coles adds that young children mix naturally, ignoring adult tensions. Teen-agers take longer, but in the course of a year begin to see "them" as individuals to be judged on personal merit. As for standards, both races generally work as hard as ever. Says Coles: "We have yet to hear a Southern teacher complain of any drop in intellectual or moral climate in a desegregated room or school."

While the pressures for integration bring a troublesome measure of controversy, reaction and disillusionment, it is a fact that every sensible effort to desegregate schools—alarmists to the contrary—is likely to improve the general level of U.S. education.

DISCRIMINATION IN PUBLIC ACCOMMODATIONS

23 : *The Struggle for Equal Service at Public Facilities*

United States Commission on Civil Rights

. . . In 1955, a group of Montgomery, Alabama, Negroes under the leadership of the Reverend Martin Luther King protested segregated seating on city bus lines. When Mrs. Rosa Parks was arrested for refusing to move to the rear of a bus, the group instituted a boycott. For twelve months makeshift car pools substituted for public transportation. Many persons walked several miles to and from their jobs. The bus company at first scoffed at the Negro protest. But as the economic effects of the boycott began to be felt, the company sought a settlement. When negotiations broke down, legal action was brought to end bus segregation. On June 5, 1956, a federal district court ruled that segregation on local public transportation violated the due process and equal protection clauses of the Fourteenth Amendment. Later that year, the Supreme Court, citing the School Segregation cases, affirmed the judgment.[1] The boycott was ended.

The success in Montgomery gave new stimulus to organizations committed to nonviolent action. The Congress of Racial Equality and the Southern Christian Leadership Conference intensified their efforts. Created in 1943, the Congress of Racial Equality (CORE), from its early beginnings, utilized the nonviolent protest to achieve its goals. The Southern Christian Leadership Conference (SCLC), a direct outgrowth of the Montgomery bus boycott, was formed to serve as a co-ordinating agency for those employing the technique and philosophy of nonviolent protest. At its organizational meeting in Atlanta in 1957, the Reverend Martin Luther King was elected as its president. The NAACP, itself a participant in direct action, the Southern Regional Council, religious groups, and various labor and civic organizations gave support and aid to those involved in direct action.

✗ Then on February 1, 1960, four students from the Negro Agricultural and Technical College of Greensboro, North Carolina, entered a variety store, made several purchases, sat down at the lunch counter, ordered coffee, and were refused service because they were Negroes. They remained in their seats until the store closed.

In the spring and summer of 1960, young people, both white and Negro, participated in similar protests against segregation and discrimination wherever it was to be found. They sat in white libraries, waded at white beaches, and slept in the lobbies of white hotels. Many were arrested for trespassing, disturbing the peace, and disobeying police officers who ordered them off the premises. As a result of the sit-in's, literally hundreds of lunch counters began to serve Negroes for the first time and other facilities were opened to them.

Thus began a sweeping protest movement against entrenched practices of segregation. In summing up the movement, Reverend King said that legislation and court orders tend to declare rights but can never thoroughly deliver them. "Only when people themselves begin to act are rights on paper given life blood. . . . Nonviolent resistance also makes it possible for the individual to struggle to secure moral ends through moral means." By 1962, the sit-in move-

[1] *Gayle* v. *Browder*, 352 U.S. 903 (1956).

ment had achieved considerable success. As a result of the sit-in's and negotiations undertaken because of them, department-store lunch counters and other facilities had been desegregated in more than one hundred cities in fourteen states in various parts of the nation.

The sit-in movement did not escape executive attention. On March 16, 1960, President Eisenhower commented that he was "deeply sympathetic with efforts of any group to enjoy the rights . . . of equality that they are guaranteed by the Constitution" and that "if a person is expressing such an aspiration as this in a perfectly legal way," the President did not see any reason why he should not do so. On June 1, Attorney General William P. Rogers met with representatives of several national variety stores and secured their promises to have their local managers confer with public officials and citizens' committees to work out means of desegregating their lunch counters. On August 10, the Attorney General announced that the national chains had made good on their promises by desegregating lunch counters in sixty-nine Southern communities.

The judiciary was soon to become involved in the sit-in's. For while some of the sit-in demonstrators voluntarily went to jail, many appealed their convictions on the ground that the ejections, arrests, and convictions by local government officials constituted enforcement of the private proprietor's discrimination and therefore constituted state action in violation of the Fourteenth Amendment. Three cases involving sixteen students reached the Supreme Court from Louisiana in the fall of 1961. On December 11, 1961, without reaching the broader constitutional questions, the Court reversed the convictions because of lack of evidence that the sit-in's disturbed the peace either by outwardly boisterous conduct or by passive conduct likely to cause a public disturbance.[2]

In November 1962, the Supreme Court heard arguments in six cases in which the arrest of sit-in demonstrators was attacked as unconstitutional. The Solicitor General of the United States, appearing as a friend of the Court, maintained that four of the criminal convictions were based on unconstitutional state laws, and the fifth on a pervasive state policy of segregation, and that the sixth

___

[2] *Garner* v. *Louisiana*, 368 U.S. 157 (1961).

should be reversed because the agent who evicted the defendants also served as the arresting officer. [The Court reversed the convictions in 1963, holding that it is a denial of equal protection of the laws for an agency of a state to require segregation in privately owned establishments. As of December 1963, additional sit-in cases were awaiting decision in the Supreme Court: *Barr* v. *Columbia, Bouie* v. *Columbia, Bell* v. *Maryland, Robinson* v. *Florida.*]

One of the most dramatic attacks on segregation and discrimination was undertaken in May 1961 by the Congress of Racial Equality. A group of CORE-sponsored "freedom riders" toured the South to test segregation laws and practices in interstate transportation and terminal facilities. The freedom riders encountered no difficulties until they arrived in Alabama and Mississippi. In Montgomery, Alabama, twenty persons were injured on May 20, 1961, by mob action. When local police failed to restore order, four hundred federal marshals were brought in to maintain order. President Kennedy said the situation was "the source of the deepest concern to me as it must be to the vast majority of the citizens of Alabama and all Americans." On May 21, after initially resisting federal authority, Governor Patterson called out the National Guard and order was quickly restored. The Department of Justice secured a temporary restraining order from the federal district court prohibiting any further attempt by force to stop freedom riders from continuing their test of bus segregation. On June 2, Montgomery city officials, together with several private individuals and organizations, were enjoined by the court from interfering with travel of passengers in interstate commerce. The city officials were also enjoined from refusing to provide protection for such travelers.

When the freedom riders rode into Mississippi, the governor called out the National Guard to escort them into Jackson. On May 24, 1961, the first contingent was arrested for refusing to obey a police officer's command to move from segregated terminal waiting-room facilities. In the following months, more than three hundred freedom riders were arrested and convicted. On July 10, the Department of Justice intervened before a three-judge federal court to halt the arrest of the riders in Mississippi. The Attorney General charged that local authorities had gone "beyond the scope of their lawful power" in making the arrests. On November 17, the court ruled that the arrests must be challenged in state courts. An application to the Supreme Court for an injunction to stay state criminal prosecutions was denied. President Kennedy, in reply to a question at his July 19 [1962] news conference, upheld the right of American citizens to move in interstate commerce "for whatever reasons they travel."

By the summer of 1962, the leaders of the direct-action movements could see results in the form of government response to their demands and favorable changes in business attitudes and policies.

The sit-in movement and the freedom riders brought the issues of discrimination and segregation in places of public accommodation back to the forefront as prime civil-rights issues. In 1875, Congress had enacted legislation to ban these practices, but the Supreme Court ruled in 1883 that the Constitution does not permit Congress to prohibit private persons from denying equal access to privately owned and operated places of public accommodation.[3] The Constitution does, however, guarantee equal access to places of public accommodation that are publicly owned and operated.[4] In the 1940's and 1950's, the Supreme Court found that discrimination in privately owned terminal facilities in interstate commerce imposes an undue burden on that commerce and is a violation of the Constitution. In 1961, the Court expanded its interpretation of "publicly owned and operated" when it held that a privately owned restaurant in a state-owned parking garage in Wilmington, Delaware, could not refuse service on the basis of race or color.[5]

In 1947, President Truman's Committee on Civil Rights recommended the "enactment by the states of laws guaranteeing equal access to places of public accommodation, broadly defined, for persons of all races, colors, creeds, and national origins." At that time, eighteen states had such laws. All had been enacted in the nineteenth century in response to the decision in *The Civil Rights Cases* that held that the federal government did not have the authority to legislate in this field. The fifty-six-year legislative lull

---

[3] *The Civil Rights Cases*, 109 U.S. 3 (1883).

[4] See *Holmes* v. *City of Atlanta*, 350 U.S. 879 (1955); *City of Baltimore* v. *Dawson*, 350 U.S. 877 (1955).

[5] *Burton* v. *Wilmington Parking Authority*, 365 U.S. 715 (1961). This decision was handed down on April 17, 1961; on June 2, 1961, Wilmington enacted an ordinance prohibiting all persons licensed to sell food for consumption on the premises from refusing to serve any person because of race, color, or religion.

was broken in 1953 when Oregon enacted a statute prohibiting discrimination in privately owned and operated places of public accommodation. This break-through was followed by Montana and New Mexico in 1955, Vermont in 1957, Maine in 1959, and Idaho, New Hampshire, North Dakota, and Wyoming in 1961. Alaska was admitted to the Union in 1959 with such a law on its books, bringing the total at the end of 1962 to twenty-eight states. In addition, several cities in states without such laws have enacted antidiscrimination ordinances concerning public accommodations.

The interest in equal access to places of public accommodation has greatly increased in recent years. On May 17, 1960, the Department of Justice filed suit to assure that a public beach constructed with funds from the federal government would be available to all the public without discrimination because of race or color. On September 13, 1961, the Department of State publicly urged the Maryland legislature to pass a bill, then pending before it, to prohibit discrimination in restaurants, hotels, and other places of public accommodation in the state. More significantly, President Kennedy spoke out on this issue. In March 1961, the Civil War Centennial Commission, responding to an appeal from the President, elected not to use segregated facilities in Charleston, South Carolina. On September 25, 1961, the President issued a personal plea for an end to discrimination "in restaurants and other places of public service."

In 1962, the executive branch of the government for the first time attacked discrimination and segregation in hospital facilities constructed or maintained with the aid of federal funds. The Department of Justice asked the federal district court in Greensboro, North Carolina, to declare unconstitutional the separate-but-equal provision of the Hill-Burton Act—the law which provides federal funds for hospital construction. The department made the request as it moved to intervene in a private suit brought to challenge the constitutionality of the separate-but-equal provision of the Hill-Burton Act. Attorney General Kennedy said the Department of Justice had specific responsibility under law to take part in the action. A judicial-procedure statute calls for the government to intervene in any suit in which the constitutionality of a federal law is questioned, but in which the government is not already a party. This was the first time the government had intervened to challenge the constitutionality of a federal statute.

24 : *Humiliation Stalks Them*

Roy Wilkins

. . . It must be remembered that while we talk here today [July 22, 1963], while we talked last week, and while the Congress will be debating in the next weeks, Negro Americans throughout our country will be bruised in nearly every waking hour by differential treatment in, or exclusion from, public accommodations of every description. From the time they leave home in the morning, en route to school or to work, to shopping or to visiting, until they return home at night, humiliation stalks them. Public transportation, eating establishments, hotels, lodging houses, theaters and motels, arenas, stadia, retail stores, markets, and various other places and services catering to the general public offer them either differentiated service or none at all.

For millions of Americans this is vacation time. Swarms of families load their automobiles and trek across country. I invite the members of this committee to imagine themselves darker in color and to plan an auto trip from Norfolk, Virginia, to the Gulf Coast of Mississippi, say, to Biloxi. Or one from Terre Haute, Indiana, to Charleston, South Carolina, or from Jacksonville, Florida, to Tyler, Texas.

Mr. Wilkins, a staff member of the NAACP since 1931, became its Executive Secretary in 1955.

How far do you drive each day? Where, and under what conditions can you and your family eat? Where can they use a rest room? Can you stop driving after a reasonable day behind the wheel or must you drive until you reach a city where relatives or friends will accommodate you and yours for the night? Will your children be denied a soft drink or an ice-cream cone because they are not white?

The players in this drama of frustration and indignity are not commas or semicolons in a legislative thesis; they are *people*, human beings, citizens of the United States of America. This is their country. They were born here, as were their fathers and grandfathers before them. And their great-grandfathers. They have done everything for their country that has been asked of them, even to standing back and waiting patiently, under pressure and persecution, for that which they should have had at the very beginning of their citizenship.

They are in a mood to wait no longer, at least not to wait patiently and silently and inactively. One of the four Negro college students who sat in at a lunch counter in Greensboro, North Carolina, February 1, 1960, was an air-force veteran and an officer of the A. & T. College Chapter of the NAACP. In an interview he said he was born and raised in North Carolina and returned there after his time in the air force to study to be a physician.

The fact that he, a veteran in his country's nonsegregated air force, after service overseas to spread and preserve democracy, could be refused a cup of coffee and a piece of pie in his home state seemed suddenly in the nineteen-sixties, to be something he just could not take any longer. He engaged in direct action to make known his views. The fact that such action has swept the country, in the North as well as in the South, is testimony enough, for those who can read the signs of the times, that this veteran's reaction accurately mirrors the reaction of millions of his fellow citizens of both races. . . .

It is contended that such legislation as is here proposed—that United States citizens be protected from humiliating racial discrimination in public places and services in their own country—is an invasion of "property rights."

It is strange to find this argument, in connection with the fortunes of this particular class of citizens, made in 1963. This was the argument of slavery time. If the United States were to free human slaves, it would be invading property rights. Today, one hundred years later, if the United States legislates to secure nondiscriminatory treatment for the descendants of the slaves, it will be invading property rights. . . .

What rights are thus being defended? Legal human slavery is gone, but its evil heritage lives on, damaging both the descendants of the slaves and the descendants of those who owned them—or those who have identified themselves with that class. Is not the "property rights" argument but an extension of the slave-ownership argument? The disclaimers would be loud and indignant if it were suggested that any senator approved human slavery; but how fine is the line between approval of slavery and acquiescence in a major derivative of the slave system?

The answer has to be that our nation cannot permit racial differentiation in the conduct of places of public accommodation, open to the public and with public patronage invited and solicited. While such establishments may be privately owned, they owe their life and their prosperity not to the personal friends and relatives of the proprietors, but to the American public, which includes today, as it has for generations, all kinds of Americans. The proprietors of small establishments, including tourist homes and gasoline filling stations, are no less obligated to render nondiscriminatory public service than are the proprietors of huge emporiums or hostelries.

The supporters of this legislation are again not greatly impressed with the timeworn admonition that this is an area which the Congress should leave to whimsy, to that great variable, men's hearts, to state and local sentiment, or to that champion among the reluctants, voluntary action.

The Negro American has been waiting upon voluntary action since 1876. He has found what other Americans have discovered: voluntary action has to be sparked by something stronger than prayers, patience, and lamentations. If the thirteen colonies had waited for voluntary action by England, this land today would be a part of the British Commonwealth. . . .

The Congress has legislated for the health and welfare of livestock. Why does it balk at legislating for the welfare of its nearly 20,000,000 loyal Negro citizens? Railroads or other carriers are prohibited by 45 United States Code, 71–74, from confining livestock for more than twenty-eight hours without unloading them into pens for at least five hours for rest, water, and feeding.

Are cows, hogs, and sheep more valuable than human beings? Is their rest, water, and feeding a proper subject for congressional legislative action, but the rest and feeding of Negro Americans in hotels, restaurants, and other public places an improper subject for congressional action? . . .

25 : *Cambridge Demonstration Resumed*

Charles Rabb

Eleven Negro and white demonstrators staged a fifteen-minute sit-down demonstration [July 9, 1963] in front of a restaurant here, less than an hour after the National Guard pulled out of this racial trouble spot on the Eastern shore [of Maryland].

One of the three white demonstrators, twenty-two-year-old Eddie Dickerson of Cambridge, who led the march to the Dizzyland, was struck in the face with eggs twice by the owner, Robert Fehsenfeld.

An unidentified white man walked through the semicircle of demonstrators several times, stepping on hands. A television sound man had a microphone jostled from his hand.

There were no arrests, although a Cambridge policeman arrived on the scene seven minutes after the demonstration began. He made no attempt to disperse the group, which was made up mostly of youths.

Afterward, Reginald Robinson of the Student Nonviolent Coordinating Committee said telegrams were sent to the Justice Department, the FBI in Salisbury, Maryland, the state police, and to

Mr. Rabb is a staff reporter on *The Washington Post*.

City Police Chief Brice Kinnamon to protest the lack of "adequate" protection.

Witnessed by scores of newsmen and local residents, the brief sit-down was the first since June 13, the night before the Guard was ordered here by Governor J. Millard Tawes.

The last of the guardsmen pulled out at 12:30 P.M. . . . and with them went all restrictions on demonstrations, the sale of liquor, and a 10 P.M. curfew. . . .

The demonstrators marched up to Dizzyland at 1:25 P.M. and tried to enter. They were prevented by Fehsenfeld, who locked the door behind him. The demonstrators sat down in front of the door.

"Get out from in front of the door," Fehsenfeld shouted and shoved several youths away from the door. They did not resist, but began singing "We Shall Overcome" and other songs of the civil-rights movement.

After they finished the first time, Fehsenfeld yelled, "Encore!" As crowds gathered on all four corners of the downtown intersection, one unidentified white man in gray work clothes stood over the singing demonstrators and yelled, "You don't know what freedom is. Freedom is when you fight.

"Put that on television," he turned and said to [a] cameraman who was grinding away.

Fehsenfeld . . . then came out with an egg and cracked it on the right side of Dickerson's face.

Minutes later, he waved a second egg in front of Dickerson's eyes and then rubbed it squarely in Dickerson's face. The huskily built Dickerson wiped the yolk off his face.

Fehsenfeld then doused Dickerson with a cup of water.

At 1:40 P.M. the demonstrators stood up and marched away, singing and clapping as they walked down the city's main street, ironically named Race Street.

26 : *Breaking the Color Line in Memphis, Tennessee*

Russell Sugarmon, Jr.

Memphis, Tennessee, in the spring of 1960, was a totally segregated Southern city. There were in existence, and had been for several years, a number of interracial agencies and organizations, which had as their objective movement in the area of rights and opportunities afforded Negroes in this city. Many Negroes felt their programs to be somewhat anemic. During this same period, across the South, a new movement, which attracted the young of the race, was beginning to catch the imagination of the Negro people. This movement has come to be called the "sit-in movement." Many in Memphis wondered whether and when this movement would come to our city. The seedbed of this movement seemed to be the dormitory colleges across the South, where young Negroes could, in nighttime bull sessions, express their frustrations and develop in themselves a frame of mind which could eventually be translated into action. In Memphis, most Negro students attending local colleges resided at home, where they were exposed to the more con-

---

Mr. Sugarmon is an attorney in Memphis and a member of the Legal Redress Committee of the Memphis NAACP.

servative influence of parents, older friends, and neighbors. Until March 18, 1960, the only overt evidence of "the movement" in Memphis was a certain restlessness among the students, with whom we had occasional communication. On March 18, 1960, however, the mood of the Negro community changed. Radio newscasts stated that several young Negroes had entered one of the downtown five-and-ten cent stores and seated themselves in an area which had been designated for white patrons only. The newscast indicated that they had remained for a brief time and then departed before the local police made any arrests. The following day, March 19, 1960, twenty-three Negro students were arrested by the Memphis Police Department for sitting in, in two separate groups, at the main branch of the local public library. They were each charged with loitering, disorderly conduct, threat to commit a breach of the peace, and disturbing the peace, the latter being a state charge. The sit-in movement had come to Memphis.

On the day of the initial arrest I received a call from the city jail which informed me that the caller was a student who had been arrested in a local library along with some twenty-odd others and that he and they desired legal assistance. Recognizing the implications of this particular call, I and one of my associates, Attorney A. W. Willis, Jr., immediately decided that we should afford an opportunity to each Negro lawyer to identify himself with the yearnings of our people by coming forward in the defense of these students. One or two of the lawyers were out of town on that day; however, at the close of the first day's trial in the city court, out of the ten Negro lawyers that then practiced law in this city, ten had participated in the legal defense of the sit-inners.

In the weeks and months that followed, similar demonstrations were held in other public facilities; i.e., the Pink Palace Museum, Brooks Memorial Art Gallery, Overton Park Shell, the zoo, and on the front seats of buses owned by the Memphis Transit Company. Private businesses also were the sites of sit-in's. During this period demonstrations occurred at lunch counters and restaurants in the following stores: Walgreen's, Lowenstein's, Woolworth's, Silver's, Shainberg's, Ohman House, Kress's, and Gerber's.

As the sequence of arrests and trials continued, certain general patterns in the handling of these incidents could be ascertained. Initially, students were arrested as soon as they occupied a seat or entered the forbidden area of the facility involved. They were transported to the local police station where multiple charges were placed against them, and then they were processed over a period of several hours. As the pattern of activities in the area of public facilities became more or less routine, the length of processing was shortened, the amounts of the fines levied by the city court lowered, and the number of charges involved reduced. This same pattern was followed when the students departed from the pattern of sitting in in public facilities and moved to the area of private facilities. In addition to the places previously mentioned, the sit-in movement also challenged the pattern of segregation practiced at the Dobbs House Restaurant in the municipal airport, and restaurant facilities in the Greyhound and Continental bus terminals.

On two or three other occasions, Negro students worshiped or attempted to worship with the congregations of white churches. On one such occasion, Negro students attended an open-air gathering sponsored by a religious denomination in the municipal shell located in one of our city parks. They were arrested and charged with disturbing a religious assembly, convicted in a criminal court of the state of Tennessee, [and] fined $200 each and sentenced to two months in jail. This particular conviction has been carried through the state court appellate procedure, and is currently pending on appeal to the Supreme Court of the United States of America.

The legal theories used in the defense of these cases were based on the Fourteenth Amendment of the Constitution. In the area of public facilities, the *Brown* case and decisions in other jurisdictions extending its reach to areas outside the field of education were argued to the courts. In the area of private facilities, the line of decisions based upon *Shelley* v. *Kraemer*, which found prohibited state action in the use of the judicial branch of government to enforce racially restrictive covenants, formed the basis for the defense. With few exceptions, in the sit-in cases the testimony adduced by the state indicated no conduct different from that of other persons using the facility involved. The rationale of our defense was based upon this fact coupled with the argument that any conviction on a case so postured could only be based on the color, not the conduct of the defendants, and therefore within the constitutional prohibition against discriminatory state action through the judicial arm of government as spelled out in the line of decisions following *Shelley* v. *Kraemer,* mentioned previously.

The number of arrests involved during the period of the local sit-in movement in Memphis eventually exceeded three hundred. At one point during the course of this episode, lawyers defending students found themselves spending their mornings trying cases, their afternoons getting more students out of jail, and their nights interviewing these students; so that they could spend the next morning trying cases.

The movement continued from March of 1960 into 1961, and may have terminated with opening of restaurants and lunch counters, in most of the downtown department stores and chain stores shortly after Christmas of that year. It's interesting to note that although civil cases in the federal district court had been initiated in several areas prior to the advent of the sit-in's, only one of them has been completed with an order directing desegregation of the involved facility by the federal district judge.

The local transit company adopted a policy of nonsegregated seating several weeks after the sit-in's focused on bus seating. Today, some fifteen Negroes are gainfully employed as bus drivers of this company. The federal civil suit directed against discrimination on the local buses has been discontinued as moot without any final order directing desegregation having been entered.

A three-judge court has heard a civil suit attacking discriminatory practices permitted by the City of Memphis in a restaurant operated by a lessee at the local airport. This case was wound up, with a desegregation order, as mentioned above, in the spring of [1962].

A civil suit attacking discriminatory practices in the operation of the public-school system was heard by the local federal district judge in the spring of 1961, and resulted in a finding that, although *de facto* segregation still exists, it was voluntary and that the school board had complied with the law by announcing a change of policy, and the adoption of the pupil-placement law, as its plan for desegregation. The court of appeals for the sixth circuit reversed this ruling and dismissed the pupil-placement law as an adequate plan for desegregation. The school board has now pending before the United States Supreme Court a petition for a writ of certiorari.

A civil suit attacking the policy of segregation in the use of the facilities maintained by the Memphis Park Commission for the citizens of Memphis resulted in a lower-court decision which found segregation, but allowed the park commission to come in with a plan of gradual desegregation of the recreation system. This was upheld by the sixth circuit court of appeals, and an appeal to the United States Supreme Court is now pending.

A suit attacking the policy of permitting lessees to practice discrimination in the seating of public gatherings in the municipal auditorium has been filed and trial [was] set for [the] summer [of 1962].

The suit attacking the policy of segregation in the operating of the Memphis Zoo [was dismissed] as moot following the voluntary desegregation of said facility after a series of sit-in's had occurred.

A suit attacking the policy of desegregation in the Memphis Public Library culminated in an order directing the library board to eliminate segregation in the rest-room facilities, which practice the board had persisted in even though use of books at the library on a nonsegregated basis had been negotiated following a series of sit-in's in the facility. . . .

27 : *The Realities of Discrimination in San Francisco*

Irving Babow

Although world-wide attention has been focused on discrimination in places of public accommodation and on protests against such practices in Southern states of the United States, there has been little inquiry into this subject in Northern cities, particularly where restrictive practices are prohibited by the state civil code, criminal code, business and professional code, administrative measures, or by court action. The present paper discusses the patterns and extent of discrimination against minority-group members in places of public accommodation in San Francisco and analyzes the evasive devices used to circumvent laws and regulations against unequal treatment. . . .

San Francisco, the birthplace of the United Nations and a symbol of cosmopolitanism, is a major seaport, convention and tourist city, a center of trade, finance, communications, and culture, and is the central city and service center for a metropolitan area with a total population of almost four million persons. Almost one of every

Mr. Babow, Lecturer in Social Welfare at the University of California at Berkeley, is coauthor of *A Civil-Rights Inventory of San Francisco*.

five San Franciscans (18.4 per cent of the total) is nonwhite; approximately one-fourth of all resident births are nonwhite, and about 30 per cent of the total population are members of some minority ethnic group such as Negro, Oriental, Mexican-American, or Jewish. Places of public accommodation play a major role in the city's economy and include approximately 3,000 restaurants, 900 hotels, 120 motels, 400 taverns, and several hundred travel bureaus. The multiplicity of establishments in this field suggests the many gate keepers for screening clientele as well as the complexities for communicating and enforcing antidiscrimination laws and policies. . . .

Although, on the whole, minority-group individuals in San Francisco have equal and unsegregated access to places of public accommodation and considerable gains have been made in recent years, . . . important "pockets" of restrictive practices still remain. . . .

When minority group persons are excluded, segregated, or otherwise treated unequally in places of public accommodation, such practices are usually covert and almost never made explicit by the management. Community sanctions against overt discrimination, the projected image of the city as an urban and urbane center of tolerance and cosmopolitanism, the fear of adverse publicity which would result in loss of business, the desire to avoid civil suits for damages under the state civil code, suspension or revocation of the liquor license, or prosecution under the state criminal code—all of these factors are involved in the institutionalized patterns of evasion or tricks of the trade which are used in a number of establishments to make discrimination difficult to prove. How to turn a person away or how to segregate him tactfully and subtly so that there is no legal evidence of unequal treatment are distortions of interpersonal competency developed to a high degree by some practitioners. . . .

The practices vary from exclusion to segregation, discourteous service, quotas, and a differential policy related to the numbers and the social status of the minority individuals involved. For instance, a hotel which provided facilities for the convention of a Negro organization nevertheless on other occasions "tactfully" did not accept individual reservations from Negroes. A restaurant which accepted reservations for a banquet of a Negro group in a "private" dining room refused reservations to Negro couples who wished to be served in the "public" dining room of the restaurant. In such restrictive and differential practices, there seems to be an assumption that segregation can be tactfully handled and concealed when occasional nonwhite groups are served apart from the main facilities. This seems to be true especially if the nonwhite organization happens to be an articulate group which might "make an issue." Furthermore, such token service permits an establishment to claim it does not discriminate because it can point to the nonwhite organization which used its facilities.

Although most hotels make rooms available to Negroes without any hesitation or qualifications, a higher proportion of first-rate hotels do so than do the hotels with more moderate rates, thereby restricting the range of selection for Negro guests who desire moderate-priced accommodations. In a sample of forty-four hotels (twelve first-rate and thirty-two moderate-priced) which were checked by telephone for reservations, twenty-nine (or approximately two-thirds) made reservations without any hesitation for a Negro couple. Seven hotels, or about one-sixth, refused reservations by claiming that no rooms were available, but a check made soon afterward by another caller who did not give any ethnic identification, revealed that rooms were actually available during the requested time period. For the remaining one-sixth (seven hotels), there were indications but no conclusive evidence that Negro guests were discouraged. One hotel, which has only male guests, made a satisfactory referral to another hotel. In San Francisco no hotel is known to admit that it discriminates and those hotels which do so generally use an evasion, such as stating that no rooms are available for the desired period or that there are only higher priced rooms.

In San Francisco, as in many other parts of the country, the number of motels has grown rapidly in recent years and many families when they travel prefer to stop at motels instead of hotels. The evidence in San Francisco is that a substantial proportion of motels are not available to Negro families. In a random sample of forty-four motels checked by telephone, twenty-six establishments or 60 per cent made reservations without any qualification for a Negro family. Fifteen motels, or approximately a third, did not give reservations —eight by an explicit statement that they did not accept Negroes, and seven by asserting that accommodations were not available for the requested date. At three motels there were indications, but no conclusive evidence, that Negro guests are discouraged. A large

number of the motels are new and undoubtedly some of the operators are not familiar with existing laws regarding public accommodations.

A telephone check of fifteen first-rate restaurants of the total 3,000
restaurants was far too small to be representative, but it suggested
what happens when Negroes try to obtain reservations. Six of the
fifteen restaurants made reservations immediately. Three restaurants
did not give reservations—one by a stated reluctance to serve Negroes, and two on the pretext that reservations were not available.
Six restaurants were found to have a doubtful practice. This was
demonstrated by such statements as: "We'll put you in a separate
corner if you like," "We usually place Negroes in a private booth,"
"We can't refuse service to anyone, but Negroes very rarely come
here." According to information from other sources, the proportion
of San Francisco restaurants which give service on a nondiscriminatory basis is probably much higher than in the small sample in
which nine out of fifteen establishments were found to have a restrictive or doubtful practice. There seems reason to believe, however, that a fairly considerable number of San Francisco restaurants
either discourage Negro clientele, or, if the Negroes are served an
attempt is made to segregate them.

Although many first-rate downtown bars and taverns serve Negroes, a substantial percentage of neighborhood taverns appears to
discriminate. Generally the management does not make any explicit
statement about restrictions in order to avoid damage suits, suspension or revocation of the state liquor license, or adverse publicity.
Some subterfuges are to claim that the tavern is a membership club,
to refuse service to Negroes by asserting they were intoxicated, to
ignore their requests for service, and to treat them discourteously.

Nondiscriminatory treatment in places of public accommodation,
as in other fields pertaining to civil rights, may be achieved by legislation, by court action, by administrative measures including antidiscrimination commissions, or by voluntary action such as by trade
associations. Action to date in public accommodations in California has been largely through legislation, by statutory provisions
in the civil code and the criminal code, and, to a limited degree, by
administrative measures. As pointed out in the 1962 American Jewish Yearbook of the American Jewish Committee, the California
legislature enacted a measure in 1961, signed by Governor Edmund

G. Brown on July 6, 1961, which extended the protection of the state's statute on public accommodations to all persons, whether citizens or not. Previously this statute protected only citizens against acts of discrimination in places of public accommodation. Several court decisions have specified certain types of establishment to be covered by the civil code. Voluntary action by trade organizations on a community or state-wide level has been negligible.

Conclusions which can be drawn from the survey are these: The considerable gains in achieving equal rights in most places of public accommodation in a Northern urban center like San Francisco have diverted attention from remaining pockets of segregation and discrimination, particularly for Negroes. Because of evasive devices (such as the "private club" device) and the covert nature of most restrictive practices, discrimination is generally very difficult to prove. Affirmative action by trade associations, by individual places of public accommodation, and by unions in service industries is rare. Many establishments have failed to adopt, communicate, and implement a firm, explicit policy of nondiscrimination and to instruct employees regarding the requirements and provisions of the pertinent statutes and administrative orders. Restrictions in employment, in union membership, in educational and vocational training opportunities, in housing, and in public accommodations appear to reinforce one another.

The experience of the many first-rate establishments which provide fair and equal treatment indicates strongly that the fears and adverse expectations of the places which discriminate are unwarranted. In San Francisco and elsewhere in California, the generally covert violations and institutionalized evasions of antidiscrimination statutes and administrative regulations are likely to continue in a number of places of public accommodation because of the relative absence of state administrative machinery for education, initiation of complaints, enforcement, conciliation, and consultation.

The findings in San Francisco suggest that legislation in civil rights is usually insufficient for social control and assurance of equal opportunity and treatment if it does not include ongoing procedure and apparatus for education and initiative for compliance. In the absence of such measures, unstructured norms prevail with many inconsistencies and evasions of legal requirements or even ignorance of the pertinent laws. . . .

It seems significant that in San Francisco the restrictive practices in places of public accommodations are applied primarily against Negroes, and that, in recent years, Chinese and Japanese Americans, who are also identifiable as nonwhite, encounter discrimination much less frequently than do Negroes. Most Negroes in San Francisco are not recent migrants to the city, but in the pecking order of discrimination they receive the most restrictive treatment. . . .

DENIAL OF HOUSING TO NEGROES

28 : *The Color Line in Northern Suburbia*

**James H. Kirk and
Elaine D. Johnson**

. . . This is the story of a city with growing pains. The city referred to in this study as "Suburbia" is Lakewood, California. It is known as an all-white city. Census reports affirm this.

Although this is a study of Lakewood, it could be the story of any one of thousands of modern American communities located just outside the central city. They are found in the North, South, East, and West. Their lily-white houses are indicative of a characteristic which is considered desirable by some, inevitable by others, although considered contrary to democratic principles by man.

Everywhere in Lakewood one notices the conspicuous absence of Negroes and orientals. The exclusion of minority racial and ethnic

Mr. Kirk, formerly Chairman of the Department of Sociology at Loyola University in Los Angeles, is with the Systems Development Corporation. Miss Johnson is a sociologist and college instructor in California.

groups is a glaring but often unrealized form of discrimination in Suburbias throughout the country.

Suburbia mushroomed in the area around the defense plants in the prewar years. The signing of the Federal Housing Act in 1939 gave new impetus to Suburbia's growth, and the area began to take on the stamp of an individual community. The beginning of the first long-range housing program got under way about 1941 and by late 1948 the population had edged near the 12,000 mark. During the war its growth was momentarily halted, but since the war it has grown even beyond the realtors' fondest dreams. The building spree reached its peak when thousands of homes were offered to veterans for nothing down and small monthly payments. Signs promised: garbage-disposal units, tile baths, stall showers, lawns, steel kitchens, venetian blinds, and many other added attractions. Real-estate salesmen did not sell—they merely took orders from people who wanted to trade the uncertainties of postwar life for the security of owning their own home.

When 1951 rolled around and the government had pulled building activity down to a slow crawl with regulation X, thousands of the planned homes had been built.

Unlike other, slower growing communities of comparable size, Suburbia grew so swiftly that it could not be afflicted with the fungus of slums. No areas could fall into the drabness of despair and decay from age and neglect. Newness was the keynote—new homes, new streets, new street lights, and new stores.

Very few of the homes in Suburbia are owned by old-timers, a stratum of Suburbia's society that lived in the area as far back as 1935. Many of these old-timers live in "millionaires row," where $50,000 mansions nestle along the edge of the country club. These are in marked contrast to the neat rows of modest homes in the new Suburbia.

Nearly all the homes in Suburbia, with the exception of millionaires row, are project homes ranging from $10,000 to $14,000. The average homes are three bedrooms, built along similar floor plans with the same square footage. There is no individuality, and no privately built homes in these projects.

Because of the financial requirements that went hand in hand with purchasing a new home, residents were largely on a common level as to age, wages, and families. The city fathers proudly state that "our population is uniformly youthful, whereas in the core of any large established city the population ranges widely in age."

Mr. and Mrs. Average are young marrieds. They are as pleasantly similar as the homes in which they live. They are in their early thirties; have three to four children. The weekly pay check is used largely for installment payments on the house, the two-year-old car, and one appliance. Nearly every home sprouts a television antenna. Mr. Average earns $4,000 a year, and works within fifteen miles of his home.

Homes in Suburbia are built to house one family—to a greater extent than elsewhere in the country. The population bears the earmarks of selection—normal, intelligent, well-established families. There is high employment among the men. There is a low percentage of women employed—and these are more concentrated in governmental, professional, and clerical positions. Employment is somewhat higher than average in proportion to the total number of persons in the age groups fourteen years and older. Because of the predominantly residential character of the area, most of the people are employed elsewhere, either in Metropolis or neighboring areas. Most of this travel must be by private automobile, because the public carriers are few and inadequate.

There is a large central shopping center, including a large branch department store with ample free parking. This shopping area serving Suburbia has caused a downward trend in department-store sales in Metropolis. The phenomenal growth of Suburbia is a far cry from the days of rabbit hunting in the bean fields which the subdividers "bought for a song and sold for a symphony."

Suburbia has an elementary-school population that is constantly increasing, while that of Metropolis is on the wane. Dozens of church- and community-sponsored youth groups collaborate to insure a minimum of delinquency and antisocial behavior.

So far, the youthful residents have concentrated all their time and energies on home decorating and landscaping. They have an intense pride in their community. While peace, for the moment, is wonderful in Suburbia, the residents hardly expect it to grow on them. If an important issue looms, they would arise to community action.

Over 95 per cent of Suburbia's youthful population are white, native-born Americans. The remainder are white, foreign-born.

Why, in the light of the desirability of Suburbia for young families, is there this conspicuous absence of Negroes and orientals?

In the light of this challenging question, two teams of sociologists made a survey of Suburbia's realtors. Each team was composed of two Caucasians and one Negro, attempting to discover what devious means, if any, are used by realtors to continue restrictive housing. What myths, if any, are perpetuated by realtors to exclude minority groups from private housing? What devious means, if any, are used by professional sellers of real estate to continue to restrict the freedom of residential movement by minority racial and ethnic groups?

The Negro, serving as the follow-up, made a request for housing comparable to that of the Caucasian couple. The follow-up had more effect on the study, since the Negro would be observing the attitude of the realtors to a Negro prospect and would learn what reasons, if any, were given or techniques were used in discouraging sales to Negroes.

Realtor 1—He offered to show the couple around. The couple was in a hurry, but accepted listings and the realtor's card. They promised to call the realtor later for an appointment to go house hunting. They were also given assurance by the realtor that there were many other homes available.

Negro Follow-up—The realtor hedged about twenty minutes. Then he started giving excuses: Realtors will not sell to Negroes; real-estate association won't allow it; their office once tried to sell a home to a Chinese family and nearly lost their license.

NEGRO: How can you enforce the restrictive covenant when it isn't legal?

REALTOR: We have a fifty-year covenant.

NEGRO: I would like to live in the Suburbia area.

REALTOR: You are the first Negro who has approached me in the eight years I have been in Suburbia. The tract offices might have some listings, and they are FHA. Why don't you try them?

NEGRO: Do you mean to tell me the tract offices will sell them without discrimination as to race?

REALTOR: There is no Negro living in the Suburbia area. You could buy in the Jonestown area. If you will come back, I will be glad to show you houses in the Jonestown area.

Realtor 2—The realtor offered to show the couple around the Suburbia area. When his offer was refused because of the pressure of time, he gave several listings in the area requested, with down payments as low as $1,000 to $1,650.

NEGRO (The realtor was very tense.): Do you have any houses with a $2,000 down payment?

REALTOR: We have nothing for less than $3,000 to $4,000 down.

NEGRO: Do you have any tract houses, GI, available?

REALTOR: Yes, for $3,000 or more down. If you will call me for an appointment, I will show you around. Is there any particular reason why you want to live in the Suburbia area?

NEGRO: Yes; I work in this area and we have all our charge accounts here. Yet we live in Smithville.

(Negro interviewer felt very sympathetic with the realtor, who was very tense and uncomfortable, and assumed it was the realtor's first contact with a Negro prospect. Then, too, there were women employees in the office who were giggling in the background and listening to the conversation. Interviewer heard one remark, "I wonder what the Negro is up to." The realtor didn't seem free to talk, as if he were afraid of ridicule from the women employees.)

REALTOR: Do you have enough money for a down payment?

NEGRO: I have $3,500.

REALTOR: I would discourage your looking for homes in this area.

(On two walls of this real-estate office were listings with addresses in the Suburbia area.)

Realtor 3—Listings for houses in the Suburbia area were requested by and were given to the couple.

It was found that the young salesman, who gave three listings, was very friendly and co-operative. The co-operation of the young salesman was so sincere that the interviewer questioned the possibility of any difficulty arising.

REALTOR: I have just come from a section of the country where the problem of segregation in housing is not acute. I will speak to my associate about you, for he is an officer of the realty association in Suburbia and may be able to help you. We have had no Negro inquiries about housing before. (The realtor shook hands, gave his card, and invited the Negro to return.) . . .

Realtor 9—The realtor stated that he had many houses available in the area at the price mentioned. He brought out a mimeographed list similar to the one shown by realtor 8. He stated there were many GI resales, and gave the couple a number of listings.

NEGRO (The realtor was very evasive at first.): I notice that you have a three-bedroom home for sale with a small down payment. You have it listed on the board in front of your office.

REALTOR: The people who owned that property have changed their minds, and withdrew the listing. I would suggest you look in the Metropolis and Smithville areas. You would be unhappy in the Suburbia area.

NEGRO: Why?

REALTOR: Because there are no Negroes here.

NEGRO: That would make no difference to me as long as the house was desirable. (When the realtor was asked for his card, the realtor walked away, entered his office, and placed a call. As he was telephoning, he fumbled in his desk drawer, drew out a card, and waved it at the Negro, which the latter "failed to see." When the call was completed the realtor handed the interviewer his card.)

NEGRO: Would it be possible to buy a house in this area?

REALTOR: The people living in the neighborhood would object.

NEGRO: Do the people listing a home for sale stipulate that it be sold to Caucasians only?

REALTOR: Of course not.

NEGRO: Is it the policy of all the realtors in the Suburbia area to refuse to show or to sell property to a Negro?

(The realtor did not answer this question. During the entire time he appeared, first, nervous, evasive; then adamant; then antagonistic because of the last question.)

Realtor 10—The procedure was reversed in this interview and the one following, with the Negro making his call before the Caucasian couple, which resulted in more information—unsolicited.

NEGRO: I would like a home from $12,000 to $14,000 with a $2,000 down payment.

REALTOR: We have no listings for less than $3,400 to $4,200 down. (The realtor didn't act cordial, nor offer a chair. However, the interviewer sat down.) No listings were given; however, the realtor gave the assurance that he would take the Negro house hunting on the next visit. As the Negro stepped out the door, he heard the realtor remark in a low tone, "—— ——!"

Couple (as husband and wife). The two realtors in the office, a man and woman, treated the couple graciously. They were assured there were many houses for sale to meet their requirements, and a large listing sheet was leafed through. The woman realtor said it included 550 listings in this area.

HUSBAND: Before you look any further, you should know that I have a criminal record. Would that have any effect on our getting credit to buy a home?

WOMAN REALTOR (gesturing with arms raised): Goodness, no; none at all. The realtors can't refuse to sell property to anyone. Your past record won't be investigated—it isn't the same as an employer checking your record.

HUSBAND: What if my wife had been a dope addict; would we have trouble getting a home here? (As wife tugs to roll sleeves below elbow as though trying to conceal needle marks.)

WOMAN REALTOR: That wouldn't make any difference; as long as you have the money required for the down payment and make this much a month, you qualify. (She figured four times the monthly payment.) I am writing out a number of listings, and here is my card. However, I would be glad to show you around.

WIFE: Dear, we had better hurry. Aren't you to report for work at noon today?

HUSBAND: Oh, well, what if I do lose this job—there are others.

WIFE: You are always so optimistic about finding work.

WOMAN REALTOR: A job is a job.

HUSBAND: Oh, well, what the hell! What's a job?

WOMAN REALTOR (aside to realtor): How did you get rid of that Negro?

REALTOR: I just yessed him to death.

HUSBAND: Any chance of Negroes moving into this area?

REALTOR: No. You won't have to worry about colored neighbors here.

WIFE: Don't you have to sell to them, though, according to law?

REALTOR: Yes; we can't refuse to show them property. But we can get people to withdraw listings. If Negroes would move into this area, the people would get up in arms and make it hot for them. They couldn't stay.

WIFE: What would happen to you if you sold to Negroes?

REALTOR: If it were known by other realtors that our office sold to Negroes, we'd be out of business.

WOMAN REALTOR: We'd be blackballed. . . .

29 : *The Struggle for Open Housing*

**Frances Levenson and
Margaret Fisher**

Any objective analysis of racial housing patterns in the United States leads to the inescapable conclusion that residential segregation—with its concomitant of segregated schools, churches, employment, and public and recreational facilities—is more widespread and more embedded as a national institution today than it was a century or a half-century ago.

A recent five-year, $400,000 Ford Foundation-financed study, conducted under the aegis of the distinguished Commission on Race and Housing (chaired by Earl B. Schwulst, president of the Bowery Savings Bank of New York, and composed of business and professional leaders of comparable eminence from every section of the country), concluded that "segregation barriers in most cities were tighter in 1950 than ten years earlier," and that we are experiencing "an increasing separation of racial groups as non-whites accumulate in the central city areas abandoned by whites, and the latter continually move to new suburban subdivisions from which non-whites are barred." The 1960 census reports clearly reveal that this picture has worsened during the last decade.

Mr. Levenson is Director of the National Committee against Discrimination in Housing. Miss Fisher is Editor of this committee's bimonthly publication, *Trends in Housing*.

It is true that in the late 1800's there were the Little Italys, the Chinatowns, the Jewish communities, Irish sections, and concentrations of other newcomers to our land. Generally poor and understandably insecure in a strange new country, the immigrants reached out for community through the common ties of language, customs, or religion.

But those homogeneous neighborhoods were formed by free choice. They continued to expand through the 1920's, but began to dwindle in the 1930's. As the newcomers or their children rose on the economic and social ladder, they were free to move wherever they chose—whether "uptown" in the city or "to the country," suburbia. Today, one must search to find a settlement with the authentic flavor of the "old country." Indeed, many observers lament that gradual dispersion has robbed the culture of our cities of diversity.

Almost precisely the reverse occurred when the color factor entered the picture. Color islands were scarcely discernible in most of our cities at the turn of the century and during the early 1900's. They became increasingly apparent in the 1930's, and continued to grow until burgeoning Black Belts were a characteristic of every major city after World War II.

The racial concentrations which form the vast American ghettos of today can hardly be described as voluntary. Their residents are generally American to the core. They and their parents and their grandparents were born on these shores. They are rich and poor; intellectual and uneducated; men of distinction and unknown laborers. No matter how they rise in status, if they want to better their living environment their only choice is likely to be between one restricted tract and another. Ninety-five per cent of these citizens who are relegated to living apart are Negro Americans.

As the United States Civil Rights Commission . . . reported to the [late] President, shelter for his family is the only major commodity on the American market which a nonwhite citizen cannot purchase freely according to his needs, his means, and his desires.

Rigid separation of Negro citizens into circumscribed neighborhoods is a relatively recent phenomenon in the United States—either in the North or the South. As late as 1934, only 5 per cent of the Negroes in Charleston, South Carolina, lived in blocks which were 100 per cent nonwhite, and more than 40 per cent lived in blocks which were more than 50 per cent white. In 1910, Negroes not only lived in practically every section of Chicago, but almost 35 per cent of them resided in areas which were less than 10 per cent nonwhite. Residential integration was customary in New England, with Negro citizens participating normally in the religious, social, civic, and political life of the community. At the close of World War I, Negro residents were scattered throughout such cities as Minneapolis, Minnesota, and Columbus, Ohio.

Many forces in our society are responsible for the formidable barriers faced by minority-group families in their quest for housing. The villains are many; the angels, few. The housing and lending industries, local "improvement" associations, individual prejudice, customs, and codes have all been part and parcel of the abridgment of one of man's most basic rights. It is not unfair, however, to lay major responsibility at the door of the United States government.

When President Kennedy sat at his desk in late November [1959] and made that long-awaited "stroke of the pen" on the executive order barring discrimination in federally aided housing, he actually laid down no new national mandate. What he *did* do was to direct the government of the United States, in the operation of its far-reaching housing activities, to start obeying the mandate of the Constitution and federal law, both of which it had been violating in its housing programs for a number of years.

The "due process" and "equal protection" clauses of the Fifth and Fourteenth Amendments to the Constitution prohibit federal or state action which discriminates against any person because of race, color, or creed. The Federal Civil Rights Act of 1866, which survives to this day, provides that "all citizens of the United States shall have the same right, in every State and Territory, as is enjoyed by white citizens thereof to inherit, purchase, lease, sell, hold, and convey real and personal property."

Even the most cursory examination of developments in the housing field shows that the requirements of the Constitution and federal law have been largely ignored, and have had little—if any—impact on the course of events.

Since the depression of the early 1930's, when the federal government first entered the housing field on a large scale, and remained as the most important single influence in the nation's housing market, it has played the roles of both architect and promoter of residential segregation. Closing its eyes to the moral and legal demands of the Bill of Rights and federal law, the government not only practiced open and overt discrimination, but it developed and presented to the private entrepreneurs a grand design for a nation composed of "homogeneous neighborhoods."

Since 1933, the housing market and the face of America have been transformed by federal housing operations. These programs have made possible the emergence of the large-scale builder, the vast new suburban subdivisions, the amortized mortgage marketable on a national basis, long-term credit and low down payment, and extensive slum clearance and renewal of our cities. In no other aspect of national life has the federal government given more aid, exercised more controls, and brought about more changes than in the field of housing. These enormous undertakings have been supported, of course, by taxes imposed on all alike. Yet their benefits have been largely denied to more than twenty million Negro Americans and to members of certain other minority groups.

From 1933 to 1938, the federal government actively promoted discrimination and segregation in much of the housing affected by its operations. A striking example is the approach of the Federal Housing Administration, which was created in 1934 to provide insurance on mortgage loans and represents the largest of the government housing programs. Charles Abrams, housing and planning expert and president of the National Committee against Discrimination in Housing, has said that FHA's official occupancy policy from 1934 to the end of 1949 might well have been culled from the Nuremberg laws. Its Underwriting Manual, which included a model restrictive covenant for inclusion in deeds, declared, "If a neighborhood is to retain stability, it is necessary that properties shall continue to be occupied by the same social and racial groups." Literally thousands of communities were developed across the nation which were restricted against occupancy by "undesirables" —American Indians, Syrians, Jews, Mexican-Americans, Puerto Ricans, Negroes, and other minorities. With FHA's benediction, the use of restrictive covenants spread through the general housing market.

In December 1949, after the 1948 United States Supreme Court decision that racially restrictive covenants were judicially unenforceable, FHA—reluctantly—bowed to the high Court's ruling. It would not, it declared, insure mortgages on any more properties subject to such covenants. However, FHA continued extending its largess to builders and developers who flagrantly denied housing to nonwhite families. Similar discrimination was practiced by the Veterans Administration.

Housing with FHA- and VA-guaranteed mortgages has accounted for the major portion of all nonfarm housing constructed in the United States since World War II. These two agencies have underwritten more than $117 billion in loans. Whole new all-white cities—the Levittowns of Long Island, Pennsylvania, and New Jersey; Lakewood, near Los Angeles; Park Forest, near Chicago— and the myriads of all-white suburban developments bear eloquent witness to government support of residential segregation. Less than 2 per cent of the new homes insured by FHA have been available to nonwhites, and the vast majority of them are in all-Negro developments in the South. VA's record is no better.

What about the other programs?

The Public Housing Administration left the question of open occupancy or segregation up to local housing authorities, and most cities—North and South—chose segregation. These low-rent projects have represented substantially all the new housing available to nonwhite families, and numerically a considerable proportion has gone to them. However, more than 80 per cent of all federally sponsored public housing is racially segregated.

Urban renewal, which provides for the revitalization of the nation's cities, has become the keystone of federal housing programs. Seven out of every ten Americans now live in urban areas. It is expected that by 1975, no less than 85 per cent of our total population will be city dwellers. Almost $2 billion in federal funds have been expended to aid 870 slum-clearance and redevelopment projects in 475 different communities. More than 70 per cent of the families displaced by urban-renewal projects have been nonwhites. Many stable, integrated communities have been "renewed" on a segregated basis. In Providence, Rhode Island, to cite one instance, the bulldozer has displaced some Negro households as many as eight times.

Shortly after its formation more than a decade ago, the National Committee against Discrimination in Housing (a federation of thirty-seven major religious, civil-rights, labor, and civic organizations) protested this scandalous misuse of federal power and funds, and launched the long, hard battle for a Presidential order prohibiting discrimination in all housing affected in any manner by government action.

But the federal government is not the only villain in the housing drama. The real-estate fraternity—the builders, brokers, and mortgage lenders—controls access to the major part of the housing supply. To a large extent, it is within the industry's power to decide who will live where. Discrimination and segregation have been the norm in the exercise of that power. Whites are shown housing only in "white" areas; nonwhites in "black" or fringe areas, or in an established integrated community which has been scheduled for all-Negro occupancy. Lending institutions, as a general rule, will grant loans to nonwhites or to whites only for homes located in neighborhoods they consider "approved" for the particular occupant.

Testimony submitted on behalf of the Mortgage Bankers Association of Metropolitan Washington before the United States Civil Rights Commission's recent hearing on housing in the capital city area stated: "Applications from minority groups are not generally considered in areas that are not recognized as being racially mixed, on the premise that such an investment would not be stable and attractive to institutional lenders."

This "premise" more often than not is accepted as fact, but there is actually no unanimity on the subject within the financial community itself. Testifying at the same hearing, a representative of the District of Columbia's largest building and loan association reported that his institution makes loans to Negroes who seek to buy in predominantly or all-white neighborhoods, and that this practice has never resulted in a loss of business. The Bowery Savings Bank of New York—the world's largest savings bank—operates on a firm policy of nondiscrimination. Mr. Schwulst, now chairman of the Bowery's board, has stated that the bank considers the "color or ethnic origin of the borrower irrelevant," and that its experience has confirmed that position.

Until recent years, the official "Code of Ethics" of the National Association of Real Estate Boards included the following specific regulation:

"A realtor should never be instrumental in introducing into a neighborhood a character of property or occupancy, members of any race or nationality, or any individual whose presence will clearly be detrimental to property values in the neighborhood."

The contention that property values must decline with the entry of a minority family into a "majority" neighborhood has been thoroughly discredited by numerous scientific studies. Yet the industry and many individual citizens cling to the myth. If white residents use common sense and resist the scare tactics of real-estate speculators who trade in creating panic for profit, the chances are about four to one that the value of their property will increase. If the market is glutted with homes for sale, for whatever reason, values will fall.

Members of the real-estate industry, in their efforts to keep their "free" enterprise in an iron grip, employ tactics that tax the imagination. A classic example was exposed recently involving the five communities which form fashionable Grosse Pointe, Michigan. For fifteen years, the local brokers association, in conjunction with a property-owners organization, operated an elaborate point-rating system to protect the Pointes from "undesirables." A private detective screened prospective home buyers and graded them on grammar, friends, dress, and complexion, as well as religion, race, and ancestry. To be approved, Poles had to score fifty-five points; Greeks, sixty-five; Italians, seventy-five; and Jews, eighty-five. Orientals and Negroes automatically scored zero. A Detroit physician, descendant of a signer of the Declaration of Independence, inventor of the electrical heart, and recipient of four national awards, did not make the grade because his father is a Jew. An ironic side light: According to an NBC-TV program aired in October 1961, a small colony of gangsters and criminals are residents and share the joys of "exclusive living" in Grosse Pointe.

Yet, in spite of the formidable barriers, some solid progress has been made in the housing civil-rights field during the last ten years. While the results of these gains are not yet statistically significant, they are an important bellwether of prospects for the future.

Antibias housing legislation has set new records in the history of civil-rights enactments. Seventeen states and fifty-five cities have barred discrimination in some area of the housing market, either by law or policy resolutions. In the last five years alone, three cities, eleven states, and the Virgin Islands have adopted fair-housing laws applying to privately financed as well as government-aided housing. These include New York City (the pioneer), Pittsburgh, Toledo, Colorado, Massachusetts, Connecticut, Oregon, California, Pennsylvania, New York State, New Jersey, Minnesota, New Hampshire, and Alaska. It is significant that this exceeds the number of civil-rights enactments in a comparable period in either the employment or public-accommodations field. Furthermore, it has been the overwhelming judgment of the courts to uphold the constitutionality of the fair-housing statutes.

While the antibias housing laws have been in operation too short a period to have caused substantial changes in residential patterns, they are unquestionably helping to lower housing barriers. They have set a new ethical standard for the entire community; many members of the real-estate and banking industries have revised their former practices and are voluntarily complying with the laws; a sizable number of minority families—predominantly middle-class —have been helped by the laws in their efforts to move out of areas of racial concentration and into the mainstream of American life.

Despite the growth of segregation as a national pattern, the number of successful interracial communities scattered over the country has increased sharply during the last five years. It is possible today to identify more than one hundred developments—both single-home and apartment communities—which have followed an open-occupancy policy from their inception. These include the giant Prairie Shores luxury-apartment development on the lake shores of Chicago; the highly profitable Glenclift community in San Diego, California; the huge Morningside Gardens co-operative in New York City; Capital Park Apartments in Washington, D.C.; the Sinaiko Homes in Madison, Wisconsin; Concord Park in Philadelphia; and the prestige-laden Eichler developments in California—to name only a few.

In addition, an endless array of communities which were formerly restricted to whites, including mammoth Stuyvesant Town in New York City and the three Levittowns, have been racially integrated for some years. The waiting list of applicants remains jammed at Stuyvesant Town, and a Levittown house purchased for $9,000 several years ago will bring up to $18,000 today.

Perhaps the most dramatic indication of progress in recent years has been the spontaneous formation of literally hundreds of voluntary fair-housing groups in many sections of the country. This proliferating movement appears to be contagious, spreading from town to town and state to state. It cuts across all economic lines: the wealthy Scarsdales have their fair-housing committees, as do the middle-class Levittowns, and the upper-class avenues and work-ingmen's sections of the inner city. These indigenous groups of "citizens for integrated living" are working to make the goal a reality in their own communities. If they live in an "all-white" section, they want it to become integrated. If they live in an interracial area, they want to keep it that way. They believe the strong arm of the law is needed to insure the right of every American to compete for housing on an open market. But they are trying to knock down the walls of exclusion whether they have the assistance of a fair-housing law or not. Some of these citizens groups have impressive records of accomplishment.

Measurable progress has also been made within the real-estate industry. The number of builders, brokers, and mortgage lenders who are now operating on an open-market basis is highly significant—and is growing steadily.

Probably the most important advance is the stirring of conscience and common sense among the American people. Housing discrimination and segregation are now widely recognized as crucial domestic issues. Like cancer, housing discrimination is now constantly discussed in public forums. The popular magazines, the press, radio and television, conferences, sermons, and political speeches spotlight the problem almost daily. The people of the United States are beginning to learn the moral, social, political, and economic costs of residential segregation: increased juvenile delinquency, human demoralization produced by slum living, disease, crime, loss of potential skills, loss of tax revenue. A Chicago official recently commented: "Always before in America, when things got too expensive, we've figured out a new way."

America is moving toward a new way in housing civil rights, but much too timidly and much too slowly. An editor of *Fortune* recently wrote that "positive discrimination" in favor of the Negro must be exercised to overcome past actions against him. One thing is certain: It will take aggressive, unrelenting, and multipronged efforts to make the right to equal opportunity in housing a reality. We can achieve this goal only when our efforts insure:

1. Effective and meaningful enforcement of the Presidential order on federally aided housing. Government sponsorship of segregation must be transformed into government sponsorship of democratic living patterns.

2. The enactment of fair-housing legislation by states and cities throughout the country, coupled with effective enforcement procedures. Law is much more than an instrument of coercion. It is a potent educational weapon in the battle for social progress.

3. A closing of the economic gap between Negro and white incomes.

4. A housing supply which is within the means of the people. "You can't have fair housing without full housing."

5. Greater understanding and active co-operation from the real-estate industry.

6. An increased drive among both Negroes and whites toward true residential integration.

America, the "land of the free," must come to grips with the hard truth that no man is free unless he can freely choose where he will live. At stake is the integrity of our democratic system, both for ourselves and before the peoples of the world.

30 : *Color Blind or Color Conscious?— Benign Quotas in Housing*

Peter Marcuse

. . . Is a [racial] quota benign [in housing] which attempts to maintain, in the development to which it is applied, the same ratio of Negro to white occupancy as exists in the community in which that development is located? Is a quota benign which measures the proportionate need in the income group in question for the particular housing involved and then allocates the housing on the basis of such a proportion? Is a quota benign which attempts to give major representation to each important ethnic group in the community, i.e., in a California community, one-third white, one-third Negro, one-sixth Chinese-American, one-sixth Mexican-American? . . . Each of these quotas is based on the fundamental assumption that when a given minority group has received its "fair share" of whatever is in question, the rights of that group have been protected. Each of these quota systems assumes that, if it

Mr. Marcuse is an attorney in Waterbury, Connecticut.

has been properly put into effect in a given development, the problem it was designed to meet is completely solved.

The theory of a true benign quota, on the other hand, as that term is here used, is that the rights of any given minority group will only be fully secured if they stand on an absolutely equal plane with all other individuals in society. Benign quotas are seen as only a step in this direction; their justification lies entirely in the belief that, were they not used, the development involved could not long remain an integrated or open one. The definition used by the American Jewish Committee and the Anti-Defamation League of B'nai B'rith is both concise and accurate, and indicates the sense in which we use the phrase in this paper: "A 'benign quota' is a system under which a fixed ratio is established in terms of race or ethnic origin for the occupancy of a housing development, for the purpose of achieving and maintaining integration."

The desirability of benign quotas may be questioned but there is no question of the seriousness of the problems they are designed to meet. The concept of the "tipping point" [is] the point at which the number of minority-group—usually Negro—families moving into a neighborhood previously racially homogeneous causes the original residents to conclude that the neighborhood is certain to become all-Negro and therefore to begin to move out. . . .

The harmful effects of passing the tipping point are, if anything, even more apparent and even more serious in public housing than in neighborhoods. The tendency for public housing to become Negro housing is widespread and accelerating. This is partially the product of the economic disadvantages suffered by Negroes as a group, resulting in generally lower wages, coupled with discrimination in most of the private-housing market, making it less possible for Negroes to obtain housing elsewhere. Above and beyond this, however, it can be demonstrated with reasonable conclusiveness that the heavy preponderance of Negro occupancy in a great many public-housing developments is caused as much by the absence of white applicants and the move-out of white residents as it is by a backlog of Negro needs for such housing.

Figures analyzed by this writer for representative northeastern metropolitan projects show that it is very rare that any project maintains a stable ratio of Negro to white occupancy when the percentage of Negro occupancy is between 40 and 80 per cent. Below 40 per cent, apparently, the tipping point has not been reached; above 80 per cent, there will always be certain white families who by virtue of economic necessity or other factors will remain in public housing regardless of its racial composition. From the figures thus analyzed, a tipping point between 30 and 40 per cent in public housing seems to be quite clearly established.

The low status to which public housing has fallen in the eyes of many in our communities is directly the result of the same factors that have caused it to become predominantly Negro-occupied. As the proportionate level of income of the occupants of public housing has diminished, as an increasing number of its occupants have been families newly arrived from rural surroundings, as an increasing number of white families in public housing are "hard core" families on welfare or otherwise unable to handle their problems with their own resources, so public housing has acquired a reputation for delinquency, noise, dirtiness, and similar characteristics.

As one method of coping with these problems, a considerable number of public-housing authorities have turned to the informal use of benign quotas to preserve the racial balance of their projects. . . . Most authorities have felt, however, that there are limitations beyond which benign quotas may not be utilized and specifically that the open use of such quotas probably would violate federal and in some cases state law. . . .

On the extreme ends of the scale, however, the legal situation as regards benign quotas in private housing is clear: in states having fair-housing laws, quotas will not be legally enforceable in the courts; on the other hand, even in such states, voluntary attempts to persuade buyers of housing at initial sales to abide by a benign quota, without refusing to sell to anyone who insists on his right to purchase, should not run afoul of any statutory or common-law provision in the United States.

In public housing the legal situation is much clearer. While one of the three decisions dealing with quotas in public housing sustained the use of such quotas, that decision relied heavily on the language of *Plessy* v. *Ferguson* and the separate-but-equal doctrine, which, of course, has since been very substantially discredited by the decisions in the school-desegregation cases. Both of the other cases held quotas in public-housing projects unconstitutional, regardless of the basis on which they were computed. The New Jersey court said flatly, "The use of any quota system in admitting Negroes to public housing projects is discriminatory." The California court held in equally strong language that, regardless of the effect of a particular quota on Negroes as a group, if an individual Negro was refused occupancy because of his race, that individual's constitutional rights were violated. . . .

That public-housing authorities may not directly use benign quotas, however, should not be taken to mean that such authorities are powerless to attempt to promote integration in their projects. Many legitimate techniques to achieve the purpose for which benign quotas are designed have been tried and found effective to varying extents. The location of projects in areas away from concentrations of minority groups, the use of selective channels of promotion and solicitation of tenants, the development of architectural styles and physical facilities uniformly attractive to all groups, and the adjustment of income limits and dependency allowances have all been used in various communities to attempt to maintain a balanced occupancy. . . .

[To turn to the policy arguments], the fundamental and overwhelming argument in favor of benign quotas of course is that they assist in the creation and maintenance of integration in housing. There is no longer any serious question that the mere knowledge that Negroes will never be in a majority in a given development has a very substantial effect in making prospective white purchasers accept more readily the idea of living in an integrated development. The extreme advocates of benign quotas go so far as to say that, under today's circumstances, if an integrated-housing development is to be built, the developer must be able to control the proportion of Negro-to-white occupancy by the use of a quota system. . . .

In many cases the type of control referred to above can be achieved by means other than the imposition of benign quotas. By judicious placement of advertisements, by working with key individuals and groups in the Negro and white community, by selecting the areas and prices and styles of the homes to be built, Negro or white interest can be stimulated or discouraged. Certainly where they are successful, these alternatives are to be preferred to the imposition of quotas; but it would be begging the question to say that quotas should only be used where other alternatives are not available. There may well be situations in which the use of benign quotas will be the key factor in determining whether or not a community will remain integrated. In such situations, should their use be recommended?

The argument against their use can perhaps be crudely summarized in one sentence: use of such quotas represents planning or manipulation of people, for an improper purpose, using an impermissible criterion, sacrificing the welfare of certain individuals for the possible benefit of a group, thus depriving such individuals of certain fundamental rights guaranteed under the Constitution. . . .

If the question were to be asked, in terms of public housing, "Can the government under any circumstances deny an apartment to a family solely because of its color?" the almost reflex answer of most thinking persons today would almost certainly be "No." This is a reaction that has been inculcated through years of fighting against prejudice and second-class citizenship, against Jim Crow buses and segregated schools, against unequal job opportunities and Negro ghettos.

But the fight in all these areas, at least on a public or governmental level, has always been a negative one. It has, at least until very recently in most areas, been to eliminate abuses, to end unfair discrimination, to combat restrictions against Negroes. . . .

Since Justice Harlan's famous dissent in *Plessy* v. *Ferguson* we have applauded the now oft-repeated phrase that our Constitution and laws should be "color blind." Where recognition of color leads to persecution, inferiority, and deprivation of rights, color blindness is much to be preferred. Color is, however, as a matter of cold fact, important in many areas of life in the United States today. Denying this fact does not change it, it only makes it harder to deal with.

If we are concerned with providing equal protection of the laws, it is necessary not only to protect equally those who are already equal, but also to achieve equality for those who are not, but should be. The law has recognized this problem in other areas: in theory, a worker on the assembly line in a Chevrolet plant in Detroit can bargain on an equal basis with the president of General Motors as to his hourly rate; as a practical matter their positions are not equal and, to remedy this inequality, the law recognizes the appropriateness of acts like the Wagner Act, which encourages union organization so that the two parties may in fact come closer to equality at the bargaining table. . . .

In the area of racial relations, the law is coming to recognize here and there that affirmative action, taking the facts of race into direct account, may sometimes be appropriate to achieve actual equality. Affirmative education of the public against prejudice based on color is recognized to be a legitimate governmental function; and the multiplication of state and city commissions and agencies charged with such responsibility shows this. Various housing arms of the federal government have their racial-relations advisors; a formal government-contracts committee attempts to enforce fair-employment practices by government contractors; special efforts are made to insure Negroes the right to vote in Southern states. . . .

Granting, then, that the use of color as a standard for governmental action does not necessarily bar the use of benign quotas, does the fact that certain individuals are directly and deliberately harmed by government action through no fault of their own make such action improper? Certainly in many other areas we are perfectly willing to accept the fact that the public welfare may require the sacrifice of individual interest. Thus a new highway will cause individual dislocations and hardships, but clearly the general good is sufficient to justify the individual harm. In the same way, certainly, integration has been found to be desirable in and of itself by most persons who are concerned with the field of intergroup relations. Both the positive values of heterogeneity and the negative impact of segregation have been documented with increasingly convincing evidence in recent years. If the sacrifice of better housing for a few members of a minority group will result in a greater benefit not only to that group but to society as a whole, such a policy should be a proper one. This is precisely the theory on the basis of which benign quotas are advocated. . . .

If a developer, with the specific aim of establishing an integrated community, should use a quota system to maintain the balance he desires, public policy is not offended thereby. If, for the same purpose, a public-housing authority attempts by a process of intelligent discussion and persuasion to convince a Negro family that it is more desirable for it to remain on the waiting list for a somewhat longer period of time than its priority of application or need dictates, such a policy may also be in the over-all social good.

[However], the attempt to enforce adherence to a benign quota [by legal means introduces] a new factor. . . . The distinction that we are drawing between permissible and impermissible uses of benign quotas is the distinction between the voluntary and involuntary use of such quotas. It may well be that there is a logical inconsistency in saying that a given policy is desirable as substantially advantageous for a large group, although detrimental to a few individuals, as long as none of those individuals object, but saying that if any one of such individuals should object, the policy becomes undesirable if insisted upon. Nevertheless, this happens to be the result of one of the basic premises on which our constitutional rights are predicated. Such rights, in American jurisprudence, are individual rights and not group rights. These individual rights are held sacred against any government interference, no matter how well motivated it may be, and our courts are protecting them also against more and more forms of private interference. . . .

The one argument in this area that is not only irrelevant but even by now harmful, and should be finally rejected for good, is the argument that governmental action must be "color blind" to guarantee effective civil rights. Like the old "melting pot" phrase, "color blindness" refers to one portion of a noble and valid ideal: that a person's color or race or national origin *should* have no relevance whatsoever to the manner in which that person is treated in a democratic society.

But this is a statement of an aspiration, not a fact, in America today; and to make the aspiration become fact it must first be recognized that there is still a difference. Recognition of the problem is the first step toward its solution; to ignore the existence of inequalities, discrimination, and prejudice does not help to erase them. One cannot effectively oppose discrimination against Negroes without knowing that Negroes are discriminated against where whites are not, and therefore that, to this extent they are in fact different. The goal of action is to make them equal, but such action must obviously comprehend the fact that they are not now equal.

When a critic of benign quotas states, "The fundamental error of a quota system is its assumption that Negroes are different from other citizens and should be treated differently," he is laying his finger on one of the strengths, not one of the weaknesses, of the benign quota. No matter what its pros or cons may be, it is at least one realistic, honest, and thoughtful effort to solve one of our country's greatest remaining social problems today. When compliance with such quotas is voluntarily achieved, they can be a major asset in the attempt to achieve integration; when the legal right of freedom from discrimination because of color is violated, however, the price that is paid, in our constitutional framework, is too high. Within these limits benign quotas can serve a real and worthwhile purpose.

DISCRIMINATION AGAINST NEGROES IN LAW ENFORCEMENT

31 : *Keeping Negroes "in Their Place" in Georgia*

United States Commission on Civil Rights

. . . The town of Dawson in Terrell County, Georgia, is approximately thirty miles south of Newton. There on April 20, 1958, James Brazier, a Negro in his thirties, suffered a beating at the hands of officers of the law (from which he later died). . . .

According to the police account, the incident started in the early evening of Sunday, April 20, 1958, when Dawson Police Officer X arrested James Brazier's father on a charge of driving under the influence of alcohol. When the elder Brazier resisted, he was subdued by a blackjack. James Brazier protested and, according to the policemen, threatened the officer who later returned with Officer Y and arrested the younger Brazier, allegedly with a warrant, for interfering with an arrest. He resisted violently and was subdued with a blackjack. Shortly thereafter he was taken to jail and examined by a local physician who found no serious injury.

Brazier died five days later at a hospital in Columbus, Georgia, from brain damage and a fractured skull. He had four to six bruised spots on his scalp from a blunt instrument which apparently also caused the skull fracture. The police claimed that Brazier was hit only once or twice at the time of the arrest.

In a sworn statement to commission representatives Mrs. Hattie Bell Brazier, the widow of the victim, claimed that this affair had actually started months earlier. Mrs. Brazier explained that she and her husband had purchased a new Chevrolet in 1956—and another in 1958. In November of 1957 James Brazier had been arrested on a speeding charge. According to Mrs. Brazier, her husband told her that Dawson Officer Y took him to jail, and that "when I first entered the door of the jail, [Y] hit me on the back of the head and knocked me down and said, 'You smart son-of-a-bitch, I been wanting to get my hands on you for a long time.' I said, 'Why you want me for?' [Y] said, 'You is a nigger who is buying new cars and we can't hardly live. I'll get you yet.' "

Officer Y then allegedly hit Brazier several more times, put his foot on the small of the prostrate Negro's back (Mrs. Brazier said she saw the footprints there later), and warned him, "You'd better not say a damn thing about it or I'll stomp your damn brains out." After his release from jail, Brazier was bleeding from his ear and vomiting blood. From this time in the fall of 1957 until the second incident in April of 1958, James Brazier was under the care of a local white doctor because of these injuries. Officer X, the policeman who accompanied Y during the arrest in April 1958, also allegedly made a remark about the new car at some time previous to the fatal incident. It appears that James Brazier of Terrell County . . . was considered an "uppity" Negro.

The story of the fatal incident in 1958 as told by Mrs. Brazier and several other colored witnesses contradicts the account given by the officers. In her affidavit Mrs. Brazier stated that her husband had been beaten brutally by the arresting officers in full view of numerous colored people, including herself and her four children. No warrant was presented by the officers, nor was any paper observed in their hands. The officers, she said, simply ran out of their car and roughly grabbed her husband. While pulling him toward the police car, Y beat him repeatedly with a blackjack. Mrs. Brazier's affidavit continued:

"[Y] then said, 'You smart son-of-a-bitch, I told you I would get you.' James said, 'What do you want to hurt me for? I ain't done nothing. I got a heap of little chillun [*sic*].' [Y] said, 'I don't give a goddamn how many children you got, you're going away from here.' . . . [Y] pulled out his pistol and stuck it against James' stomach and said, 'I oughta blow your goddamn brains out.' "

Then these events allegedly occurred: James Brazier's ten-year-old son pleaded with the officers to stop beating his father and was knocked to the ground by Y; the victim was thrown onto the floor of the police car with his legs dangling outside; Y kicked him twice in the groin; slammed the car door on his legs; threw a hatful of sand into his bloody face, and drove off.

When Brazier reached the jail, he was bloody but conscious and apparently not seriously injured by the beating he had received. Yet, when he was taken to court the next morning, he was virtually unconscious. The question that arises is whether Brazier was beaten during the interval between his arrival in jail at approximately 7 P.M. and his appearance in court at approximately 9 A.M. the next day. There is evidence that he was. It comes from several witnesses, one of whom has since died and may be identified— Marvin Goshay, a Negro who was twenty-three years of age when he signed an affidavit on August 24, 1960, during an interview with commission representatives in Albany, Georgia. Goshay was in jail on a charge of assault and battery when Brazier was incarcerated. The story, as Goshay saw it, is as follows: When James Brazier was brought into the jail he was fully dressed in suit, shirt, tie, and shoes. He talked coherently to Goshay (describing his arrest consistently with Mrs. Brazier's later testimony). Several hours later—probably around midnight—he was ordered out of the cell by Officers X and Y. "They took Brazier out again," Goshay stated in his affidavit. "He asked them to wait because he wanted to put on his shoes. The police said, 'You won't need no shoes.' " This was the last time that Goshay saw him that night. Goshay next saw Brazier on the following morning. His affidavit continued:

He had on pants, a torn undershirt, no coat, no tie, no white shirt. The last time I saw him, he had on a blue suit, white shirt, and tie. He looked worse on his head than when I saw him also. . . . It was beaten worse than when I first saw him. On his back were about four long marks about a foot long. They looked reddish and bruised. His head was bleeding. We had to carry [him] to the car because he couldn't walk. He was slobbering at the mouth. When we got to the car, James, who was dazed but not completely out, didn't know enough to get in the car. Mr. [Z—a Dawson police officer] said if he didn't get in, he'd beat him with his blackjack.

More than a year after Brazier's death Sheriff Z. T. Mathews of Terrell County allegedly made the following statement to Mrs. Brazier: "I oughta slap your damn brains out. A nigger like you I feel like slapping them out. You niggers set around here and look at television and go up North and come back and do to white folks here like the niggers up North do, but you ain't gonna do it. I'm gonna carry the South's orders out like it oughta be done." Also, Sheriff Mathews told reporter Robert E. Lee Baker, "You know, Cap, . . . there's nothing like fear to keep niggers in line. I'm talking about 'outlaw' niggers."

No local disciplinary or criminal action was taken against any of the officers involved. The attitude of local authorities toward police was protective in this and several other cases of alleged brutality that occurred within a brief period in Dawson. Indeed, there was indignation when Negroes claimed they were "living in an atmosphere of fear." . . . [The] Department of Justice was sufficiently impressed with the results of an FBI investigation to authorize Civil Rights Acts prosecutions. From August 4 to 8, 1958, the local United States Attorney presented witnesses to a federal grand jury in Macon and requested indictments in five cases of alleged police brutality against policemen X, Y, and another Dawson officer. The grand jury returned no indictments. . . .

Not long after Brazier died, police officer Y was promoted to Chief of the Dawson Police Department. Z. T. Mathews at this writing [1961] is still sheriff of Terrell County. . . .

32 : *Police Tactics in Mississippi*

**Mississippi Advisory Committee,
United States Commission
on Civil Rights**

. . . We . . . believe that a pattern exists in our state that leads
to the denial of constitutional rights and, in some instances, to
brutality and terror. From the moment a Negro adult is hailed as
"boy" or "girl" by a police officer, through his arrest, detention,
trial—during which his Negro lawyer is treated with contemptuous
familiarity by the judge and other officers of the court—and even-
tual imprisonment, he is treated with a pernicious difference. This
difference is incompatible with Christian ideals about the dignity
of man and with the principles of Anglo-Saxon criminal law.

How often this atmosphere produces actual terror and brutality
is a question that demands further investigation. We feel strongly
that we have probable cause to believe that police brutality is a
continuing problem in at least certain sections of our state, and
that a formal investigation into this problem must be undertaken.
The cases that follow give some indication of the severity of the
problem. The names, places, and dates have been omitted to protect the witnesses. All incidents reportedly occurred in Mississippi
in the last three years.

EXAMPLE E: A NEGRO MAN

"On . . . about 11:30 A.M., I, ———, was trailed about three miles by a highway patrolman, immediately after leaving ———. Knowing that I was being followed, I took extreme caution in my driving.

"When the officer decided to stop me he blew his siren, and I pulled to the side of the road and stopped.

"At this point the officer got out of his car, walked to the rear of my car and demanded that my friend remain in the car and I come to the rear. When I approached the officer he asked me for my license. As I began looking through my belongings for my license, I asked the officer what were the charges. The officer replied, 'Nigger you keep your damn mouth shut, I'll ask the questions.' At which time the officer raised his blackjack and began hitting me on the head and the shoulders. In an attempt to protect myself from him I threw my arms up. The officer, still trying to hit me on the head, demanded that 'you move them damn arms boy, move them god-damn-it.'

"Because I did not move my arms from around my head, the officer drew his gun and declared, 'Damn you, nigger, I'm going to kill you.' I begged him not to shoot me and he told me, 'Shut up nigger,' and hit me, with his gun on me, declared, 'I will make you move them arms, nigger, put your arms out here,' at which time he handcuffed me, and hit me several more times, pushed me to the side of his car, opened the door, pushed me in, hit me on the head and told me to 'sit there you black b—— and shut up.' The officer then walked over to my car where my friend was sitting.

"With his pistol in his hand, he pulled the door open and demanded that he get out and get in the car. When the officer got in his car, I informed him that I had dropped my wallet, and asked him could I get it. At that moment, again he began hitting me as he was saying, 'I thought I told you to shut your damn mouth. Move your hands, you damn nigger, god-damn-it, I'm going to kill you.' After he had finished beating me, he placed his gun under his left leg and proceeded to drive.

"On our way to the police station he asked me, 'Where were you going, boy?' I told him we were just riding. Then he asked me, 'What are you going this way for, boy?' I told him I had planned to visit some friends, where he said, 'You are telling me a damn lie, boy,' and then asked my friend where he was going. My friend said he just came along with me, then the officer asked, 'You mean you just go along with people, without knowing where in the hell you are going?' In reply my friend said, 'He is my friend —I don't have to ask him where he is going; if he was a stranger I would have.'

"When we reached the station he demanded us to get out of the car and head for those two doors on the right, he was walking behind us. Upon entering the building, he demanded my friend to sit down in the hall and continued to trail me into the clerk's office.

"Before we had reached the center of the room he began hitting me with his blackjack on my head and arms, as he was saying, 'Boy, I am going to kill you'—'this damn nigger scratched me'— 'I'm going to kill this nigger.'

"There were eight or nine other men in the room and I pleaded with them to stop him from hitting me, but not a one said a word, as the officer continued his inhuman attack.

"When the officer did stop, I asked to use the phone and was told by the officer, 'You ain't using nothing.' The desk clerk, wearing glasses, took a leather strap out of a drawer (a brown strap about 4 or 5 inches wide and about 2½ or 3 feet long) and said, 'Let's take him down.' When my friend got up to come along, he was told to stay there.

"The officer that brought me in, the desk clerk, with the glasses on, the warner (*sic*) and two other men escorted me to a little room in the building where the cells were.

"With the five men standing around me the clerk said, 'Drop your pants, nigger.' I did as he said and some of the other men began instructing me, how to lay across a chair. My hands were handcuffed around the foot of the chair as I lay across the back of it.

"After I was in a position to please them the clerk said, 'If you holler, nigger, we will kill you.' The officer said, 'Nigger, we are going to tear your a— off,' and hit me again on the head with his blackjack. As all of them took turns beating me with the strap I could hear statements as, 'Let's kill this nigger'; 'This nigger knows what he has done wrong'; 'A nigger going to hit an officer.'

"This beating continued while two men held my legs and one my hands.

"The officer asked the jailer did he have anything to keep me from swelling? In reply the jailer stated he had some whisky and poured some over my back and legs.

"During that time the clerk said, 'Get up nigger, you are lucky you are not dead.' As the other men began leaving the room the officer said, 'What is your name, nigger?' When I told him my name he said, "Wipe the whisky on your a— nigger, and pull your pants up.'

"After I had dressed, the jailer carried me to a cell. I again asked to use the telephone, but he said, 'No, not now, maybe later.'

"During my 28½ hours in jail I asked the jailer for four times, each time he brought my meals, to let me use the phone, and he said, 'Later.' " . . .

FINDINGS

1. The first finding of this committee is that justice under law is not guaranteed for the Negro in Mississippi in the way that it is for the white man. This is true to the extent that much of the basic meaning of being an American citizen is denied to nearly half the citizens of the state. The idea of the dignity and worth of every individual is fundamental to the American way of life and to the Christian code of ethics on which our system is based. These concepts are systematically violated and an injustice done to us all when 42.3 per cent of the citizens of this state must either accept an inferior station in life and an attitude of servility or endanger themselves and their families by protesting. All Mississippians are thereby denied the privilege of living under the best and fairest form of government yet devised. We find that terror hangs over the Negro in Mississippi and is an expectancy for those who refuse to accept their color as a badge of inferiority; and terrorism has no proper place in the American form of government.

2. The second finding of this committee is that the state government of Mississippi is not sufficiently concerned with the task of protecting the rights of all citizens of Mississippi. Even if police brutality were less severe and widespread than we have believed, a responsible state government would take energetic steps to ascertain the facts and punish the wrongdoers. A firm position on this

matter by the state government would reduce the tendency of lesser officials to abuse their authority and would enhance the respect of the people for the state government. As matters stand today, we are forced to report that the attitude of the state government, rather than being one of protection, has been one of obstruction of the realization of the rights of our citizens. Sections 2155.4–2155.6 of the Mississippi Code are an indication of the current official attitude. These sections make a conviction for perjury in a civil-rights case easier to obtain than in any other perjury case. Since Negroes represent the overwhelming majority of persons likely to be forced to make sworn statements in order to secure basic rights, this 1960 legislation seems designed to intimidate or punish those of the Negro race who would assert these rights.

3. While this committee feels that the accounts of its meetings in the press of the state have usually been fair and objective, we find that in general the press is failing to meet its obligation to our society. When an element of government exceeds or neglects its proper role in a free society it is the duty of the press to alert the people to the situation. The people of Mississippi are largely unaware of the extent of the problem of illegal official violence and the press is partly to blame. It is a zealous crusader against governmental injustice when the federal government is believed to be at fault, but closes its eyes to state or local official mistreatment of Negro citizens.

4. This committee finds that the federal government has not provided the citizens of Mississippi the protection due them as American citizens. The Department of Justice has acted in good faith, but the present interpretation of the function of the Civil Rights Division of the Justice Department is unduly and unwisely narrow and limited. This may be due to the inadequacy of funds available to the division for staff and the like, and it may be due to a reluctance to bring cases to trial under existing Civil Rights Acts in view of the prospect of facing an all-white jury likely to return a verdict in favor of a white law-enforcement official accused by a Negro. Whatever the reason, the fact that police officers are rarely tried on civil-rights charges has led the public to believe that few serious charges are ever made, and has reinforced the belief among offending peace officers that they may treat or mistreat Negroes as their whims direct them. . . .

33 : *Segregated Justice in Birmingham*

Charles Morgan, Jr.

(A) For that in the City of Birmingham, Alabama, according to the 1960 Federal Decennial Census, there are 205,260 white people and 135,113 Negro people.

(B) For that in the County of Jefferson, Alabama, according to the 1960 Federal Decennial Census, there are 415,035 white people and 219,542 Negro people.

(C) In the County of Jefferson, Alabama, according to the 1960 Federal Decennial Census, there are 312,479 persons over the age of twenty-one years; 120,205 of whom are white males; 136,114 of whom are white females; 51,961 of whom are Negro males and 64,199 of whom are Negro females.

(D) Boaz Sanders, a Negro man, is accused of the crimes of both murder and robbery of a white man, the alleged acts having occurred on, to wit, the third day of June 1962. He was arrested on the fifth day of June 1962, by a white policeman or policemen, employed by the police department of the City of Birmingham, Alabama, the entire membership of which is composed of white men and women, Negroes being systematically excluded from em-

Mr. Morgan, a white lawyer in Birmingham, was appointed by the Circuit Court of Jefferson County, Ala., to represent the defendant in the case described here.

ployment therein because of their race or color. He was thereafter transported to the Birmingham city jail in a racially segregated patrol car or paddy wagon, such racial segregation existing under and by virtue of the terms and provisions of Rule 327 of the Police Manual of the City of Birmingham, Alabama, which provides: "He shall not transport white and Negro prisoners or male and female prisoners or juvenile and adult prisoners in the same *compartment* of the patrol wagon." (Emphasis supplied.)

He was then incarcerated in the city jail of the City of Birmingham, all of the wardens, matrons, clerks, and employees of which are white, Negroes being systematically excluded from employment therein because of their race or color. In such jail he was placed and confined in a cell set apart for Negroes, racial segregation being practiced in the housing of prisoners thereat. He was thereafter transferred and transported in racially segregated circumstances and facilities to the Jefferson County jail by a deputy sheriff employed by the sheriff's department of Jefferson County, Alabama, Negroes being systematically excluded from employment in such sheriff's department because of their race or color. He was then incarcerated in the Jefferson County jail (Birmingham Division), all of the wardens, matrons, clerks, and employees of which are white, Negroes being systematically excluded from employment therein because of their race or color. In such jail, he was placed and confined in a cell set apart for Negroes, racial segregation being practiced in the housing of prisoners thereat.

A warrant for his arrest (which was never served on him) was sworn out against him (after he had been confined to the city jail) said warrant being issued from and returnable to the Jefferson County court of misdemeanors which is presided over by a white judge, all of the bailiffs, clerks, and employees thereat being white, Negroes being systematically excluded from employment therein because of their race or color.

He was then indicted by the grand jury for the tenth judicial circuit of Alabama (Jefferson County, Birmingham Division), Negroes having been systematically excluded from membership thereon solely because of their race or color. Presentation of evidence to the grand jury was under the control of and conducted by the office of the circuit solicitor of the tenth judicial circuit of Alabama (Birmingham Division) Jefferson County, Alabama, Negroes being systematically excluded from employment therein because of their race or color. At the time of arraignment, he was brought to the courtroom by a white bailiff or other white court employee in the courtroom, there being no Negro court employees in the Jefferson County (Birmingham Division) courthouse, Negroes having been systematically excluded from employment therein because of their race or color. Approaching the said courtroom, he must pass by rest rooms marked "Colored Men" or "Colored Women" or "White Men" or "White Women." He also must pass drinking fountains labeled "Colored" and "White." On the sixth floor, he must pass by an elevator leading to the law library of the Birmingham Bar Association, which such bar association systematically excludes Negroes from membership therein and which such law library has in the past been racially segregated, Negro attorneys having been allowed in the past to acquire books from any room, but being confined to the use of only one room for the reading thereof, such practice having been discontinued in the last three (3) months.

The audience in the courtroom will be racially segregated, such custom and practice not having been altered up to and including the date of the filing of this motion. The trial will be held before a white petit jury, Negroes having been systematically excluded from listing on the rolls or being placed upon the cards from which the membership thereof will be drawn because of their race or color. At his trial, a white judge (there being no Negro judges in the entire state of Alabama) will preside and a white circuit solicitor or deputy or assistant circuit solicitor (there being no Negro circuit solicitors or deputy or assistant circuit solicitors in the entire state of Alabama) will prosecute him, his counsel being white and all court employees being white.

In the event that one or more Negroes appeared on the petit jury in this or any other criminal case tried in Jefferson County (Birmingham Division), they would be required to use segregated rest rooms, water fountains, eating facilities, and overnight accommodations. Indeed, it would be impossible for a racially mixed petit jury to be kept together overnight in that there are no hotels, motels, restaurants, or other sleeping and eating places in Jefferson County, Alabama, whether publicly or privately owned, whereat a Negro member of a jury could be housed overnight and fed with other jury members who were white, except perhaps, they could eat together at the Greyhound Bus Station, no jury ever having done so in the past. Ordinances of the City of Birmingham and the custom and practice in Jefferson County, Alabama, forbid this. Negroes could sit without physical barriers between them and whites in the jury box.

In the event he were convicted, and was not sentenced to death or placed on probation and no appeal were taken from such conviction, Boaz Sanders would be transported to the state penitentiary by a white man in racially segregated transportation facilities and circumstances. He would thereafter be incarcerated in a racially segregated penitentiary. In the event he receives the death penalty, he will be confined in Kilby Prison on death row, which is racially segregated. The wardens, matrons, clerks, and employees of the Alabama State Penal Institutions are white, Negroes being systematically excluded from employment therein because of race or color.

Boaz Sanders, if convicted, and sentenced to death, will have an automatic appeal to the Supreme Court of Alabama, which appeal would be opposed by an attorney employed by the office of the attorney general of Alabama, all employees thereof, attorneys and clerical and other lay assistants being white, Negroes being systematically excluded from employment therein because of race or color.

All justices of the Supreme Court of Alabama are white as are all of their clerks and employees.

Assuming failure in the Supreme Court of Alabama, Boaz Sanders would then appeal to the Supreme Court of the United States, each of the justices thereon being white.

If he receives the death penalty there, he will then be given a last meal by his white guards, visited by a white chaplain, shaved by a white barber, and taken by white guards to a yellow electric chair in Kilby Prison (the yellow electric chair being the only facility in Alabama justice which is and has always been desegregated, there being but one such electric chair in existence in the Alabama State Penal Institutions). A button or switch will be pressed or pulled by a white man, before white witnesses, and the condemned man will die. Being in indigent circumstances, he will thereafter be taken by white men and buried in a potter's grave in a racially segregated cemetery, provided by the state of Alabama.

As further proof of a system of segregated justice in the City of Birmingham and Jefferson County, Alabama, Boaz Sanders offers as fact:

(A) That the civil-service system in Jefferson County, Alabama, is responsible for the filling of vacancies and positions of employment for Jefferson County and all municipalities therein, of over five thousand (5,000) population, Birmingham being but one of these, and the County Health Department, such vacancies and positions of employment including all nonelective governmental positions relating to the system of justice such as bailiffs, clerks, typists, and policemen and policewomen, deputy sheriffs, and jail personnel, elective positions being circuit clerk, circuit solicitor, police commissioner, sheriff, and circuit judges, and the said civil-service system is administered by a white director, the personnel board itself is composed of white men only, the Citizens Supervisory Commission, with the power to revoke rules, recommend rules, elect members of the personnel board and remove them, and remove members of the staff of the board, is composed of white persons only, and each and every one of the employees of said personnel board are white.

(B) That all recorders courts of the City of Birmingham and all inferior civil courts and the probate court in Jefferson County, Alabama, are presided over by white judges and have white clerks and employees.

(C) That the clerks of the recorders court of the City of Birmingham and of the tenth judicial circuit (Jefferson County, Birmingham Division) are white men, as are all employees in such offices.

(D) That the jury board of Jefferson County, which is charged by law with acquiring the names of persons eligible for jury duty and making jury rolls and lists, is composed only of white persons and has no employee who is not white.

(E) That the laboratory facilities provided by the state of Alabama for use in the investigation of crime is [sic] staffed in administrative and professional positions by white people.

(F) That the Alabama State Highway Patrol employs no Negroes in professional or technical positions, all of such personnel being white.

(G) That the office of city attorney of the City of Birmingham,

Alabama, employs no Negroes, all of its staff and personnel being white.

(H) That all state toxicologists are white.

The State of Alabama does not now and has not for many years (at least during this century) provided a system of justice other than the one set out herein which is based on absolute racial segregation, a segregation which permeates the entire system from the cradle to the grave; one from which Negroes are and have been systematically excluded in every respect except as defendants. . . .

34 : *Police Inaction and Anti-Negro Violence*

United States Commission on Civil Rights

"One charged with the duty of keeping the peace cannot be an innocent bystander where the constitutionally protected rights of persons are being invaded. He must stand on the side of law and order or be counted among the mob."

These words, written by a federal circuit judge almost ten years ago, constitute a lucid statement of the major premise underlying this section on . . . "private" violence that has some direct or indirect governmental sanction—as when policemen intentionally fail to protect a person from mob attack; when they fail to take proper steps to protect prisoners in their custody from private violence; or when they connive in private misconduct by failure to arrest its perpetrators. . . .

JACKSONVILLE: 1960

On Saturday, August 27, 1960, there were a series of attacks by white men on Negroes in Jacksonville, Florida. This soon developed into a race riot which continued for several days. For some weeks prior to the outbreaks, Mayor Haydon Burns explained to a commission representative, members of the NAACP Youth Council had staged peaceful sit-in demonstrations in downtown Jacksonville. On Friday, August 26, Mayor Burns (who is also the police commissioner) received reports that violent white attacks might take place on the next day. He so informed the chief of police at midnight on August 26. Both the mayor and the chief of police arrived at police headquarters at 6:45 the next morning. They went before the squads going on duty at 8 A.M. and apprised them of the situation. According to the mayor, the policemen were told to concern themselves only with preserving the peace—that as long as they could do so they were not to make any wholesale arrests.

Several eyewitnesses stated that at approximately 8 A.M., August 27, they saw a group of white men milling about in Hemming Park, which is in downtown Jacksonville. Some had axe handles and baseball bats in their hands and two white men were seen cutting the wire from around a bundle containing perhaps fifty new axe handles. These were passed out to the waiting crowd. At approximately 9:30 A.M., the mob marched in a column of two's toward the nearby downtown stores.

Most carried axe handles or baseball bats over their shoulders military-style. Some had Confederate battle flags attached to their weapons. When they found Negroes they proceeded to attack them with the clubs.

This had all the earmarks of a carefully planned assault. At the beginning it was not a race riot but an attack by violent white men on peaceful Negroes, many of whom had nothing to do with the sit-in demonstrations. Negro witnesses were of the opinion that many of the assailants had come into the city expressly for this attack.

Jacksonville policemen observed the apparently disciplined group forming in Hemming Park. They saw the axe handles being passed out. They watched as the crowd marched toward the stores and the Negroes. Only when the white men began attacking Negroes did some policemen intervene.

Even after the mob attacked, according to several eyewitnesses, not all of the policemen attempted to control it. An officer directing traffic allegedly looked on while whites beat a Negro teen-age boy near the corner of Hogan and Duval streets. Instead of help-ing the boy, he talked and laughed with a white man who was armed with an axe handle. This was one of several similar incidents reported.

Chief of Police Luther Reynolds explained that there were too many armed white men—approximately sixty—for the few police-men present to disarm and control and that police reserves did not arrive in time to prevent the violence. . . .

A Negro minister reported that when he saw the white men as-sembling in the park, he asked the three policemen on duty to take the clubs away so as to prevent violence. He said they refused to do so but advised him to call the chief of police. When the minister did so about 9 A.M., he was reportedly told that the situa-tion was well in hand.

A white reporter informed the commission that a uniformed police lieutenant made a frantic call to headquarters in the pres-ence of newsmen "and begged whomever it was he talked to for permission to stop the incipient trouble." The lieutenant was said to have "told the person on the other end of the wire he was well aware that his request was almost insubordination, but that unless they did something about it the newsmen would blast the whole police force for not taking some affirmative action." This conver-sation allegedly took place at approximately 11 A.M., at least two hours after the mob began assembling in Hemming Park. . . .

No section of the nation has a monopoly on racial violence. In the North and West the breeding places for discord have been the cities where large concentrations of Negroes and whites are in direct competition for employment and housing. Following mass Negro migrations, racial tension erupted in Detroit, Los Angeles, New York, and in other cities during the early 1940's, causing severe loss of life and property damage. A study published by the Inter-national City Managers Association reported that "in both the Los Angeles and Detroit riots the minority peoples involved were convinced that they could not depend upon the respective police departments for protection." Despite the progress in police con-trol of mob situations, in recent years there have also been claims of police passivity or other involvement in such situations.

The now famous Trumbull Park Housing Project riots started in

July 1953, in the South Deering section of Chicago. As soon as
Negro families began moving into the previously all-white project
the residents of the neighborhood started rioting. During the next
four years whites committed numerous acts of violence against the
few Negroes in the project. Negro tenants had to travel to and
from their homes under police guard. On some occasions 1,200
policemen were assigned to cover the housing project area during
the course of a twenty-four-hour period. Criticism was leveled at
the police for laxity. On numerous occasions, it was alleged, the
police allowed crowds to form when their prompt dispersal might
have prevented violence. While some policemen acted vigorously,
there were persistent reports that whites attacked Negroes in full
view of white officers who did nothing.

On April 5, 1954, for instance, it was reported that a Negro
police officer attempted to arrest a man who had just thrown a
piece of steel at a Negro's window in the project. When the man
resisted, the officer struck him on the forehead with his night stick.
The man got away when three women from a gathering mob
attacked the Negro policeman. It was reported that white policemen nearby did not assist the officer, nor did they attempt to
arrest the man or the three female assailants.

Another such incident allegedly occurred on April 17, 1954. Two
Negro women and a small boy drove through the Trumbull Park
project and were met with a vicious mob assault. Bricks and bottles
were thrown at the Negroes' car, and it was purposely hemmed in
by drivers of two other cars. The women escaped injury only by
smashing the car in front out of the way. They did not report this
incident to the Chicago Police Department they said, since the
stoning occurred in full view of several policemen who did nothing
to protect them. Negroes complained that the only time the police
took vigorous action was when a Negro appeared ready to retaliate.
One Negro claimed that a white policeman said he wasn't there "to
protect us but to protect the grounds." A Negro officer, who was
present during these disturbances, was of the opinion that seventy-
five aggressively led policemen could have "cleared up" the matter
in a few days. Other responsible Chicago citizens share these
sentiments.

In the summer of 1957, rioting began again near the South Deering area. This time the issue was the use of Calumet Park by

Negroes. The police did not prevent crowds numbering several thousand persons from gathering outside the park on consecutive Sundays; from throwing rocks at Negro motorists; or from attacking Negro pedestrians. For several weeks the situation was tense and hundreds of police were required to keep it from getting worse. Again the police were criticized for passivity toward the violence —for their refusal to disperse crowds before they became mobs. It was claimed that policemen on the scene continually refused to arrest white hoodlums who attacked Negroes. After strong protests from civic groups, two Park District policemen were suspended for brief periods.

Since these disturbances, there has been evidence of more effective riot-control practices on the part of Chicago policemen. For example, another incident took place when a Negro family bought a house on West Jackson Boulevard in the summer of 1959. Crowds gathered; rocks were thrown; and threatening telephone calls made. The police acted promptly and effectively, cordoning off the area for two blocks around the house. Loud-speakers were used by the police to inform the crowds that either they would disperse or face arrest under a state antiriot statute. Within a short time numerous arrests were made, and the crowds disappeared. The courts held the arrested persons under high bond. Many were found guilty and fined the maximum amount, $500, allowed by the statute. Within a few days no more incidents were reported from the area.

Two minor disturbances occurred during the summer of 1960. One was at a beach, the other in a city park. Both were prompted by Negroes using swimming facilities. In each case, however, vigorous work by teams of racially integrated police coupled with arrests and heavy fines kept the situation under control.

In the summer of 1961 new instances of interracial violence erupted in Chicago. Although there was criticism of police action in a few situations, it was generally conceded that the Chicago Police Department took vigorous action to quell trouble. Therefore, when Mississippi Congressman John Bell Williams asked the Department of Justice if it intended to dispatch federal marshals to Chicago as it had to Alabama in May, the reply was that this would not be done because local officials were taking the necessary action.

35 : *Keeping Negroes "in Their Place" in Detroit*

United States Commission on Civil Rights

. . . Jesse Ray, a Negro, had been an officer in the Detroit Police Department for thirteen years. He resigned on June 25, 1960—several months before he gave this sworn testimony at the commission's Detroit hearing on December 15, 1960.

. . . I, myself, personally have experienced two assaults by police officers. The facts in both incidents happening to me are very similar to the things that I have learned are happening to other Negro citizens. In both cases there was no reason for the officer to hit me or punish me or to take the law in his own hands. In both cases the attitude of the officers of the department, that is, the superior officers, was to protect the policemen instead of trying to find out actually what happened and prevent future brutality. In both cases the officers claimed that there was some provocation, which there wasn't.

The first incident that occurred to me was in 1955. I went to a house on a routine gambling investigation and knocked at the rear door. [Mr. Ray was on vice-squad duty but in plain clothes.]

As I knocked at the door, the lady turned the light out. I knocked and remained on the porch for a few minutes and started down the steps. When I got to the last step, the lights were turned on again. I turned to see why and the [white] police officer charged down the steps and proceeded to whip me with his pistol.

This was the alleged reaction of Ray's superiors to this incident:

I was then taken to the fifth precinct where statements were made, and the sergeant, my sergeant, and the police sergeant at the precinct asked me to co-operate with the organization, that it was an unfortunate thing but they didn't want any adverse criticism and they would appreciate my co-operation. Being a member of the organization, I agreed to co-operate. At that time I was confined to receiving hospital for about five days. About a year and a half later some blood clots developed in my eye, and I went back to the hospital, and this was diagnosed as a ruptured blood vessel in my eye causing these clots from the blow I had received. The doctors told me this was something I would have to learn to live with, which I am trying to do. . . .

The second incident occurred on November 13, 1960, after he had resigned from the force. Ray testified:

I was stopped by two officers, two white officers, who ordered my car pulled over to the curb. One of the officers snatched my door open, after calling me a name that I really shouldn't use, unless—

Chairman Hannah: Go ahead.

Mr. Ray: He called me a black son-of-a-bitch and ordered me to the curb. I pulled over to the curb and he opened my door and ordered me out of the car. I got out of my car and told the officers to take it easy; I had been beaten by them once before. The officer then pushed me against my car and stepped back and reached for his blackjack. When he did this, I pushed him back in an effort to try to explain what I meant. He proceeded to hit me on the head. The other officer, his partner, hit me on the head, and then a third officer came up behind me and choked me, cut my wind off, and the two other officers beat me to the ground, and then took my arms and twisted them around behind me and handcuffed me and put me in the scout car.

While I was in the scout car I asked the officers if they would mind getting my hat out of the street. They had knocked my hat off just before. One of the officers told me to shut my so-and-so mouth, and during this time he hit me in the stomach with his fist.

Taken first to the thirteenth precinct, Ray was later transferred to receiving hospital. Although he was identified as a retired police officer, the police shackled him to the hospital bed all night. He was denied a request to call his lawyer, he said, but managed secretly to get a message to him.

At his later trial on a charge of reckless driving, Ray's defense was that the charge was laid against him only as a cover for the senseless brutality of the officers. He explained that he blew his horn at the officers in a friendly greeting as he drove by their parked cruiser. In his opinion, the policemen thought he was a "wise guy," chiding them for being double-parked which is a violation of the law in Detroit. The officers ordered him over to the curb in order to reprimand him, he reasoned at his trial. When he protested—"Take it easy . . ."—the officers simply started to beat him. Mr. Ray further alleged that he was not driving recklessly and had never had a traffic ticket in his life—even during the years when he was not a policeman. The jury rendered a verdict of acquittal on the charge of reckless driving. . . .

36 : *Negroes and the Police in Los Angeles*

Loren Miller

. . . The problem of police brutality—to use the common term—
is a recurrent one in urban areas, especially in those cities in which
there has been a rapid growth of the Negro population. The five-
fold growth of Los Angeles' Negro population since 1940 carried
with it an almost built-in guarantee that incidents between police
and citizens would flare out. Historically, the relations between
Negroes and law-enforcement officers in the Southern states has
not been a happy one. Custom has barred Negroes as peace officers
in the South since Reconstruction days. The white law-enforcement officer has been charged with the duty of enforcing segre-
gatory laws in that section; the Negro has regarded these laws as
denials of his citizenship rights and has vented his resentment on
the officers who enforced them. And, of course, there is the more
serious matter of unequal law enforcement involved in the situation where the Negro has been unable to secure redress of his own
grievances where they were invaded by a white person and the re-

Mr. Miller, a lawyer and newspaper publisher in Los Angeles, is a national vice-
president of the NAACP.

verse of that situation in which a mere charge against a Negro by a white person was tantamount to conviction. Out of this background there has emerged the stereotype of the law-enforcement officer as an enemy, rather than a protector.

On the other hand, the police officer reflects the attitude of his own community. This commission has heard the story of the spatial expansion of the Negro community and of the manner in which white neighborhoods have been displaced. This contest for living space inevitably bred conflict; Negro residence in a hitherto white community is always referred to as an "invasion." Police officers, or some of them, are bound to share that view to some extent. The tavern keeper, the restaurant owner, the proprietor of any other place of public accommodation who has customers moving away and being displaced by another group was bound to harbor certain resentments toward the strangers who had harmed his business investment, and his attitude was often transmitted to his police officer, neighbor, and patron.

There is a formidable literature on what is described as Negro criminality . . . purporting to prove that Negroes are innately criminal. Fortunately, that gross attitude has been supplanted to a great extent, but there is a multiplicity of data to show that Negroes commit crime out of their proportion to population. . . . The point I want to make here is that the police officer, the average officer, is apt to carry his own stereotype of the Negro as a highly suspect person.

Thus, stereotype confronts stereotype. The result is mistrust at best, conflict at worst.

Racial segregation is a device to keep the Negro "in his place." It is significant that public facilities for Negroes are always described as "separate schools," or "separate parks," etc. The residential segregation that pervades Los Angeles maintains a "place" for the Negro. The Negro's "place" in our society is a subordinate one. He lives in some of the worst areas of our city. Public facilities and public services tend to compare unfavorably with similar urban services in other parts of the city. I think we have to face up to the fact that most Americans, and that includes police officers, are a little resentful of the Negro who doesn't want to "stay in his place"—that is, in his physical place and in his psychological place—stirs resentment. The Negro who resents being questioned by the police officer, or who becomes angry when police insist on a search of his dwelling, or who talks about his constitutional rights at the point of arrest or interrogation is out of his "place" in the minds of many police officers. He may have to pay for his—the common phrase is "uppityness"—by an arrest, whereas meekness and humility might have resulted in his release.

Residential segregation breeds another species of conflict between the Negro citizen and the police officer. I have a son who is now in law school who was stopped by police at what I suspect was a fairly late hour in a community in which no Negroes lived some years ago. He, and some other Negro companions, had taken a white fellow athlete home. They were forced to face a wall and were searched for contraband, a rather humiliating experience. My son tried out a little influence peddling by saying that his father was a lawyer. One of the officers told him in effect that the officers knew no Negroes lived in the community; that it was late; that there had been burglars at work; and that, as a matter of course, young Negroes riding around in an automobile were suspect. The Negro who is found in a "white community" runs the risk of police interrogation and, again, resentment may land him under arrest. Association of Negro males and white females offends many officers, just as it offends many other Americans and it, too, may lead to police interference.

[However] no police arrests have been made in the more than two dozen cases of vandalism that have flared out against Negro occupancy of housing in formerly white areas in the past two years. Some four or five years ago we had a bombing in a similar situation, and that offender was not arrested. Here, the shoe is on the other foot. Police officers profess inability to protect Negroes in a situation in which popular opinion runs against the Negro even though he is exercising a citizenship right. On the other hand, I cannot make myself believe that, if Negroes had directed a similar number of acts of vandalism against white persons for one reason or another, there would have been no arrests and no prosecutions. I do not think this failure to make arrests reflects a deliberate policy of encouragement for vandalism, but I do think it reflects a significant failure on the part of police in the area of equal protection of the law.

Equality before the law is an ideal toward which we must constantly strive, but equality in the enforcement of the law will never be an absolute as long as the badge of race, or color, or nationality is an indelible stamp of a subordinate status in society. We ought not delude ourselves into the belief that the disadvantaged person in our society, whether that disadvantage flows from an economic or social status, can get that equality of treatment which is our ideal. And we ought never cease striving toward that ideal.

Let's turn to the matter of gambling, which has had a great deal of publicity in our city recently. Police statistics show that about 84 per cent of those arrested for gambling in Los Angeles are Negroes, who are some 15 per cent of the population. Of course, Negroes gamble in Los Angeles. So do other people. My common sense and a little experience with human beings tell me that Negroes don't do 84 per cent of the gambling in this city. The kind of gambling Negroes do may make police detection a little easier, and a police officer who raids an alley crap game has an easier task than one who sets himself the task of raiding an exclusive-membership club. The epitome of this situation was pointed out by a Pasadena judge who handed out suspended sentences to a group of Negroes with the tart observation that every time he went to his club he saw fellow members gambling and no arrests were made. Arrest statistics have little relevance to gambling on a racial basis; what they do demonstrate is the vulnerability of Negroes to arrest for gambling.

For crime statistics in general, I suspect that they prove far less than we ordinarily think they do. Wholesale comparisons of one racial group with another necessarily leave out of account the economic status and the racial background of individual offenders. If one group is more advantaged than another, I think we have a right to expect that fewer of its members will commit certain kinds of crime. If members of a social strata of one group were compared to members of that same social strata in another group, the figures would assume some meaning, but even then they would not measure acculturation and the psychological factors that might arise from the fears and frustrations to which one group or another might be subjected. I understand that police justification for racial identification of prisoners or suspects is based on the belief that such identification may help in detection of the suspect. There is some merit in that view although the mere description of a person as a Negro may mean that his color ranges from blond to very dark; that his eye color may vary from blue to black; and that his hair may be either very straight or very kinky. Here, again, I doubt very much that the police are going to rise above social customs and traditions and that, as long as societal judgments rest on race judgments, police officers are apt to follow the same pattern.

It is against that social background I have just outlined that the problem of the conflict between citizen and police must be judged. No good can come out of the pretense that there is no problem. I understand that police statistics show that there were eighty complaints of police brutality made by citizens in 1958 and that two of these complaints were found to be justified by the police investigatory body. There were twenty-one complaints of invasions of civil rights in that same year. None was found to be justified. The percentage is remarkably low. However, in general, one-third of the general complaints were sustained. . . .

PART IV

THE TECHNIQUES OF THE

CIVIL-RIGHTS

STRUGGLE

37 : *Boycott in Philadelphia*

Hannah Lees

When four hundred ministers in one city advise their congregations not to buy something, a lot of whatever that something may be goes unbought and the company that makes it is quickly aware of the fact. . . .

These periods of mass inaction have been the result of a joint decision reached [in May of 1960] by the pastors of those four hundred churches. They call it their Selective Patronage Program, and their purpose is simple and forthright: to persuade—they reject words like "force" or "demand"—one company after another in Philadelphia to employ more Negroes in prestige jobs.

Their method is equally simple and forthright. A delegation of ministers—sometimes five, usually four—calls on whatever company the group has decided to investigate and politely inquires how many Negroes it employs and in what jobs. The companies have given this information willingly . . . , and they might as well; the ministers usually already know, unofficially. The first meeting is always exploratory, but a second meeting is then requested a week or two later. At this meeting, the ministers, though still quiet, still polite, are specific about what they want. At first it was not

---

Miss Lees is a free-lance writer who has contributed several articles to *The Reporter*.

very much. Lately, as with the . . . Sun boycott, it has become a good deal. Whether they are now asking too much only time will tell.

With the Tasty Baking Company, the second firm they visited and the first one where they encountered opposition, the ministers asked the company to hire two Negro driver salesmen, two Negro clerical workers, and three or four Negro girls in the icing department, where the workers had traditionally all been white. They were not interested in the fact that the Tasty Baking Company already had hundreds of Negro employees. What they were interested in is placing Negro workers in positions of dignity and responsibility. Their aim is to change the public image of Negro workers. The Tasty Baking Company did not have any Negroes driving trucks or working in its office.

"UNTIL FURTHER NOTICE"

When Mr. Pass, the personnel manager of the company, and Mr. Kaiser, the president, pointed out that they had no need, just then, for more driver-salesmen or clerical workers, the minister said politely but firmly that they still hoped these people could be hired within two weeks. If not, the four hundred ministers they represented would have to advise their congregations on the Sunday following not to buy any Tasty cakes or pies until they were hired.

Mr. Kaiser understandably felt pushed and resistant. The Negro driver-salesmen and clerks and icers were not hired within the two weeks, and the ministers did tell their congregations not to buy any Tasty cakes or pies until further notice. Printed advertisements to this effect mysteriously appeared in bars, beauty parlors, and barbershops. Nobody knows how many thousand dollars' worth of sales the Tasty Baking Company lost during those summer months, but there are 700,000 Negroes in Philadelphia and a large proportion have some connection with those four hundred churches. When the boycott was officially called off two months later from four hundred pulpits, the Tasty Baking Company had in its employ two Negro driver-salesmen, two Negro clerical workers, and some half-dozen Negro icers.

The Pepsi-Cola Company, which was called on in September [of

1960], was also resistant to the ministers' requests. On October 2, a boycott was called from four hundred pulpits. Two days later the spokesman of the delegation received a telegram saying that Pepsi-Cola had hired the requested personnel. But the boycott lasted two weeks, because it is a policy of the ministers not to call a boycott off until the new employees are actually at work.

Gulf Oil, which was approached last winter at the height of the heating season, showed no interest in meeting with the ministers. When three weeks had gone by without an appointment being arranged, a boycott of Gulf products was called the next Sunday. The day after that the switchboards at Gulf were jammed with calls canceling oil contracts. Gulf then moved so quickly to meet the ministers' demands that the boycott lasted only a week. But here a new factor entered: the union. One of the ministers' stipulations, that the new Negro employees must not be the first to be laid off, conflicted with seniority provisions in Gulf's union contract. Union officials met with the ministers and explained that they were sympathetic with their aims, but not when they collided with union bargaining. Three Negro truck drivers had been hired and after thirty days joined the union. All has been serene, but seasonal layoffs have begun by now. If drivers with seniority are laid off first, the union is not likely to take it lying down. The ministers may decide to finesse that one. . . .

The origin and operation of the Selective Patronage Program are somewhat shrouded in mystery. It acknowledges no leaders, and no one will say who called the first meeting. "Some of us just got together," they say, "and decided we could not in good moral conscience remain silent while our congregations patronized companies that were discriminating against Negroes." The names of the ministers who have called on the various companies are on public record, but there is a different delegation for each company and a different spokesman. . . .

But no one will say who makes up the priority committee, which meets—always at a different place—to decide on the next target and what they will ask for. They have, they say, no officers, no by-laws, no minutes, no dues, and no treasury.

"But it is the best-organized unorganized program you ever saw in action," one of them said to me. "We can call a boycott of a quarter of a million people within twenty-four hours and call it off within twenty-four hours." A quarter of a million is probably not too high. Lined up solidly behind the ministers are fraternal organizations, social clubs, insurance agents, bartenders, beauticians, the NAACP, and the Negro newspapers. Even local dealers whose sales have been hurt by the various boycotts seem to go along with the program.

. . . A consistent complaint of both liberals and conservatives has long been that Negroes did not do enough for themselves, did not exercise enough leadership in solving their own problems. These Negro ministers exercise leadership . . . with impunity. The Tasty Baking Company consulted both the Chamber of Commerce and their own lawyers to see if any counteraction were possible. The conclusion seemed to be that it would be pretty hard to take a group of unorganized ministers to court, and even if they could it would not help Tasty's position much.

The ministers point out that some three thousand Negro boys and girls graduate from Philadelphia high schools every year and usually end by taking the jobs that nobody else wants because they are the last to be chosen. Many of them, the ministers admit, are not as highly qualified as they should be, but even the qualified ones have to fight the preconceived idea that they are not qualified. This, essentially, is the battle the ministers are trying to fight for them.

There are some new elements to the Sun Oil boycott now in progress. The ministers are feeling their strength and pushing harder than ever before. They may be pushing too hard, but perhaps they have to, to find out how far and how fast they can move. They phoned Sun at the end of January [1961] and requested a meeting. Sun arranged a meeting for February 3 in a very relaxed mood. A year ago, Sun had asked the Reverend Leon Sullivan and Dr. Jerome Holland, president of Hampton Institute, to advise it in setting up a program of increased Negro employment in white-collar jobs. At that time it had hired two Negro clerks. It had records of hundreds of Negro employees at its Marcus Hook refinery, some in responsible supervisory jobs. It had just decided to include three Negro colleges in its yearly talent search. Sun felt it was in the clear.

The ministers didn't agree. They were not interested in the number of Negroes working in the refinery. Negroes had always held jobs like that. "You hired two Negro clerks a year ago, but none since," they said. "Two in an office force of fifteen hundred isn't much, is it? And you have no Negroes driving trucks. And even though you plan to include Negroes in your talent search, you haven't actually hired any."

Sun said business had fallen off. They had had to move more slowly than they planned, but were now going ahead as fast as they could.

At the second meeting, two weeks later, the ministers quietly dropped what must have seemed to Sun a bombshell. They wanted Sun to hire twenty-four Negro employees: nineteen additional office workers, three permanent truck drivers, and a motor-products salesman. When? Within the next month.

Sun said that was not possible, not within a month. There would not be anywhere near nineteen new job openings in the office in that time. And how could it hire three new truck drivers when they were just about to lay off thirty-five as the heating season ended? . . .

Sun has not, so far, asked the ministers to recruit for them, but it has been in touch with the Urban League. By March 16, the last meeting before the boycott deadline of Sunday, March 19, Sun had interviewed nineteen Negro applicants for clerical work and had hired one of them. The others, they said, did not have the necessary qualifications. Sun had also hired one Negro salesman and upgraded one man from mechanic to truck driver. The ministers had accepted Sun's stand that it could not take on new truck drivers while about to lay off old ones and said they would settle for upgrading to truck driver three of their men who were already employed by Sun.

The boycott was called on March 19 and [as of May 1961] is still in progress. As of late April, Sun had hired about half the workers requested by the ministers. There were seven more Negro girls in the home office, there were two Negro salesmen, and three drivers had been upgraded from work in the garage and the refinery. Sun [said] that from [then] on it [would] hire people as needed, interviewing both white and Negro applicants without discrimination. When asked about the loss in business, spokesmen for the firm shrug and say it is hard to estimate. They seem unruffled and without resentment, but say flatly that they cannot do more. And there is no reason why they should if they can get along without Negro customers. The ministers estimate, however, that Sun is losing some $7,000 a week. And the number of Negro customers Sun may have to get along without seems to be increasing.

Those four hundred unorganized ministers . . . plan to spread their boycott progressively, first across the state and then, they say, across the country if necessary. On Sunday, April 9, they began the first part of what they call the second phase of their program. All the Negro Masonic lodges across the state announced a boycott of Sun products. Their members number twenty-five thousand, and they claim to be able to influence several times that many. Perhaps they can. If Sun [had] still not hired the requested twenty-four Negro workers in another couple of weeks, the ministers [said] the boycott [would] spread to all the churches across Pennsylvania, and after that to all the men's and women's clubs. And after that they will go beyond Pennsylvania.

"Would it not have been more logical," I asked, "to start with all the churches in Pennsylvania?"

"A boycott of the Masons is easier to control," I was told, "and easier to call off in a hurry if Sun fills its quota. We could easily call on a boycott of all the churches, but it might take a while to call it off. We don't want to hurt Sun. We aren't mad at anybody. We just want to see our boys and girls in decent jobs."

. . . George Schermer, executive director of the Philadelphia Commission on Human Relations, has been glad to see these Negro ministers exercising leadership. As long as they can function in this amorphous state, he is all for them, he says, but if they can make good on this spreading boycott, it may be hard not to develop an overt organization with leaders and factions and ultimate corruption. At the very least, any real organization could sooner or later run into some sort of conspiracy suit. These are the dangers ahead of the crusading ministers.

"Power corrupts, you know the old saying," I reminded one of the ministers. "Aren't you afraid that all this mushrooming power may land you in trouble?" He smiled gently. "No, honey," he said, "because we haven't any heroes to feed on that power, we haven't any leaders or bosses. And we aren't going to have any. As long as we can make out without them, we'll do fine." As long as they can, he is probably right.

38 : *Picketing in Rochdale Village*

William H. Booth

The recent, successful march on Washington—for jobs and free-dom—was preceded in Jamaica, Long Island, New York, by a local demonstration for the same goals. We picketed an under-construction six thousand family state-financed co-operative—Rochdale Village—because of the scarcity of Negroes working at the site.

There were over two thousand workers at Rochdale Village in June 1963, of whom only about one hundred and fifty were Negroes. In the highest paying trades, there were no Negroes employed; of 115 electricians, of 60 plumbers, of 50 steamfitters, of 40 metal lathers, of 20 elevator installers, there was not a single Negro. These facts had been determined by surveys conducted in June by NAACP and CORE investigating teams. The reasons for this im-balance were numerous; chief among them, however, was the closed door policy of the respective unions. The contractors could not hire nonunion workers, and the unions would not open their mem-bership rolls, or their apprenticeship training programs, to Negroes. And some of the same unions were "respected" members of the United Housing Foundation, owner-sponsor of the development under construction!

Many in the Jamaica branch had for a long time considered jobs

---

Mr. Booth, an attorney, is President of the Jamaica Branch of the NAACP.

and the complexities of securing them the rallying point for our community. Our area is largely a white-collar one, and there had been general apathy to civil-rights causes in spite of the large number of Negroes concentrated there. Now, the question was raised as to whether the "bread and butter" issue, employment, would arouse the community.

At an NAACP meeting on July 22, 1963, the call went out for picketeers for July 23, 1963. The same call had sounded forth from church pulpits on July 21, 1963, and at a CORE meeting during the previous week. To the credit of Jamaica, the people responded; over two hundred pickets joined the lines at Rochdale Village (there were three gates of entry to the site that had to be picketed), and our demonstration was under way.

At a meeting that night in a local church, the group decided to continue the demonstration. However, a mass rally was planned for the following Sunday to raise funds for bail (twenty-seven persons had been arrested on the first day, including the president of NAACP, local director of CORE, and the pastor of a local church; these had been designated leaders of the movement) and printing, sound-equipment rental, and permits. Picketing was suspended until after the rally.

The rally, held in an open parking lot, attracted a large number of people on a hot Sunday afternoon and a war-pot of $750 was collected. On the following day, July 29, 1963, the demonstrations recommenced, with about two hundred persons again and has continued daily thereafter. . . .

Every night since the picketing began, we have held inspirational meetings at different churches and other meeting rooms at which exploration of the day's activities was carried out and determination was made as to future plans. Also, each Sunday, we have held mass rallies in various parts of the community at which funds were collected to carry on the fight. . . .

It is now expected that the governor and the mayor will take action to withdraw the state and municipal aid which Rochdale Village enjoys and to prosecute the unions for violations of state and municipal laws and ordinances forbidding discrimination.

Until such time, however, as the governor and mayor act, we can point to many positive side effects as the direct result of our demonstrations:

(1) Local banks (three) have hired Negro personnel where never before hired.

(2) Local finance companies (two) which have considerable Negro business now have hired Negroes where never before hired.

(3) Local insurance companies (two) have set up training programs for agents and have requested Negro applicants for other positions.

(4) A local union has set up an attractive in-service training program for higher paying jobs within the union membership.

(5) Two local Negro contractors have negotiated well-paying contracts for work at Rochdale Village.

(6) A local newspaper has hired Negro printers, apprentices, and writers.

(7) A local bakery has requested Negro applicants for jobs in various categories.

Meanwhile, the picketing continues daily from 6:30 A.M. to 3:30 P.M. with nightly meetings at 8:00 P.M. and mass rallies on Sundays until our goals have been fully realized.

39 : *Freedom Ride—Washington to New Orleans*

James Peck

Little did I realize that my second interracial bus trip through the South would end in a mob beating which almost cost me my life. Such a trip had been contemplated even before the 1947 journey of reconciliation was over. Several years thereafter, Billie Ames of the St. Louis CORE group started to organize one, but it never materialized. In the winter of 1961, riding aboard a bus together, Thomas Gaither . . . and Gordon Carey, CORE field director, broached the subject in earnest and devised the term "freedom ride." The idea was accepted enthusiastically by the next national CORE council meeting. The ride would take place in the spring.

What made the timing particularly opportune was that, in December, the United States Supreme Court had issued a decision in the Bruce Boynton case extending the Irene Morgan ruling which had been the basis for the 1947 journey. The Morgan decision had outlawed segregation of interstate passengers only aboard the vehicles on which they traveled. The Boynton decision extended

Mr. Peck is Editor of *Corelator*, the publication of CORE, and author of *Freedom Ride* (1962).

that ruling to cover facilities used by interstate passengers outside the actual vehicles. This meant waiting rooms, rest rooms, terminal restaurants, rest stops, and so on. The freedom ride would test all these facilities, not merely the seating aboard buses.

Also, the freedom ride would penetrate the deep South, not merely the upper South as had the 1947 journey. The route decided on was Washington to New Orleans. The starting date was May 4. Gaither traveled the entire route, as Houser had traveled the journey's route, setting up meetings and arranging housing for the overnight stops.

Applications for participants went out from the CORE office. It was made clear that the policy in event of arrest was to remain in jail rather than pay fines or bail out. The first two volunteers were Jim Farmer, one of CORE's founders who had become national director, and myself. The group which assembled May 1 at Fellowship House in Washington for training totaled thirteen. It was a very different type of group from the one which had gathered in Washington fourteen years previously for the same type of project. It included a number of what has become known as "the new Negro"—Southern students who took part in the sit-in movement and for whom arrest or the threat thereof had become commonplace. Most of the group were young people in their twenties. Very few of them were pacifists. I was the only participant who had been on the 1947 journey, and was therefore in a good position to make contrasts or comparisons with the trip fourteen years before.

The outstanding contrast, and most heartening to me, was that, aboard the buses, desegregation had become a reality. On the journey, members of our group had been the only passengers to sit unsegregated. On the freedom ride, even in the deep South, ordinary Negro passengers no longer confined themselves to the rear seats.

The outstanding comparison was that, in the terminals and at the rest stops—even in Virginia's larger cities where the white and colored signs had been removed—segregation still prevailed as it had aboard the buses in 1947. Our freedom riders were about the only persons to wait, wash, and eat unsegregated in these terminals.

It was disheartening to me that in a city such as Richmond, which is not far from the nation's capital and where the color signs had been removed, Negroes were sticking to the formerly separate and grossly unequal colored waiting rooms and restaurants. This was true both in the Greyhound and Trailways terminals.

The first white and colored signs encountered were only fifty miles south of Washington—atop the rest-room doors at the Greyhound stop in Fredericksburg. Charles Person, a Negro student from Atlanta, went into the white rest room and I went into the colored rest room without incident.

In Farmville, center of Prince Edward County, where school closing had left Negro children schoolless since 1959, the white and colored signs were painted over but still visible. Freedom riders were served without incident.

While there were no color signs in the Lynchburg Trailways terminal, there was a divider in the middle of the counter, making persons on one side virtually invisible to those on the other.

Danville, Virginia, was the first place where testers were refused service. At the colored counter, Ed Blankenheim, a white, sat for ten minutes until his bus was ready for departure. Genevieve Hughes, a white, and I, aboard a later bus, were at first refused service but we—and Walter Bergman—finally got refreshments after a brief discussion with the manager.

Greensboro, though reputed for its liberalism, was the first city where the color signs started to become the rule. The first greetings to arriving bus passengers were oversized signs all around the building with arrows pointing to the colored waiting room. On the other hand, the colored lunch room, which was no bigger than a good-sized closet and equally gloomy, had been closed permanently a week before our arrival. A Negro in the colored waiting room told me he was amazed when on entering the colored lunch room one day, he was advised to walk around to the formerly white restaurant. . . .

Charlotte was the scene of the trip's first arrest—and the birth of a new "in," the shoe-in. Charles Person climbed onto a shoe-shine chair and, after being refused service, remained seated until a cop with handcuffs arrived. Person then left, since no policy regarding shoeshines had yet been decided by the group and, as on the journey, each step and who was to take it would be decided at group meetings before every lap of the ride. When Person went for the shine, he did not even think of it as a test. He simply looked at his shoes and thought they needed a shine. It was then hastily decided by the group that Joe Perkins should make a test and stay in the shoeshine chair until arrested. The trip's first arrest came within minutes. Attorney Thomas Wyche won an acquittal on the basis of the Supreme Court's Boynton decision, and Perkins rejoined us a day later.

Violence against the freedom riders erupted for the first time in Rock Hill, South Carolina, where the press had headlined our arrival and where hoodlums had recently attacked lunch-counter pickets. In fact, several of the hoodlums waiting at the Greyhound station were recognized as the same individuals who had assaulted the local student pickets.

As the Greyhound contingent of riders arrived, some twenty of these ruffians were waiting. When John Lewis, who is Negro, approached the entrance of the white waiting room, he was assaulted by two of them. Three started slugging Albert Bigelow, a white, who was next in line.

Aside from their commitment to nonviolence, these two freedom riders were as dissimilar as any two individuals could possibly be. Lewis is a short, muscular divinity student. Bigelow is a tall, gray-haired, ex-naval commander. Lewis is taciturn. Bigelow is articulate. Lewis is one of ten children born on a southern Alabama farm—the only one to finish high school. Bigelow's family background is blueblood New England. Lewis got his extensive nonviolent training during the lunch counter sit-in's in Nashville, where he was studying for the ministry. Bigelow became a pacifist in revulsion over his World War II experiences as a naval commander and had, like me, participated in protest actions against nuclear tests and war. Had it not been for the freedom rides, these two would never have met. Yet, here they were together, being slugged in front of the Greyhound terminal in Rock Hill, South Carolina, and remaining completely nonviolent.

In the course of the slugging, Genevieve Hughes, who was behind Lewis and Bigelow, was pushed to the ground. At that point, the police, who had been standing by but taking time in performance of their duty, arrived. The police captain asked Lewis and Bigelow whether they wanted to press charges against any of their assailants. They declined. Thereupon, the riders entered the white waiting room unmolested.

When the group with which I was riding arrived at the Trailways terminal a few hours later, some of the hoodlums were waiting in cars. However, they did not attack, but only drove after us a few blocks toward Friendship Junior College. The Trailways terminal building was completely locked up. Its eating facilities had been closed since Friendship students had conducted sit-in's there. . . .

When we left the next day, the Trailways white waiting room was open, and a test team sat there unmolested. The same was true at the Greyhound station. The hoodlums did not stage a repeat performance.

Our Trailways group left Rock Hill about lunchtime. At what was supposed to be the lunch stop in Chester, "closed" signs had been hastily put on the doors.

The lunch stop turned out to be Winnsboro, an ultrasegregationist little town. Here occurred the freedom ride's first arrest of lunch-counter sit-inners. It all happened so quickly it seemed like a film being reeled too fast.

Henry Thomas, a lanky Negro student, and I entered the white lunch room and sat at the counter. The restaurant owner dashed away from the counter to phone the police. Within two minutes a police officer who was a stereotype for such a role in Hollywood, stepped over and drawled to Thomas, "Come with me, boy!"

I stepped over to ask about my teammate and was also promptly arrested. We were driven away in a police car before the bus had left the rest stop. Aboard the bus, there was no outspoken reaction, as we learned later from others in the group. Mrs. Bergman, an elderly woman, who had been designated as our observer, got off the bus and braved the hate-filled town alone, trying to find out what the authorities intended to do with us.

We were segregated in the jail and unable to communicate with each other. It was several hours before we were told what the charges against us were. The officer who booked us had been overanxious to fill in that section but the cop who drove us had kept insisting, "Don't write anything down before we talk with the chief." The charge against Thomas turned out to be "trespass," and that against me, "interfering with arrest." However, after eight to ten hours in jail, we were released and the charges dropped. Local officials apparently concluded that our cases would not hold in view of the Supreme Court's Boynton decision.

Thomas was released in the middle of the night, as carloads of hate-filled segregationists still roamed around town. One of them had parked directly in front of the jail with his car's headlights glaring into my cell. I did not know that Thomas had been released. By the time I was set free, it was dawn. Jim McCain had driven over from his home in Sumter to give me a ride. I learned for the first time that Thomas had gotten out.

After his release, Thomas went to the bus station. A cluster of segregationists was there, and it was too late for a bus. "Go in the nigger waiting room," one of them ordered. Thomas entered the white waiting room, bought a candy bar, and walked out past the gaping segregationists. Such is his boldness. Some call it foolhardiness. An aunt in Georgia, whom he sometimes visits, prays that God guide him to cease these hazardous activities. But Thomas is determined to make the world better than the one he knew as a youth. He was raised along with nine other children by a drunken stepfather in an overcrowded Georgia shack. While still attending the separate and very unequal school, he worked as a road laborer and cotton chopper. He finally managed to win a scholarship at Howard, where he was studying when he joined our freedom ride. . . .

In Atlanta, we were welcomed at the Greyhound terminal by a large group of students, many of whom had participated in the local lunch-counter picketing and sit-in's. The terminal restaurant was closed but we used the waiting room and rest rooms. The Trailways terminal restaurant was open, and two of our teams tested it on departure without incident. . . .

Our experiences in traveling through Georgia were clear proof of how segregation can come peacefully in a deep South state, providing there is no deliberate incitement to hatred and violence by local or state political leaders. . . .

The most nightmarish day of our freedom ride was Sunday, May 14, Mother's Day. I identify the date with Mother's Day because when Police Chief Connor was asked why there was not a single policeman at the Birmingham Trailways terminal to avert mob violence, he explained that since it was Mother's Day, most of the police were off-duty visiting their mothers. That there was going to be a mob to meet us had been well known around Birmingham for several days. Reverend Fred Shuttlesworth told me so when I phoned to give him the scheduled arrival times of our two buses.

However, we did not know in advance that a similar mob was waiting in Anniston, a rest stop on the way. Our first contingent, aboard Greyhound, learned of this when their bus stopped just outside of Anniston and their driver conferred briefly with the driver of a bus going the other way.

When the Greyhound bus pulled into Anniston, it was immediately surrounded by an angry mob armed with iron bars. They set upon the vehicle, denting the sides, breaking windows, and slashing tires. Finally, police arrived, and the bus managed to depart. But the mob pursued it in cars. One car got ahead of the bus and prevented it from gathering speed. About six miles out, one of the tires went flat, and the bus was forced to pull over to a gas station.

Within minutes, the pursuing mob was again hitting the bus with iron bars. The rear window was broken and a bomb was hurled inside. Suddenly the vehicle became filled with thick smoke. The passengers, including the freedom riders, ducked toward the floor in order to breathe. A few climbed out of a window. Some tried to get out the door, but it was being held shut from the outside.

As Henry Thomas tells it, he shortly succeeded in pushing the door open. As he stepped out, he walked toward a man who looked friendly. Suddenly the man wielded a club from behind his back and struck him over the head.

All the passengers managed to escape before the bus burst into flames and was totally destroyed. The extent of the destruction was shown in the grim newspaper photos of its charred interior and exterior. Policemen, who had been standing by, belatedly came on the scene. A couple of them fired shots in the air. The mob dispersed and the injured were taken to a local hospital. The freedom riders were finally transported to Birmingham in cars dispatched by Reverend Shuttlesworth.

When the Trailways bus carrying our contingent arrived in Anniston an hour later, the other passengers learned of what had happened to the Greyhound bus and discontinued their trip. While waiting for the bus to proceed, we heard the sirens of ambulances taking the injured to the hospital, but we did not know what had happened.

We learned of it only when eight hoodlums climbed aboard and stood by the driver as he made a brief announcement. He concluded by stating that he would refuse to drive on unless the Negroes in our group moved to the formerly segregated rear seats. They remained quietly in their front seats. The hoodlums cursed and started to move them bodily to the rear, kicking and hitting them at the same time.

Walter Bergman, who is a retired professor, and I were seated toward the rear. We moved forward and tried to persuade the hoodlums to desist. We, too, were pushed, punched, and kicked. I found myself face downward on the floor of the bus. Someone was on top of me. I was bleeding. Bergman's jaw was cut and swollen. None of us realized that he also had received a crushing blow on the head which would bring him close to death four months later. Following an appendicitis operation, he suffered an almost fatal stroke which attending doctors attributed to a "preexistent condition of brain damage" resulting from the Anniston assault. They notified police, because had Bergman died, it would have been a case of murder. Fortunately he recovered.

Mrs. Bergman, who observed the beating, commented later, "I had never before heard the sound of human flesh being hit; it was terrible!"

Finally, all of our group—whites and Negroes—and one Negro passenger who had not gotten off, had been forced to the back of the bus. The hoodlums—together with a pregnant woman whom they had brought aboard—sat in the very front. The seats in between remained empty. At that point the driver agreed to proceed to Birmingham. Some of us doubted whether he would really head there or turn up some obscure side road for another mob scene. For the entire two-hour ride to Birmingham, the hoodlums craned their necks to make sure we did not move into any of the empty rows of front seats.

Upon arrival in Birmingham, I could see a mob lined up on the sidewalk only a few feet from the loading platform. Most of them were young—in their twenties. Some were carrying ill-concealed iron bars. A few were older men. All had hate showing on their faces.

I looked at them, and then I looked at Charles Person, who had been designated as my teammate to test the lunch counter. Person, a slim youth, quiet and determined, had been jailed-in for sixteen days during the campaign to desegregate Atlanta lunch counters. On our overnight stop in Atlanta he visited his parents—reluctantly, he said, because he knew they would try to dissuade him from continuing the freedom ride. At departure time, one of us wondered whether the parents had prevailed. Most of us were confident that they had not, and sure enough, just as we were leaving for the bus station, Person appeared.

Now we stood on the Birmingham unloading platform with the segregationist mob only a few feet away. I did not want to put Person in a position of being forced to proceed if he thought the situation too dangerous. When I looked at him, he responded by saying simply, "Let's go."

As we entered the white waiting room and approached the lunch counter, we were grabbed bodily and pushed toward the alleyway leading to the loading platform. As soon as we got into the alleyway and out of sight of onlookers in the waiting room, six of them started swinging at me with fists and pipes. Five others attacked Person a few feet ahead. Within seconds, I was unconscious on the ground.

I learned only later that the mob went on to assault Tom Langston of the Birmingham *Post-Herald* and smashed his camera. Langston had been sufficiently quick-witted to remove his film, and the photo of my beating, clearly showing the hate-filled expression of my assailants, appeared in next morning's *Post-Herald* and in many newspapers throughout the country. Then, Clancy Lake, a radio newsman, was attacked as he sat in his car, broadcasting an account of the onslaught.

When I regained consciousness, the alleyway was empty. Blood was flowing down my face. I tried to stop the flow with a handkerchief but it soon became soaked. A white soldier came out of the waiting room to see whether I needed help. I declined, because I suddenly saw Bergman coming from the loading platform. He helped me to get a cab. The first two refused to take me, but a third agreed. I told the driver to go to the home of Reverend Shuttlesworth, which was our Birmingham headquarters.

The first thing Reverend Shuttlesworth said to me as I got out of the cab was, "You need to go to a hospital." He called an ambulance. While waiting for it to arrive, I looked for Person among the assembled Negro onlookers. I finally found him and we shook hands. He had a gash in the back of his head and his face was swollen, but he did not require hospitalization. I did not realize how seriously I had been hurt. My head required fifty-three stitches. X-rays were taken to determine whether my skull had been fractured and whether my ribs were intact.

I was on an operating table for hours. The doctor who was sewing my stitches had to leave periodically to attend to other emergency cases. During one of these interruptions, reporters arrived. Hospital regulations required that I sign a paper permitting them to interview me and snap photos. I did. Although I was feeling weak and nauseated, I answered their questions to the best of my ability.

Finally, after eight hours in the hospital, I was discharged, my face and head half hidden by bandages. . . . I must have looked sick for, next morning, some of the group insisted that I should fly home immediately. I said that for the most severely beaten rider to quit could be interpreted as meaning that violence had triumphed over nonviolence. It might convince the ultrasegregationists that by violence they could stop the freedom riders. My point was accepted, and we started our meeting to plan the next lap, from Birmingham to Montgomery. We decided to travel in a single contingent on a Greyhound bus leaving at three in the afternoon.

Reverend Shuttlesworth and two members of his church drove us to the terminal, but the bus never left. Drivers of both Greyhound and Trailways had determined to refuse to drive the freedom riders. We waited more than an hour on the loading platform as the mob started to gather. We recognized some of their faces. We sat down in the white waiting room. As evening approached, it became clear that we would not get out of Birmingham in time to make our scheduled meeting in Montgomery—and that in fact we might not get a bus out of Birmingham for several days. We decided to fly to New Orleans to make sure of being at the mass rally there marking the end of the freedom ride on May 17, anniversary of the Supreme Court's key antisegregation decision.

In cars supplied by Reverend Shuttlesworth, we rode from the bus terminal to the airport and got reservations on an Eastern Air Lines plane leaving about an hour later. No sooner had we boarded it than an announcement came over the loud-speaker that a bomb threat had been received, and all passengers would have to debark while luggage was inspected. Time dragged on and eventually the flight was canceled. The mob started to gather in the airport. Dressed in T-shirts and dungarees and clustered in groups, they were obviously not airline passengers. Near the doorway to the loading gates, I heard a youth tell his girl friend, "We're going to get them as they come through this way." What deterred the ever-growing mob from staging a repeat performance of the previous day's assault was that, this time, police were present in sizable numbers.

One heartening incident occurred. A white man approached us and introduced himself as a resident of Birmingham. He said he was sorry about what had happened to us there and wanted us to know that there were some whites in the city who thoroughly disapproved.

We got reservations aboard a Capital Airlines plane, which was the next flight to New Orleans. That flight was canceled also, though no public announcement was made of a bomb scare.

By about 10 P.M., police cleared the mob out of the airport and set up a roadblock nearby to prevent them from returning. We finally took off on an Eastern Air Lines plane at eleven, after six tense hours in the airport. An hour later we landed in New Orleans. A deputation of the New Orleans CORE group was at the airport to welcome us. A battery of newspaper photographers snapped photos as we walked from the plane into the waiting room. The first freedom ride had ended.

40 : *Biracial Committee in Knoxville*

Wilma Dykeman and James Stokely

Negroes have served notice on white America that they intend to be part of a community dialogue. The massive resistance to change on the part of whites in the past has led to massive resistance on the part of Negroes today. If they are not allowed to communicate their deep-seated anger and compelling needs by negotiation, they will communicate them by demonstration. Local leaders everywhere are becoming aware of this fact. To many it is not welcome, but common sense compels them to act in the face of a challenge that threatens the entire fabric of the American community.

One important answer to this challenge is the formation of biracial committees, examples of which are being created almost daily throughout the South. These committees have a very real function. They offer an alternative to those who shout, "We'll do nothing and we'll do it tomorrow," and those who demand, "We want

The authors, Mr. and Mrs. James Stokely, have coauthored *Neither Black nor White* (1958), *Seeds of Southern Change* (1962), and frequent articles on racial matters.

everything and we want it yesterday." Between these two defiant positions stands the majority group of each race. The biracial committee helps them to create a full, meaningful exchange.

Recent and continuing developments here in Knoxville provide an example of how local leadership and biracial responsibility may mobilize to achieve progress with a minimum of open conflict and its aftermath. Because Knoxville has neither the intransigence of the deep South nor the complacency of the North, its experience has significance for cities both North and South.

Two facts are fundamental to understanding the situation that existed in Knoxville at the beginning of last May. First, white residents of the city had been served notice that the Negro citizens of the city were not satisfied with the *status quo*. Lunch counter sit-in's [in 1960] and, more recently, student picketing of segregated restaurants near the desegregated University of Tennessee and demonstrations at a downtown movie theater had pinpointed some of the Negro grievances. They had also shown that Negroes were ready to take direct action if that was necessary to abolish segregation. (Although the lunch counter sit-in's had been resolved when department and variety stores desegregated their counters, the other sources of resentment remained and led to almost nightly demonstrations during the spring of 1963.)

Second, and even more important, Negroes were making their demands known at another level, through conferences among community leaders. The Knoxville Area Council on Human Relations, the interracial Fellowship House, and the ministerial association had provided channels for discussing integration and the achievement of certain limited goals of desegregation. The weakness of these groups was that they were not part of the community's economic and political decision-making power structure.

Then the violence in Birmingham, Alabama, occurred. Faced with a reappraisal of the critical situation throughout the South and in their own city, some thirty-five white business, political, educational, and social leaders of Knoxville came together on May 16 to discuss immediate desegregation.

"We were running scared because of Birmingham," one member of the group admitted, but another added, "Knoxville at least had the sense to profit from Birmingham's experience. We know we couldn't let it happen here."

An editorial which had appeared in the Knoxville *News-Sentinel* the previous afternoon gave these men confidence. Editor Loye W. Miller had issued this challenge: "Let's Make Knoxville an 'Open City.'" Citing its recent award as an All America City, Mr. Miller urged open facilities for all Americans. "This means admit everybody to every place that caters to the general public—to the movies, the stores, the hotels, motels, and to the 'private' hospitals. And let's do it by common consent and not by force. This calls for leadership from Knoxvillians of all races and faiths."

The editorial appealed to civic pride and helped create an atmosphere of what one resident called pragmatic idealism. It paved the way for the statement the thirty-five civic leaders publicly endorsed the following afternoon: "Believing in the equal rights of all people and what is morally right is economically sound—and in observing the law of the land—we pledge ourselves to work peacefully for the prompt and orderly desegregation of all public facilities."

Hugh W. Sanford, Jr., an industrialist in the group, concluded, "Getting everyone's name out in the open was important. We wanted to make public opinion public, get leadership focalized out in front."

An executive committee of eight men was named. Beside Mr. Sanford, it included Mayor John Duncan; former mayor and industrialist George R. Dempster; Dr. Charles A. Trentham, minister of the First Baptist Church; chamber of commerce president E. B. Copeland, Jr., and three other prominent businessmen—Robert G. Chapman, John Hart, and W. B. Neill. It met with a committee of the city's Negro leaders—Dr. James A. Colston, president of Knoxville College; Dr. William T. Crutcher; and the Reverend Robert E. James.

The first of a series of biracial meetings was held in one of the public assembly rooms of a leading downtown hotel. Most of the participants were already acquainted with one another, but within a few weeks they would realize just how superficial this previous acquaintance had been. "I know I have developed the greatest respect for this Negro leadership," one of the white businessmen says, "since I've seen these men under pressure and witnessed their maturity and judgment and their commitment to the community." And one of these Negro leaders says, "I know working with this executive committee has helped bring problems of white leaders into sharper focus for me. We've all learned a lot."

Although the two groups sat down together in an atmosphere of goodwill, there was tacit understanding that the Negroes were staking their reputations on the good faith and the ability of the white participants to deliver results. If the Negro leaders could not return to their people and say, "Negotiations won us these specific gains," they were in real danger of being shunted aside for leaders who might prefer belligerent protests to less dramatic progress.

They were asked to spell out what the Negro community wanted. As immediate steps toward the ultimate goal of total participation in the life of the city, they listed: desegregation of hospitals, hotels and motels, theaters, and restaurants and improved job opportunities.

"We'll get to work on it," the white leaders promised. But they soon discovered that what was needed as much as better communication between the races was improved communication within the white group. At this point, Knoxville began to adapt the workings of the biracial committee to its own local needs. The white executive group became completely flexible in handling each phase of desegregation, working on a biracial basis in its meetings with Negro leaders to learn what Negro citizens wanted in specific instances, operating unilaterally in its approach to certain businesses and white groups which had to be won over to the "open city" idea.

This procedure had the approval of the Negro leaders. "We feel," says one, "that this is the best approach they could have used. These were not crusaders or people of another race asking for something; these were fellow businessmen talking good business and the progress of our city."

The task of talking good business was not easy. Not all of the establishments faced with the demand for immediate desegregation were controlled locally; the owners or regional managers of at least two of the key enterprises were in other states. Attitudes varied sharply from businesslike adaptation to the inevitable to outright hostility toward any discussion of change.

"One fellow was hardnosed as the Devil," a committee member says. "He grew pretty hot on the phone and so did I. 'Look here, I'm not trying to tell you how to run your business,' I finally said to him, 'I'm just trying to help you save it.' He saw our point after a while and agreed to have a talk with us, and now Negroes are welcome in his establishment."

One important result of the first meeting of the biracial committee had been that eroding Negro trust in the good faith of the white community was considerably shored up. This had important consequences for the work of the white executive group. As one member confided recently, "First we found that some businesses wouldn't even discuss desegregation if they were under any pressure. By having the good faith of the Negro leadership, we were able to halt some of the pressure, at least momentarily, until we could talk. One of the businessmen felt that he had been singled out for demonstrations. We could see his point. So, although we had planned at first to start in only one or two fields at a time, we decided we had to attack segregation across the board."

Within a week, three Knoxville hospitals (St. Mary's, Baptist, and Presbyterian) had agreed to desegregate that summer. (The other, University Hospital, already accepted Negro patients.) "We must follow the example of the Great Physician, who ministered to all people, if we are to be consistent in our practice of Christianity," Dr. Trentham insisted.

A few days later, downtown hotels and several major motels announced their desegregation. As public endorsement of the open city declaration began to grow—the chamber of commerce received more than 4,500 signatures within a few weeks—confidence among both Negroes and whites increased.

On June 22, an International Visitors Center for entertaining foreign observers of the TVA was opened in one of Knoxville's leading hotels. (Financed by a grant from the Edgar Stern Family Fund in New Orleans, this center is the first of its kind in the country and has been acclaimed as a symbol of Knoxville's awareness of its role in building or damaging America's image abroad.)

Desegregation of downtown theaters began a little later. As the committee worked on this, one Negro was heard to remark, "I fought in Korea to preserve the ideals of this community. And yet when I go to buy a ticket to 'Ben Hur' or 'The King of Kings,' they turn me down. I don't want to marry the cashier; I just want to learn about the life of Christ." Ex-Mayor Demster summed it up in committee meetings: "I know a lot of good Christian people who are looking forward to spending two billion years in heaven with Negroes but won't spend two hours at the show with them."

Opening restaurants to Negroes required considerable negotiation. Without the efforts of the biracial group, no one can even hazard a guess as to when, or at what cost in violence, the city's restaurants might have been desegregated. During the weeks the committee was at work, there were no restaurant demonstrations.

"Even the most radical Negroes knew we were putting our best effort into this," one man says, "and they helped us and themselves by keeping faith with their leaders and providing an atmosphere in which we could negotiate." On July 5, 1963, the overwhelming majority of Knoxville's restaurants—about sixty-five—including all major downtown ones, desegregated.

With the municipal auditorium and libraries, city golf courses, parks, the swimming pools, and public schools all integrated without incident, desegregation of Knoxville's restaurants was the latest, but not the last step in the march toward an open city.

Plans for the opening of the restaurants were no sooner completed than the committee set up a meeting to consider equal employment opportunities. White and Negro members alike agree that this is the longest, hardest step of all. Some progress is being made: Negro sales clerks in certain downtown stores, Negro bus drivers for the city transit system, upgrading of Negroes in industries where they are employed. But as Frank Gordan, a Presbyterian minister and state president of the NAACP, observes, "This committee is opening better opportunities for us to spend our money. Now we need better opportunities to earn money. Before long we want a real breakthrough on jobs."

"I went down to eat in one of the big hotels last week," a Negro student confides, "but I won't be going again soon. I can't afford it, and neither can most Negroes in Knoxville and east Tennessee. What we need is jobs."

But in Knoxville and the surrounding area, many white people are also waiting for a breakthrough. Most of these unemployed are unskilled. It is possible that as the committee searches for a solution to racial difficulties, it will also gain new insights into other problems in the region. To some observers this would involve the healthiest sort of integration: the co-operation of Negro and white citizens in an attack on the common enemies of poverty, inadequate education, and cultural deprivation.

A key figure in Knoxville's program has been the chamber of commerce's President Copeland. A native of Birmingham, he is committed to avoiding repetition of that city's upheaval. "What we try to do," he says, "is dig out the reason why a man won't go along on this and then we try to show him where his course is unrealistic or more likely to bring him trouble than orderly desegregation would."

"We haven't got a completely open city yet," another Knoxvillian said last week, "but the door's swinging wider all the time. No matter what anybody says or thinks, there's no magic wand we can wave and solve this problem. What we've all got to do is settle into the harness in our own towns and communities for a long, hard pull. I believe that's what we're doing here and I believe we're getting somewhere."

"Some people say that Negroes must earn the right to participate in democracy," another commented. "Well, we all have to earn that right, and those of us who are white must earn it now by participating in a search for a solution to our racial crisis."

Other cities have noted the Knoxville program. Even Mississippi's Governor Ross Barnett is aware of its influence. Mayor Duncan tells of a late evening telephone conversation with the Governor. "He asked me what we were trying to do up here," the Mayor recalls. "He wanted to know if I was from the South. He said the South had to stick together now. Finally I told him that Mississippi would have to work out its problems and we would work ours out."

Because of their vulnerability and accessibility, both Mayor Duncan and Editor Loye Miller have received most of the anonymous threats and obscene messages from rabid segregationists. There has been little real opposition to this drive for desegregation, however. A White Citizens Council which flourished briefly has sunk into oblivion.

Reports from all parts of the South reveal that biracial committees are achieving solid results in many communities. The most effective committees have certain characteristics in common—small size, informal procedures, unassailable civic figures as members. One factor for success remains constant: Negro members of the committee must be truly representative of the Negro community and not mere reflections of white opinion. An interracial committee exists to listen to ultimate demands and extreme defiance; then it has to work out a course by which both may be kept from tearing the community apart.

"The art of the whole thing," says a philosophic Southern editor in summation, "is recognizing and including the spectrum on this committee and in its thinking. Negroes are fragmented as well as whites. In fact, isn't that the story of our whole civilization today—man's fragmentation, his loneliness?"

41 : *The Sit-in Comes to Atlanta*

C. Eric Lincoln

. . . One morning last March, sophisticated Atlanta was rudely jarred by the realization that it was like New York in ways it had never particularly noticed before: its Negro minority was not at all timid about expressing its dissatisfaction and demanding action in no uncertain terms. In fact, there in the morning Atlanta *Constitution* was a full-page advertisement entitled "An Appeal for Human Rights," and the list of rights the Negroes said they wanted ranged all the way from the right of attending the public schools of Georgia on a nonsegregated basis to being admitted to hospitals, concerts, and restaurants on the same basis as anybody else. The home-bound commuters got the same message in a full-page advertisement in the evening *Journal*, which, according to its masthead, "Covers Dixie like the Dew."

The advertisement, signed by six Negro students representing the six Negro colleges in Atlanta, said in part:

> We, the students of the six affiliated institutions forming the Atlanta University Center—Clark, Morehouse, Morris Brown,

Mr. Lincoln, Professor of Social Relations and Director of the Institute of Social Relations at Clark University in Atlanta, is the coauthor of *Black Muslims in America* (1961).

and Spelman colleges, Atlanta University and the Interdenominational Theological Center—have joined our hearts, minds and bodies in the cause of gaining those rights which are inherently ours as members of the human race and as citizens of the United States. . . .

We do not intend to wait placidly for those rights which are already legally and morally ours. . . . Today's youth will not sit by submissively, while being denied all rights, privileges, and joys of life. . . .

The reaction in Atlanta, a city known for its more-or-less amicable race relations, was swift and vigorous. In the white community there was genuine amazement over the dissatisfaction of the Negro students. . . .

Predictably, white reaction polarized along urban-rural political lines. Mayor William B. Hartsfield, whose qualifications as a hard-headed Southern liberal are rated high by many of the most militant advocates of Negro rights, praised the statement and said that it "performs the constructive service of letting the white community know what others are thinking."

But a few blocks away in the state capitol, Governor Ernest Vandiver denounced the student appeal as a "left-wing statement . . . calculated to breed dissatisfaction, discontent, discord and evil." The Georgia governor had been elected on a platform of total segregation by a predominantly rural electorate voting under Georgia's so-called county-unit system. . . .

FIRST SKIRMISHES

. . . A mass meeting at Atlanta University early last March resulted in the formation of a Committee on Appeal for Human Rights, which several days later drew up the statement enumerating their grievances and calling on "all people in authority . . . all leaders in civic life . . . and all people of goodwill to assert themselves and abolish these injustices."

To test the receptiveness of white Atlantans to the attempted desegregation of public and semipublic facilities, the students sought to attend a musical at the city auditorium with tickets for orchestra seats ordered in advance; and they "sat in" for service at a lunch counter at Rich's, the largest department store in the

Southeast. At the municipal auditorium they were permitted to occupy the seats for which they held tickets, but the section in which
they sat was promptly designated a Negro section by the management, and seating continued on a *de facto* segregated basis. At
Rich's the students were served on March 3 and 4, but thereafter,
and without prior notice, they were refused. The Appeal for Human Rights followed, but neither the newspaper advertisements
nor attempts at negotiation with Rich's and the other major downtown stores produced results.

At Rich's—which stretches almost a full block on either side of
Forsyth Street—one can buy anything from a packet of pins to a
passage to Paris. It is generally assumed that from 70 to 90
per cent of the Negroes in Atlanta's business and professional class
have maintained accounts there. When no satisfactory agreement
could be reached with the management of the store, the students
threw picket lines in front of it and urged all Negroes to cancel
their accounts and practice "selective purchasing"—that is, to spend
their money somewhere else. This was to be the first in a series of
skirmishes with the giant store, a kind of field maneuver in preparation for an all-out campaign in the fall.

By the time the colleges were closed for summer vacation, the
student movement had taken on some of the aspects of a permanent organization. . . . A Student–Adult Liaison Committee had
been established to interpret the student movement to the Negro
community and to enlist its support. On this committee were business executives, college presidents, professors, lawyers, other Negro
leaders, and students. The adult members of the liaison committee
also served in an advisory capacity on request, but they were excluded from all student meetings dealing with policy and strategy.
. . . Nonetheless, the sit-in's got overwhelming support from Negro
adults, both direct and indirect. . . .

The summer "maneuvers" were directed mainly at units of Colonial Stores and at some smaller businesses located in areas with
from 95 to 100 per cent Negro patronage. When the stores refused
to negotiate with the students on the question of hiring Negroes
above the level of menials, picket lines were organized and a selective purchasing campaign was urged on Negro housewives. The
chief target, a Colonial store near the heart of the Negro business
district on the city's northwest side, suddenly "closed for remodel-

ing." A few days later it reopened with Negroes upgraded in three departments. Shortly thereafter a second store in the Colonial chain hired a Negro cashier and a Negro butcher. . . .

LOGISTICS AND DEPLOYMENT

What came to be referred to as the "Fall Campaign" got under way immediately after the reopening of the colleges in mid-September. This time the main sit-in targets were in the heart of the Atlanta shopping district. . . . Accommodations were requested at *all* facilities—lunch counters, rest rooms, and, in the case of the department stores, restaurants and dining rooms.

The stores refused to negotiate with the students, and beginning on October 19 a succession of sit-in's harassed the downtown merchants and brought out scores of extra police and plainclothes detectives. By Friday, October 21, hundreds of students had launched attacks in co-ordinated waves. Service to *anyone* at eating facilities in the stores involved had all but ended, and sixty-one students, one white heckler, and Dr. Martin Luther King were all in jail. Under a truce called by Mayor Hartsfield everyone was out of jail by Sunday morning except Dr. King. Negotiations between the merchants and the Student–Adult Liaison Committee were promised on the initiative of the mayor. When the truce ended thirty days later, no progress had been made in settling the impasse, and on November 25, the all-out attack was resumed. . . .

Both the Atlanta police and the merchants had been baffled by the students' apparent ability to appear out of nowhere armed with picket signs, and by the high degree of co-ordination with which simultaneous attacks were mounted against several stores at once. . . .

Much of the credit for the development of the organizational scheme belongs to Lonnie King, a Morehouse student who is the recognized leader of the student movement in Atlanta, and his immediate "general staff." Policymaking is done by a board of about fifteen students, constituting the Committee on Appeal for Human Rights, which interprets and tries to make effective the wishes of the students of the six colleges who are loosely joined together in what is known as the Atlanta Student Movement. The committee is cochaired by Lonnie King and Herschelle Sullivan, a twenty-two-year-old senior at Spelman College. Its executive officer has the rather whimsical title of "le Commandante." *Le Commandante* is Fred C. Bennette, a pretheology student at Morris Brown College. . . .

By 8:00 A.M. the first contingent of volunteers for the day's assignment has arrived; there may be anywhere between twenty-five and a hundred students present. There is a brief devotional period, which usually concludes with a prayer that the white people of Georgia and throughout the United States will learn to overcome their prejudices and that the students will be restrained, nonviolent, and loving in their attempts to establish human dignity in Georgia. . . . They are then likely to scatter about the church looking for places to study until they are summoned for duty.

Meanwhile, *le Commandante* and his staff are in conference. . . . Telephoned reports from Senior Intelligence Officer Daniel Mitchell, a Clark junior (already at his post downtown), will describe the nature of the flow of traffic at each potential target.

"ALL RIGHT, LET'S GO"

The general staff having concluded its deliberations, a number of pickets selected on the basis of their class schedules and the nature of the day's objectives will be assembled and briefed. . . . Assignments fall into three categories: pickets (called by the students "picketeers"), sit-in's, and a sort of flying squad called "sit-and-run's." The objective of the sit-and-run's is simply to close lunch counters by putting in an appearance and requesting service. When the merchants discontinue service to all rather than serve the Negroes, the sit-and-run's move on to another target. The group designated "sit-in's" are prepared to contest their right to be served and are willing to go to jail if need be. Those volunteering for sit-in duty agree not to request bail if they are arrested.

By now it is 9:00 or 9:30 A.M., and transportation has arrived. . . . The deputy commander provides each driver with a driver's orientation sheet outlining in detail the route to be followed by each driver and the places where each of the respective groups of students are to be let out. . . .

Meanwhile, Field Commander Otis Moss is checking a communications code with Ernest Brown, an eighteen-year-old Morehouse junior, or one of the five other licensed radio operators who man a short-wave radio set up in the church nursery. When this has been attended to, Commander Moss climbs into an ancient automobile equipped with a short-wave sending and receiving unit and heads for the downtown shopping district. . . .

. . . Reports from the field and area commanders begin to trickle in by radio and telephone. As the lunch hour nears, the volume of reports will increase to one every two or three minutes. The reports are typed and dated and placed on the desk of *le Commandante* by a corps of young women who serve as communications aides. Duplicates are posted on the bulletin board and the students remaining at headquarters crowd around to watch the fortunes of their colleagues downtown. Here are two actual reports taken from the files and approved for publication by the Security Officer:

11/26/60   11:05 A.M.
From: Captain Lenora Tait
To: le Commandante
Lunch counters at Rich's closed. Proceeded to alternative objective. Counters at Woolworth's also closed. Back to Rich's for picket duty. Ku Klux Klan circling Rich's in nightgowns and dunce caps. "Looking good!"

From: Gwendolyn Lee
To: le Commandante
Sign has been torn from the back of one of our white picketeers. He got another sign and returned to the line. Morale of white picketeers very good. Known heckler, an old man in a gray suit, is on the scene. White opposition increasing. Plain-clothes detective made co-ordinator keep moving. All picketeers now in front of Rich's.

The white pickets referred to were from Emory University, a segregated Methodist college in Atlanta. White students from the University of Georgia have also joined the Negro students in the picket lines. . . .

ALLIES AND MORALE

The sit-in's continue, a somber prelude to the school desegregation problems Atlanta will have to face September [of 1962]. Support from adult Negroes is firm and consistent, and professional men and women have joined the students in the picket lines. . . .

In some cases the students have been encouraged by white clerks and other personnel working in the very stores against which the sit-in's are directed. . . . A white woman who had been watching the New Orleans spectacle on television called an official at one of the Negro colleges to ask that the Negroes continue to pray that the white race be forgiven for its behavior toward Negroes and that the students be encouraged to continue their efforts.

There seems little doubt that the efforts will be continued. The Negro students and their white and black allies are determined to keep on sitting in, sitting and running, and picketing until their battle is won.

42 : *Court Victory in New Rochelle*

Irving R. Kaufman

New Rochelle, a suburb of New York City, is, as we know, located in southeastern Westchester County. In late 1960, a class action was initiated in this court by several Negro children enrolled in the Lincoln School, a public elementary school operated by the Board of Education of the City of New Rochelle, which was named as one of the defendants. In this action, the plaintiffs charged that Lincoln School, situated in central New Rochelle, then with an enrollment of approximately 94 per cent Negroes, had been deliberately created and maintained by the board as a racially segregated school in violation of the Fourteenth Amendment to the Federal Constitution. After a trial, this court found [1] that the school board, in 1930, had gerrymandered the district in which the Lincoln School was located in order that a large portion of its white students would be excluded and permitted to attend the nearby Webster and Mayflower schools; that within the four years following, the boundaries of the Lincoln district were manipulated so as to incorporate the ever-increasing Negro population; that until 1949, the board assured the continuance of Lincoln School as a Negro

---

Judge Kaufman is a judge of the United States Court of Appeals, Second Circuit.

[1] 191 F. Supp. 181 (S.D.N.Y. 1961).

school by permitting white students resident within the district to transfer to schools outside the district; and that after 1949, when further transfers were forbidden, the school board did nothing to alter the *status quo* or to ameliorate the serious racial imbalance in the Lincoln School which it had caused to be brought about.

It followed, therefore, that this court was constrained to find that the deliberate efforts to maintain the Lincoln School as a segregated educational institution worked a deprivation of the equal protection of the laws constitutionally proscribed by the Fourteenth Amendment as interpreted by the Supreme Court in *Brown* v. *Board of Education, supra.* As I noted at that time, "The conduct of responsible school officials has operated to deny to Negro children the opportunities for a full and meaningful educational experience guaranteed to them by the Fourteenth Amendment." [2]

In order to cure this social illness, this court directed the board to present a plan to remedy the illegality. The board proposed such a plan which, with considerable modification, was adopted as the decree of the court in May 1961.[3] In essence, the decree provided for a completely optional transfer of all Lincoln students to any schools having sufficient room to receive them without the imposition of any requirements for minimal academic achievement or emotional adjustment. Further provisions were incorporated in order fully to effectuate the spirit of the optional transfer plan; but, the decree provided that the board was under no obligation to furnish transportation to pupils transferring under the terms of the decree. The decree concluded with the provision that "The court shall retain jurisdiction over this case to assure full compliance with this decree."

. . . On the date of the commencement of this litigation, Lincoln School had an enrollment of 483 students, of whom 454, or 94 per cent were Negro. As a result of the transfer of Lincoln students to the city's eleven other elementary schools, the percentage of Negro students dropped immediately to approximately 89 per cent. A year and a half later, in April 1963, the entire student population at Lincoln School was less than half what it was when this court entered its decree; only 210 pupils had chosen to remain enrolled at this antiquated school, constructed sixty-five years ago.

[2] 191 F. Supp. at 182–193.
[3] 195 F. Supp. 231 (S.D.N.Y. 1961).

The economic and social impact of this mass exodus has been perceptively analyzed and extrapolated by the present forward-looking school board. The operation of Lincoln School has become economically unfeasible due to the greatly diminished size of the student body; as of April of this year, although the average annual per capita cost of education in all the New Rochelle elementary schools was approximately $877 per student, the cost of educating a student at Lincoln was somewhat more than $1,057. As the student body will continue to decrease, the cost per Lincoln School student will increase. It has become obvious to the present board that the Lincoln School must be closed and permanently shut down.

But more at the heart of this proceeding is the school board's fear—grounded in a sincere desire to conform not only with the letter but with the spirit of this court's decree—a fear that the continuation of the plan of free optional transfer, pursuant to the terms of the decree, will result in an unbalanced racial population in schools adjacent to the Lincoln district. The board in effect urges that strict compliance with the original decree, now that Lincoln School is being closed down, will pose a serious threat of de facto racial segregation in those contiguous schools, if the remaining students at Lincoln are permitted to exercise a free choice of school to be attended.

The school board and its enlightened superintendent of schools, Dr. David G. Salten, a nationally recognized organizer—after holding two public hearings in May of this year, at which 1,300 and 900 citizens, respectively, were in attendance and ninety-eight speakers heard; after attending many meetings of PTA groups, and civic and neighborhood associations; and after consulting with experts in the field and with those representing the interests of the Negro population of the Lincoln district—therefore ask this court to amend and modify the letter of the decree in order that its spirit may best be perpetuated. . . .

With the closing of the Lincoln School and the accompanying need for enlightened placement of the students living within the Lincoln district, the board proposes to provide bus transportation to these students on a basis identical to that provided throughout New Rochelle—that is, transportation to any school destination within one and one-half and ten miles of the student's home. As the school board has stated in its report on its proposed plan to the citizens of New Rochelle: "Transportation will be a key factor in our efforts to maintain an ethnic balance in our elementary schools and to prevent the emergence of segregated schools." This report further states: "Any solution for the problems at Lincoln must be resolved on the basis of what is good for the school system and the community as a whole. Closing the school and transporting its students to outlying areas fulfills this criterion because it avoids tipping contiguous schools and enables students in outlying as well as in the central schools to attend an integrated school."

I have been advised that the additional cost to each of the residents of New Rochelle once the benefits of bus transportation are extended to the students in question will be insignificant. It must also be noted that, pursuant to state law, 90 per cent of the transportation costs incurred in the city of New Rochelle will be borne by New York State in the 1963–64 and successive school years, and only 10 per cent by the city. In short, the burdens resulting from the implementation of the proposed transportation plan are infinitesimal when compared to its benefits.

I am convinced that the closing of Lincoln School, conjoined with free bus transportation for former pupils there to other schools within the city will have a salutary influence in securing true equality of educational opportunity for all parties before this court. . . .

The more fundamental modification of the decree proposed by the school board is the deletion of paragraphs one and two which deal with the optional transfer plan and the substitution therefor of a provision designed to permit the board to assign students residing within the Lincoln district where necessary to secure or maintain racial balance within the elementary school system. Such a provision would repose in the board's discretion in the assignment of pupils in order best to effectuate the principles announced in the original opinion of this court. Viewing this proposed modification in light of the school board's demonstrated genuine support for those principles, this court has decided to so modify its decree. Compliance therewith will be insured if ever necessary, by this court's continued retention of jurisdiction over the case. . . .

And so, as the board in its "Comprehensive Plan for Educational Excellence—A Report to All Citizens of New Rochelle," dated

May 14, 1963, stated: "The eyes of the entire Nation are fixed upon our community and our special difficulties have received national attention." The nation will now observe how men of compassion and foresight have faced up to the racial problem of their community and with courage undertaken the task of solving it.

43 : *Marching on Washington*

Murray Kempton

The most consistent quality of white America's experience with the Negro is that almost nothing happens that we—or perhaps even he—expects to have happen. Faithful to that tradition, Washington waited most of the summer for the avenging Negro army to march on Washington for jobs and freedom; what came [in the march of 200,000 whites and Negroes to the Capitol on August 28, 1963] was the largest religious pilgrimage of Americans that any of us is ever likely to see.

When it was over, Malcolm X, the Muslim, was observed in the lobby of the Statler. It had, he conceded, been something of a show. "Kennedy," said Malcolm X, "should win the Academy Award—for direction." Yet while [Kennedy] may have triumphed as director-manipulator, he was also deftly manipulated by those whom he strove to direct.

"When the Negro leaders announced the march, [Kennedy] asked them to call it off," Bayard Rustin, its manager, remembered the next day. "When they thumbed—when they told him they wouldn't—he almost smothered us. We had to keep raising our demands . . . to keep him from getting ahead of us."

Rustin and A. Philip Randolph are men who had to learn long

Mr. Kempton is an editor of the *New Republic* and a former columnist for the *New York Post*.

ago that in order to handle they must first permit themselves to be handled. The moment in that afternoon which most strained belief was near its end, when Rustin led the assemblage in a mass pledge never to cease until they had won their demands. A radical pacifist, every sentence punctuated by his upraised hand, was calling for a two dollar an hour minimum wage. Every television camera at the disposal of the networks was upon him. No expression one-tenth so radical has ever been seen or heard by so many Americans.

To produce this scene had taken some delicate maneuvering. Randolph called the march last spring at a moment when the civil-rights groups had fallen into a particularly painful season of personal rancor. Randolph is unique because he accepts everyone in a movement whose members do not always accept one another. His first support came from the nonviolent actionists; they hoped for passionate protest. That prospect was Randolph's weapon; the moderates had to come in or be defenseless against embarrassing disorder. Randolph welcomed them not just with benevolence but with genuine gratitude. When President Kennedy expressed his doubts, Randolph answered that some demonstration was unavoidable and that what had to be done was to make it orderly.

It was the best appeal that feeling could make to calculation. The White House knew that the ordinary Negro cherished the Kennedy brothers and that the larger the assemblage the better disposed it would be not to embarrass them. When [Kennedy] finally mentioned the march in public, he issued something as close as possible to a social invitation. . . .

If the march was important, it was because it represented an acceptance of the Negro revolt as part of the American myth, and so an acceptance of the revolutionaries into the American establishment. That acceptance, of course, carries the hope that the Negro revolt will stop where it is. Yet that acceptance is also the most powerful incentive and assurance that the revolt will continue. The children from Wilmington, North Carolina, climbed back on their buses with the shining memory of a moment when they marched with all America—a memory to sustain them when they return to march alone. So it was, too, for all the others who came from Birmingham, Montgomery, Danville, Gadsden, and Jackson—places whose very names evoke not only the cause but the way it is being won.

GRAY FROM JAIL, HAGGARD FROM TENSION

The result of such support—the limits it placed on the spectacle—was illustrated by the experience of John Lewis, chairman of the Student Nonviolent Co-ordinating Committee. Lewis is only twenty-five; his only credential for being there was combat experience; he has been arrested twenty-two times and beaten half as often. The Student Nonviolent Co-ordinating Committee is a tiny battalion, its members gray from jail and exhausted from tension. They have the gallant cynicism of troops of the line; they revere Martin Luther King (some of them) as a captain who has faced the dogs with them and they call him with affectionate irreverence, "De Lawd." We could hardly have had this afternoon without them.

Lewis, in their spirit, had prepared a speech full of temerities about how useless the civil-rights bill is and what frauds the Democrats and Republicans are. Three of the white speakers told Randolph that they could not appear at a platform where such sedition was pronounced, and John Lewis had to soften his words in deference to elders. Equal rights for the young to say their say may, perhaps, come later.

Yet Lewis' speech, even as laundered, remained discomfiting enough to produce a significant tableau at its end. "My friends," he said, "let us not forget that we are engaged in a significant social revolution. By and large American politics is dominated by politicians who build their careers on immoral compromising and ally themselves with open forums of political, economic and social exploitation." When he had finished, every Negro on the speakers' row pumped his hand and patted his back; and every white one looked out into the distance.

So even in the middle of this ceremony of reconciliation, the void between the Negro American and the white one remained. Or rather, it did and it didn't. At one point, Martin King mentioned with gratitude the great number of white people (about 40,000 to 50,000 out of an estimated 200,000) who had joined the march. There was little response from the platform—where it must have seemed formal courtesy—but as the sound of those words moved across the great spaces between King and the visitors from the Southern towns, there was the sudden sight and sound of Negroes cheering far away. Nothing all afternoon was quite so moving as the sight of these people, whose trust has been violated so often in the particular, proclaiming it so touchingly intact in the general.

We do not move the Negro often, it would seem, and we do it only when we are silent and just standing there. On the speakers' stand there were the inevitable Protestant, Catholic, and Jew without whom no national ceremony can be certified. Is it hopeless to long for a day when the white brother will just once accept the duty to march and forego the privilege to preach? Dr. Eugene Carson Blake of the National Council of Churches told the audience that the Protestants were coming and "late we come." It was the rarest blessing—an apology. We have begun to stoop a little; and yet it is so hard for us to leave off condescending.

We cannot move the Negro by speaking, because the public white America seems to know no words except the ones worn out from having been so long unmeant. Even if they are meant now, they have been empty too long not to *sound* empty still; whatever our desires, our language calls up only the memory of the long years when just the same language served only to convey indifference.

Yet the Negro moves us most when he touches our memory, even as we chill him most when we touch his. August 28 was to many whites only a demonstration of power and importance until Mahalia Jackson arose to sing the old song about having been rebuked and scorned and going home. Then King near the end began working as country preachers do, the words for the first time not as to listeners but as to participants, the intimate private conversation of invocation and response. For just those few minutes, we were back where this movement began and has endured, older than the language of the society which was taking these pilgrims in, but still fresh where the newer language was threadbare.

The Negro comes from a time the rest of us have forgotten; he seems new and complicated only because he represents something so old and simple. He reminds us that the new, after which we have run so long, was back there all the time. Something new will some day be said, and it will be something permanent if it starts from such a memory.

44 : *Blockades in New York*

Peter Kihss

More than two hundred civil-rights demonstrators were arrested in Brooklyn [July 22, 1963] and twenty-six others were taken into custody in Manhattan as a result of efforts to block public construction until Negroes and Puerto Ricans get more jobs.

Police officials said they believed the mass arrests here were the highest since five hundred persons were jailed in the Harlem riot of August 1, 1943, when five persons were killed.

At least ten ministers and church officials were detained in the Brooklyn demonstrations, outside the Downstate Medical Center. In wave after wave for nearly eight hours, Negro and white sympathizers darted in front of incoming construction vehicles to sit down or lie down in the roadway. They were picked up and taken away in patrol wagons—a dozen at a time.

In Manhattan, seven ministers were arrested for locking their arms to obstruct construction vehicles trying to enter the Rutgers Houses project on the Lower East Side. There the demonstrations led to scuffling between other pickets and policemen trying to move them. The demonstrations were over within a quarter hour.

The Reverend Dr. Gardner C. Taylor, a spokesman for the Brooklyn demonstrators, said last night that he and three other spokesmen

---

Mr. Kihss is a reporter for *The New York Times*.

would meet with Mayor Wagner at City Hall at 11:30 A.M. today. However, he said demonstrations at the $25,000,000 state project would resume at 7 A.M.

"While we talk, walk!" Dr. Taylor told two thousand supporters at a rally [that] night in the Corner Stone Baptist Church, at 574 Madison Street, in the Bedford-Stuyvesant section of Brooklyn.

All the Brooklyn defendants were charged with disorderly conduct. A total of one hundred and ninety-two were arraigned, and all were released on their own recognizance, pending varying hearings. . . .

Section 722 of the State Penal Law provides that disorderly conduct is any of a dozen specified acts committed "with intent to provoke a breach of the peace and under circumstances whereby a breach of the peace may be occasioned." These include acting "in such a manner as to annoy, disturb, interfere with, obstruct or be offensive to others" and congregating with others on a public street and refusing to move on when ordered to by the police.

Dr. Taylor estimated that 1,250 persons had taken part in the Brooklyn picketing. Three-fourths or more of the participants were Negroes.

The clergymen arrested were both whites and Negroes.

PART V

AREAS OF TENSION
WITHIN THE
CIVIL-RIGHTS MOVEMENT

45 : *A Debate over "Compensation" Programs*

Domestic Marshall Plan

Whitney M. Young, Jr.

In 1948, by instituting the Marshall Plan to aid the war-torn countries of Europe, the United States took a step unparalleled in history. Recognizing the special need of the nations shattered by World War II, the people of this country committed some $17 billion in money, machines and technical aid to help our neighbors overseas to take their place again in the community of free nations.

This rightful action was in keeping with the long tradition of America's moral, political and economic credo. We have long given special, emergency aid to the oppressed, the sick, the handicapped and deprived. In recent years, we have seen this concept put into action through our aid—in employment, education, and welfare—to Hungarian and Cuban refugees. We see it annually carried out in the form of emergency help to "depressed" and "disaster" areas,

---

Whitney Young, Jr., is the Executive Director of the National Urban League.

suffering from joblessness or devastation by hurricanes, drought, and other misfortunes. The "G. I. Bill of Rights" after World War II was, in a sense, a recognition of the special need of our discharged veterans for education, housing, employment, and other benefits.

Recently, the National Urban League has attracted nationwide attention with its proposal for a temporary "more-than-equal" program of aid for Negro citizens. In the current drive for civil rights, with its demonstrations, marches and sit-in's, this proposal has confused many white Americans. They ask: Is the Negro not to be satisfied by equality alone? Or, is he seeking, not equality, but preference? In the face of these questions, our history should teach us that what the Urban League proposes is not only directly in the American tradition, but has the arguments of racial justice, economic practicality, and morality—secular as well as religious—behind it.

On an economic level, the hard but simple fact—borne out by comparative statistics on unemployment, income, mortality rates, substandard housing, and education—is that the past of the Negro exists in the present. Citizens everywhere must realize that the effects of over three hundred years of oppression cannot be obliterated by doing business as usual. They must know, too, that in today's complex, technological society, a strong back and a will to succeed are no longer sufficient to break the bonds of deprivation, as was the case with minority groups in the past. For, in addition to the ordinary forces affecting one's way of life, the Negro's struggle into America's mainstream has been thwarted by the barriers of discrimination and denial based on the color of his skin.

The facts speak for themselves. Today, the average Negro family earns $3,233, as compared with $5,835 for the white family—a difference of 45 per cent. This gap has widened by two percentage points in the last decade alone. It has widened because the Negro started receiving too little, too late. More than 75 per cent of Negro workers are found in the three lowest occupational categories —service workers, semi-skilled workers, and unskilled and farm labor—the categories most affected by the geometric growth of automation. These same categories include less than 39 per cent of white workers.

By the same token, one out of every six Negro dwellings is substandard, as compared with one in thirty-two white dwellings. One in every four Negro women with preschool children is working away from home. Of the school dropouts, 21 per cent are Negro; only 7 per cent of high-school graduates are Negroes. Unemployment rates for Negroes are from two and one-half to three times higher than those for white workers.

To overcome these conditions the National Urban League declares that the nation must undertake an immediate, dramatic, and tangible "crash program"—a domestic Marshall Plan—to close this intolerable economic, social, and educational gap, which separates the vast majority of Negro citizens from other Americans. Unless this is done, the results of the current heroic efforts in the civil-rights movement will be only an illusion, and the struggle will continue, with perhaps tragic consequences.

In its plea for such a domestic Marshall Plan, the Urban League is asking for a special effort, not for special privileges. This effort has been described as "preferential treatment," "indemnification," "special consideration," "compensatory activity." These are "scare" phrases that obscure the meaning of the proposal and go against the grain of our native sense of fair play.

We prefer that our recommendations be seen as necessary and just corrective measures that must be taken if equal opportunity is to have meaning. They are necessary, because only by such means can the majority of Negro citizens be prepared to assume the increased responsibilities that they will face in a more integrated society. They are just, because such an effort alone can repair the devastation wrought by generations of injustice, neglect, discrimination, and indifference based on race.

To put it another way, the scales of equal opportunity are now heavily weighted against the Negro and cannot be corrected in today's technological society simply by applying equal weights. For more than 300 years the white American has received special consideration, or "preferential treatment," if you will, over the Negro. What we ask now is that for a brief period there be a deliberate and massive effort to include the Negro citizen in the mainstream of American life. Furthermore, we are not asking for equal time; a major effort, honestly applied, need last only some ten years. This crash program must be a co-operative effort by all agencies, institutions, and individuals, public and private.

The elements of the crash program, or domestic Marshall Plan, would include:

Education. For the deprived child—Negro as well as white—provision for first-class schools, with the most modern facilities and the best and most experienced teachers. These are necessary to help him realize his potential and prepare him to take advantage of greater educational opportunity. Necessary also is intensified remedial instruction in the lower grades for culturally deprived and retarded pupils. Schools and colleges must find new ways to seek out Negro youths with undeveloped talents. Similarly, adult education programs must be expanded and geared to the needs of citizens lacking the basic literary and technical skills.

Employment. A planned effort to place *qualified* Negroes in all categories of employment, at all levels of responsibility. This would mean that employers would consciously seek to hire qualified Negro citizens and would intensify apprenticeship and training programs to prepare new Negro employees and upgrade those already employed. Labor unions, too, must make a conscientious effort to include Negroes in their membership and training programs.

Further, where Negroes have not been employed in the past at all levels, it is essential that there be conscious preferment to help them catch up. This does not mean the establishment of a quota system—an idea shunned by responsible Negro organizations and leaders. But, because we are faced with the hypocrisy of "tokenism," where the presence of two or three Negro employees is passed off as integration, we are forced, during the transitional stages, to discuss numbers and categories. We demand, in all fairness, that the Negro not be expected to bear the brunt of unemployment.

Housing. Racial ghettos eliminated by providing genuine housing opportunities on the basis of need and financial ability. Programs of redevelopment and relocation, planned to provide both low-income housing and a racial diversity, are needed throughout our communities. This will require the active participation of real estate brokers as well as homeowners.

Health and Welfare. Public and private agencies seeking to provide the best personnel and facilities in low-income neighborhoods, and increased counseling services to troubled families. Here, particularly, the churches and schools must combine efforts to help Negro families develop a deeper sense of parental and community responsibility.

Finally, qualified Negro citizens should be sought and named to public and private boards and commissions, particularly those which shape employment, housing, education, and health and welfare policies. In achieving this objective, we would develop strong, responsible leadership within the Negro community. Also, we would prompt private foundations, business and government to reassess the extent and aims of their financial contributions to established Negro leadership and organizations.

The program outlined here has a simple, practical aim: to provide the Negro citizen with the leadership, education, jobs, and motivation that will permit him to help himself. It is not a plea to exempt him from the independence and initiative demanded by our free, competitive society. It makes practical economic sense as a measure to reduce unemployment and welfare costs and to increase our productivity and national income by including Negro citizens in the benefits of our rich society. President Kennedy's economic advisers estimated that our gross national product could be raised 2.5 per cent, were the Negro worker's earnings commensurate with the nation's average.

This program makes historical sense as a rehabilitation of the damage inflicted upon the Negro by generations of injustice and neglect. He, too, has given his blood, sweat, and tears to the building of our country; yet, where the labor and initiative of other minority groups have been rewarded by assimilation within the society, the black American has been isolated and rejected.

The domestic Marshall Plan has profound moral and religious justification. Our country is in dire jeopardy as long as it has within its body politic a socially and economically deprived group of citizens, whether they be actually enslaved or denied the full benefits of equality and freedom by an insidious economic and psychological slavery. In this sense, the crash programs that we propose are not an effort to impose the guilt and sins of a past generation on our present white community. This is an appeal for all Americans, working together, to rid present-day America of its sickening disease and its moral shame.

The Negro is in revolt today, not to change the fabric of our society or to seek a special place in it, but to enter into partnership in that society. It is a revolt with which every American should sympathize. Already a few educational and business institutions are working with intensified effort, special consideration, if you will, in solving this problem. We have the material and spiritual resources as a country to meet the challenge and accomplish the urgent task ahead. All we need is the will to act and the spirit of decency and sacrifice which abounds in our land.

Parity, Not Preference

Kyle Haselden

An increasing number of Negro and white Americans agree that securing complete freedom and total equality for the Negro is this nation's No. 1 domestic issue and that justice for the deprived one-tenth of the nation's population is the end toward which the whole society should move speedily. Unanimous in this agreement, they nevertheless disagree as to the permissible and effective means to that end.

Varied in their temperaments, their religious convictions, their sense of what is prudent and practical, these Americans prefer one or another of the various strategies which seek racial justice. The options range from the doctrine of violent rebellion against white domination at one extreme to a patient yet active appeal to the nation's creeds, congresses, and courts at the other. Between these extremes fall various nonviolent strategies and schemes, each with its own supporters.

Unfortunately there are, in the ranks of men and women genuinely committed to racial justice, some who insist that unanimity of purpose requires uniformity of plan. They insist that whites and Negroes who share their objective also adopt their methods—however unruly, eccentric and impractical those methods—or accept vilification for Uncle Tomism. This absolutist, autocratic spirit believes that justice for the Negro is the ultimate criterion of all human action and that this end validates any means, whatever practicality or religious principle may dictate to the contrary.

Mr. Haselden is Managing Editor of *Christian Century* and author of *The Racial Problem in Christian Perspective* (1959).

This is a dangerous mood. It divides those who seek justice for Negroes; it alienates influential moderates unnecessarily; and, most serious, this authoritarian spirit lures the Negro into activities which corrupt his purpose and defeat his ultimate hope.

In the struggle for racial justice a technique is not valid simply because it annoys the white man or because it promises some temporary advantage to the Negro. It is valid only if it honors the moral ground on which the Negro makes his claim for justice, respects the right of all men to the same justice, preserves in the human relationship values which are equivalents of justice, and promotes rather than prevents the Negro's progress.

The idea of compensation, which has been suggested as a device to equalize competition between whites and Negroes, fails these crucial tests. By compensation—in the passive rather than the active sense—is meant compensation *for* the Negro rather than *by* the Negro. It has been proposed that the Negro cannot succeed in his search for freedom and equality unless there is an arbitrary—in fact, artificial—removal of the academic, cultural, and professional lag forced upon him by over two centuries of slavery and by another of exploitation. It is argued further that the Negroes' years of involuntary, payless servitude established a collectible claim against the descendants of those who enslaved and exploited him.

How can this debt be paid? The proposal is that the Negro be given preference in employment wherever a vacancy occurs, a premium in salary, and a quota system guaranteeing that one-tenth of all people hired by firms, professional enterprises, and industries be Negroes. Even though this proposal is obviously unfeasible, what shall we say of it as a theory?

Compensation must be rejected as an equalizer of competition between Negroes and whites for several reasons, all of which rest on the grounds to which the Negro appeals in his demand for freedom and equality.

First, compensation for Negroes is a subtle but pernicious form of racism. It requires that men be dealt with by society on the basis of race and color rather than on the basis of their humanity. It would therefore as a public policy legalize, deepen, and perpetuate the abominable racial cleavage which has ostracized and crippled

the American Negro. Racism, whoever may be its temporary bene-
ficiary, should be eliminated from the social order, not confirmed
by it.

Second, preferential economic status for Negroes would penalize
the living in a futile attempt to collect a debt owed by the dead.
The twentieth-century white man is no more to blame for the fact
that his ancestors bought and held slaves than are twentieth-century Negroes for the fact that some of their ancestors captured and
sold slaves. This is the ironic tragedy of exploitation. It leaves with
the descendants of the exploiters a guilt they cannot cancel and
with the descendants of the exploited a debt they cannot collect.

Third, a scheme which gives Negroes preference in employment
and a premium in salary would bestow on Negroes the debilitating
social status which has for centuries cursed the initiative and enterprise of the white man in the South. Preferred status for the Negro,
however much society may owe him a debt, will inevitably destroy
in him the initiative and enterprise required of a minority people
in a highly competitive society. Slavery corrupts ambition and self-
reliance; so, too, does patronizing social status.

Fourth, compensation for Negroes would be unfair to other minorities handicapped by their history or by rapid social and industrial change—Puerto Ricans, Mexican-Americans, migrants of all
races, Indians, coal miners, and others. Negroes are entirely right in
demanding that they be hired, paid, and promoted on their merit
and in boycotting those enterprises which discriminate on a racial
basis. But they are not right in demanding an artificial scheme
which is unworkable, racist, destructive of initiative, and unfair to
other struggling Americans.

Our goal should be parity, not preferment, and there are three
things we must do, none of them pleasant, none easy, if we are to
attain it.

First, there must be a total, across-the-board desegregation of
American society. Wherever the white man will not voluntarily surrender the psychic and material advantages of racial discrimination, the Negro must use the law, his power as a consumer, his increasing political leverage, and coercive nonviolent protests to assail
and destroy the color structures of our society.

Equality of opportunity is an elemental civil right specifically
declared in the sacred documents of the United States. Withhold-

ing that right from any people because of their race profanes every tenet in the political and religious creeds of the American people. Denying that right encumbers and humiliates twenty million American citizens. The first business of the nation is the total elimination of racial discrimination and its component, racial segregation.

Such liberation, however, would leave the Negro still handicapped by centuries of poor schooling and by his long exclusion from most trades and professions. A desegregated society would open to the Negro opportunities which are rightfully his and should be granted to him but for which centuries of neglect and abuse leave many of his race inadequately prepared. Even though all racial bars were removed, most Negroes could not, in a free and impartial society, compete on equal terms with most white people for jobs and preferments.

But this, as we have noted, is a handicap which Negroes share with another one-tenth of the population, whose competitive strength has also been sapped by an unfortunate history or by the entrapping eddies of industrial development.

Our second task, therefore, is to undertake a nationwide crash program for the education, training, and employment of the underprivileged, underdeveloped one-fifth of the nation, a domestic Point Four which would give to the employable a fair chance and to the unemployable qualifying education and training. Such a program would be based not on race but on need. Negroes would of course be the chief beneficiaries of an educational and economic crash program, because of the predominant number of deprived Negroes. But a domestic Point Four program aimed at the needs of *all* the nation's backward peoples would close rather than widen the nation's racial cleavage.

Finally, irritating as it may be, the fact might as well be faced that no immigrant or minority group has ever made its way into the mainstream of American life without studying and working harder and longer than the general population. This is the third task as it now confronts the Negro.

During their long pilgrimage through slavery and semislavery, most Negroes did not have an incentive for the kind of active self-compensation by which other minorities have climbed out of humiliating servitude into respected equality with other ethnic groups. Slavery and peonage do not generally encourage ambition. Even now the Negro must divert himself—his native abilities and his acquired skills, his initiative and enterprise, his devotion and endurance, his ablest leadership—from the pursuits followed by free men to the claiming of those dignities and opportunities which are the birthright of every American citizen. Yet the hard historical fact is that self-compensation is essential if he is to escape that social substratum into which a cruel history and an arrogant, avaricious white man have coerced him.

Along with several million Caucasian Americans, most Negroes need a lift from their government if they are to overcome the handicaps of a tragic history. More than that, however, Negroes need to throw off the white man's domination if they are to discover at last what they can do for themselves unencumbered in an open society.

46 : *The Negro and Labor Unions*

Daniel Bell

Some years ago, an older friend, an official of one of the out-of-town locals of the International Ladies Garment Workers Union and a Socialist, complained to me about the apathy of most of the members in his local, and, in some cases, the resentment of a minority against the union leadership. "I don't understand it," he said. "I work hard for them. I spend long hours negotiating for them. I don't let the boss get away with a nickel. But they don't appreciate it."

I was reminded of his remarks recently on reading the charges made by Herbert Hill, the labor secretary of the NAACP, of racial discrimination in the Garment Workers Union, and the outraged rejoinders by David Dubinsky and other ILGWU officials. . . .

Hill's statement, compiled originally for a congressional subcommittee, stated that Negroes were excluded from the higher paying jobs in the garment trades (specifically in the cutters' local); that certain locals excluded Negroes; that a predominantly Negro local (composed primarily of shipping clerks) was attached to a larger local of pressers and was thus deprived of full citizenship rights in

Mr. Bell is Professor of Sociology at Columbia University, former Labor Editor of *Fortune* magazine, and author of *Work and Its Discontents* (1956) and *The End of Ideology* (1961).

the union; and that Negroes and Puerto Ricans were underrepresented in the union's leadership, which was, and remains, predominantly Jewish.

The ILGWU's answer, which appears in the fall 1962 issue of *New Politics,* was prepared by Gus Tyler, the union's political director. It is, I think, quite convincing as a rebuttal to the specific charges. Hill's statement was sloppy (Local 89, accused of rebuffing Negroes, is an Italian-language local, and accepts only Italian members—a hang-over from an early organizational structure), his figures were often incorrect, and his portentous social analysis (e.g., that the Jewish labor leaders have more in common with the Jewish employers than with the rank-and-file membership) was a piece of pseudo sociology.

It also seems clear that the original occasion for the statement was unfortunate, since the congressional hearings were being conducted, in New York rather than in Washington, during a primary campaign by a congressman who had been denied endorsement by the ILGWU-dominated Liberal party in New York. And for anyone who has known the long devotion to liberal causes of such men as Charles Zimmerman, the manager of the union's Dress Joint Board, the idea of their condoning overt racial discrimination, even for reasons of expediency, did not ring true.

Yet, wrong as Hill's charges are in detail, deeper problems remain, problems that have been obscured by the stridency of charges and replies. The first is symbolized by my friend's observations about the apathy and ingratitude within his local. But this is only part of a broader, more vexing issue: the propriety of attacking one's friends, rather than one's enemies, as the Negro organizations are now doing. And this, in turn, is part of a still larger question which few persons have cared to discuss openly: whether in his fight to overcome second-class status, the Negro should receive not merely equality of opportunity but, in order to establish himself as a full citizen, preferential treatment as well.

The first problem (which has been caricatured by the charge of racial discrimination) is really, in its way, the familiar family chronicle of the original generation that built an institution (or a business or a store) and won't let go for the next one. The telling phrase in the complaint that my old Socialist friend made was the reiterated "for them." He was doing a good job, for them. He was honest and conscientious, for them. He had negotiated a good contract, for them.

But as I tried to tell him at the time, sometimes people like to do things for themselves, even if they do them less well. His reply, on reflection, was that the workers could not negotiate a contract: They did not possess the skills, the boss would outmaneuver them, they would be too exorbitant in their demands, they did not understand the economics of the industry, etc. When I asked him if they could not learn—after all, *he* had come up from the shop—his answer was that they were not interested, that in his generation the talented people had gone into the shop because there was nowhere else for immigrants to go, but now the more educated ones did not go into the union, and so on.

My friend was no fool. He knew all about Robert Michels' "iron law of oligarchy," had read Will Herberg on union bureaucracy, was aware of the growing gulf between the leadership and the rank and file, and his reply reflected an awareness of being trapped in this disparity. "Besides," he said, "I am fifty-five years old. Am I supposed to get out of the union now, after thirty years of service, because the new membership, which had little to do with building the union, is ethnically different from me?" He had helped build a useful social institution and had identified himself so completely with it that he found it hard to conceive of its continuing without him and others like him.

And in a way he was right. Once the older generation passes, the ILGWU will be a different union. The tragedy is that the change is going on now, amid circumstances of growing resentment rather than of honor. Clearly, there is no easy answer.

The other problems are of equal difficulty, going far beyond the dilemmas of the ILGWU. It is startling to realize that in the quickened pace of the Negro effort to gain higher status in this country, the liberals (Dubinsky, Walter Reuther, and even George Meany), rather than the reactionaries, are the ones who find themselves under the gun in the Negro community. Why does the NAACP pick on us? a friend in the needle trades recently asked me. Why doesn't it go after the building trades, the electrical unions (apart from Local 3 in New York), and other places where Negroes can't even get jobs, let alone leadership positions, because of union discrimination? One reason, he said, answering his own question, is that the NAACP is itself under fire from the more militant sections of the Negro community, and to maintain its own position it picks on the liberal unions because they are more vulnerable.

Wasn't this, I asked, exactly the reaction that the Jewish employers in the needle trades had fifty or more years ago, when the ILGWU was first trying to get a foothold in the industry? The Italian bosses run worse sweatshops, they said, yet the unions pick on us because they can shame us in the Yiddish press. But precisely because the ILGWU was able to do so, the union succeeded in winning such victories as the establishment of arbitration councils under Louis D. Brandeis and other prominent Jewish spokesmen. Such tactics are bound to be repeated, and they are understandable.

What is it, then, that the Negro community wants, and why so much more demandingly from its liberal friends? The fact is—and this is the "bite" in Hill's charges—that the Negroes are under-represented in the leadership of many of the unions where they form a significant proportion of the membership. In the case of these unions, what the Negroes want is "recognition" at the level of top leadership and a growing share of the spoils of office.[1]

Demands such as these are usually voiced behind closed doors rather than openly, because they fly in the face of the American mythos that all individuals are equal and there is no such thing as a group identity. And they usually provoke the response (which Reuther, for one, has articulated) that this is Jim Crow in reverse, that a man ought to be judged on the basis of individual merit and not for any "extraneous" capacity. Yet there is a curious paradox in this "democratic" response. For one thing, the realistic political process in the United States, at least in the Northern urban centers, has been one of ethnic groups advancing themselves precisely in this fashion: by organizing on bloc lines, electing their

---

[1] A few years ago, the ILGWU did begin to make a more determined effort to bring Negroes and Puerto Ricans into leadership positions. But, ironically, the union found that leadership training enhanced the market value of its best candidates and, because the ILGWU pays relatively poorly, it "lost" the trainees to other unions or to government, where they could command more money and status.

own kind, and using the patronage system to enhance the wealth and status of their group.

A second, more complex fact is that the basic existence of the labor movement is rooted in the conception of "group" rather than individual rights. Legally, the individual's protection on the job—where, for example, a union shop exists—is based on the "collective" contract, not on his individual right. (Thus, under an old NLRB ruling, employers are forbidden in certain circumstances to give individual workers merit wage increases on the ground that this may be a form of favoritism and would violate the group's rights.) How far down does the group right extend *within* the union? Often a union recognizes certain "functional" groupings (for instance, the skilled trades in the United Auto Workers) as legitimate claimants to its own rights of representation. Does the Negro community—if it so organizes itself—have a legitimate claim for representation in group terms?

This has to be answered in a still wider context, which is the unspoken premise that "equality of opportunity" is an inadequate springboard from which the deprived sections of the Negro community—that is, the overwhelming majority—can advance economically and educationally. The phrase "equality of opportunity" has meaning if the competitors are roughly equal from the start (which is why there are handicaps in a horse race). But in many instances, even if a genuine equality of opportunity—for jobs, school places, and the like—prevailed, the Negro would still lose out, with harmful social consequences for the community, simply because of extra, inherited handicaps he bears.

Admission to an elite public school like New York's Bronx High School of Science, for example, is by competitive examination, a matter purely of merit. Yet the number of Negro children in that school is scandalously low, and this failure to get on the first step of the educational escalator becomes a self-reinforcing vicious cycle as regards future opportunities. The solution is not necessarily a double standard, wherein Negro children with lesser qualifications are admitted on a quota basis; it may require the creation of special classes to coach bright but culturally deprived Negro children, in order to allow them to compete on a better footing.

But why even blink at the "double standard?" Why should intellectual merit alone be the determining basis for entry into an elite school? Ivy-league colleges such as Harvard, Yale, and Columbia maintain geographical quotas in order to gain a representative national student body, on the ground that such mixtures are more valuable to the educational process than those selected by grades or college-board scores alone. On the same basis, a larger proportion of Negro children in the elite schools would act both as a spur to these children and "broaden" the experience of the other students.

All this may seem a far cry from my opening story; yet there is a consistency and a connection. The implicit demand of the Negro community today is for special efforts and even special treatment in order to win basic social rights. It arises for the same reason that de Tocqueville noted in all revolutionary movements: Increasingly radical demands are made not when one's lot goes from bad to worse, but when it goes from bad to better. For what may have been formerly accepted as destined and inevitable now, with the possibility of improvement in sight, becomes intolerable; and the demand for improvement quickens.

But the demand for special treatment is nothing new in the United States. It is the very basis for the existence of the labor movement. The preamble to the Wagner Act points out that equality of bargaining is a necessary aspect of social justice, and in order to redress unequal power, the workers have to be given the added protections of the law to organize, to compel the employer to bargain, and so on. Farmers receive price supports, subsidies, mortgage insurance, and the like. In economic and educational opportunity, the Negro is in a position of inequality, and the government is bounden to help him move ahead. But doesn't the trade-union movement have a *special* obligation to help redress the balance?

To return to my original tale, the tragedy of old institutions is that they are like Cheshire cats: the image remains after the body has disappeared. In the end, the image without the body is insubstantial, and quickly fades away. Or, to change the metaphor, and make the issue more plain: The "genius" of American democracy is that the society survived because the older ruling groups learned to share their power instead of resorting to class war, most notably in the acceptance by employers of collective bargaining in the factories. How curious that the labor leadership which benefited from that historical lesson should so plainly fail to see the virtue of applying it to its own institutions.

47 : *Negro–Jewish Relations*

Will Maslow

Relationships between the eighteen million Negroes and the five-and-one-half million Jews in the United States are limited almost exclusively to their organizational leaders. Any close contact between the average Negro and the average Jew is rare. The American Jew today is primarily a part of the middle class engaged in business or trade or is a self-employed professional; the younger Jew is likely to be a college graduate. The American Negro on the other hand is at the bottom rung of the economic ladder, largely uneducated and unskilled. Discriminatory housing patterns accentuate the rigid separation between them.

It is indeed remarkable therefore that the relations between "defense" organizations of each group, e.g., the National Association for the Advancement of Colored People (NAACP) and the American Jewish Congress, have been so close, cordial, and co-operative. I cannot recall an important issue during the fifteen years in which national Jewish and Negro groups took opposite positions. In every civil-rights battle of the period—for fair-employment practice legislation, against housing discrimination, against Negro disenfranchisement, and for reform of the obstructive rules of pro-

Mr. Maslow, a lawyer, is Executive Director of the American Jewish Congress and author of several articles on civil-rights issues.

cedure of the United States Senate—both groups have fought side by side. Nationally, both groups, together with trade-union and church bodies, are united in the Leadership Conference on Civil Rights which directs the recurring national campaigns for civil-rights legislation. The historic March on Washington received the endorsement of almost every national Jewish organization interested in human rights and Dr. Joachim Prinz, president of the American Jewish Congress, was one of the so-called "Big Ten" leaders who organized the march.

The scope of concern of Negro organizations is, however, far narrower than that of Jewish agencies. Negro associations rarely display any interest in international affairs, church-state matters, or civil-liberties questions. Co-operation between Negro and Jewish groups is confined therefore to civil-rights issues.

In politics, too, there are few issues which separate the Negro and Jewish voter. The Negroes in the North, concentrated in metropolitan centers, are concerned about civil rights, welfare legislation, and "bread-and-butter" issues. Negro voters who shifted from the Republican to the Democratic party during the great depression of 1929–33 have ever since remained solidly in the Democratic camp. The five Negro congressmen from New York, Chicago, Philadelphia, Detroit, and Los Angeles are all Democrats. Jewish voters, by and large, do not vote their pocketbooks but, following a liberal-internationalist line, also tend to vote Democratic. According to the best estimates, about 80 per cent of Jewish voters pulled down the Democratic levers in the last seven presidential elections. The only Republican Jew in the United States Congress is Senator Jacob Javits, but his voting record continues to shock hard-core Republicans.

The organizational picture in the South is bleak. The 265,000 Jews of the Solid South are a tiny minority in a region inhabited by thirty million white Christians and ten million Negroes. Southern Jewry organized in local Jewish welfare funds and community-relations councils have almost no contact with Negro associations and have rarely offered any formal or public support in the struggle against segregation and the white supremacy system. A few courageous rabbis and Jewish individuals have supported the Negro demand for equality but organized Southern Jewish communities have by and large remained silent. On the other hand, only a handful of Jewish businessmen have joined White Citizens Councils formed to resist the drive for equality.

An economic gulf separates the rank-and-file Negro and Jew. Until recently, the average Negro rarely encountered the Jew, except as landlord, employer, or shopkeeper. When the relationship between Negro and Jew is exclusively commercial and where inevitably there is a suspicion of exploitation or sharp dealing, distrust, hatred, and fear are generated by such encounters. The grim consequence is that the Negro image of the Jew tends to be that of the exploiter.

The Negro attitude is based in part upon disappointment. He had hoped that a minority group, with a history of vilification and persecution that indeed was longer and as bitter as his, would be more sympathetic to his plight. Although many Southern Negroes appreciate the exposed position of the Southern Jew, they had nevertheless expected that the Jew would have spoken out more forcefully than he has against exploitation and oppression.

The sharpness of the Negro reaction was manifest in the recent controversy between the NAACP and the International Ladies Garment Workers Union, a respected progressive organization whose leadership is predominantly Jewish. The NAACP had charged that certain New York City locals of the ILGWU were "lily-white"; but what particularly embittered David Dubinsky, president of the ILGWU, was the purported explanation that the top officials of the union were of a different "ethnic" group than the Negro complainants. To round out the picture, it must be pointed out that the ILGWU contributed $5,000 to help organize the historic March on Washington.

In recent years, a Negro middle class has been emerging. Negroes are applying for civil-service jobs, making careers in the labor movement, opening shops in Negro neighborhoods, beginning to practice law and medicine and other professions, and seeking political patronage by the ballot or appointment. The Secretary of Labor reported in 1960 that the number of Negro workers employed in professional, clerical, sales, and skilled jobs had doubled in the last twenty years. In New York City in 1961 about 35,000 Negroes and Puerto Ricans were working in civil-service jobs, or 14 per cent of the total staff of the city, according to a Negro Civil Service Commissioner. He added that there were over 150 Negro and Puerto Rican executives with salaries ranging from $10,000 to $34,000 a year. In cities like New York (inhabited by two million Jews), conflict between this emerging middle class and its Jewish competitor is inevitable.

The growing Negro militancy has been accompanied by an increased awareness of race that often degenerates into an unabashed anti-Semitism. The Black Muslim movement, a Negro cult emphasizing the Negro's African background and repudiating Christianity as the white man's religion, is openly anti-Jewish, fostering the latent anti-Semitism of their followers. This racism in reverse is not confined to cultists like Malcolm X, former leader of the Black Muslims and founder of a new black nationalist party. Adam Clayton Powell, chairman of the House Committee on Education and Labor, has a long history of anti-Jewish utterances. He has complained that Jewish (and Italian) gamblers control the policy racket in Harlem (Mr. Powell apparently prefers that his congregation be victimized by Negro racketeers). Stung by editorial attacks on him by *The New York Times*, he remarked that it was unfortunate that it was owned and operated by a "minority group" and to make his point clearer sneered that he doubted "whether the editors of the *Times* even go to their own synagogue." But Powell speaks only for himself. He has repeatedly been denounced by the NAACP and today is a "loner" with diminishing influence even in Harlem, once the seat of his power.

More serious was the publication by the *Amsterdam News*, a New York City Negro weekly, of a front-page article on March 9, 1963, headlined "Secret Study Says Jews Control City's Top Jobs." (In response to protests from Negro and Jewish organizations, the *Amsterdam News* two weeks later gave equal prominence to a reply by the American Jewish Congress which described the so-called survey as "inaccurate in fact and bigoted in tone.") On the other hand, other Negro weeklies like the *Chicago Defender* and the *Pittsburgh Courier* have on numerous occasions in recent years demonstrated attitudes of respect, if not admiration, for Jewish organizations and Jewish causes. An editorial in the *Pittsburgh Courier* (January 16, 1960) entitled "Let Us Fight the Beast" declared, "Not only have Jews stuck their necks out for us—they have fought gallantly and intelligently for social justice for everybody. The Jews are a people to be emulated, not despised." The

Chicago Defender editorialized in 1963 that "the Negro people have just as deep anxieties about the revival or attempted revival of anti-Semitism as do the Jewish people themselves. . . . Negroes and Jews belong to the same fraternity of the persecuted."

Needless to say, leaders of the top Negro organizations, like Roy Wilkins for the NAACP, and the Reverend Martin Luther King, Jr., for the Southern Christian Leadership Conference, have repeatedly denounced anti-Semitic utterances and sought to remind their followers of the support they have received from Jews and Jewish organizations. The truth is, as Wilson has put it: "Anti-Semitism is not widespread among Negroes nor is it nourished and passed on as a working creed. More often than not it is a spite thing, used to assuage a particular failure or to spur a particular effort."

The racial crisis of 1963 manifested by the scores of demonstrations throughout the country culminating in the March on Washington has spurred the Jewish community to an examination of its own practices. At the annual assembly of the Council of Jewish Federations and Welfare Funds, the leaders of Jewish communal institutions throughout the land were repeatedly urged to use their investment funds, construction contracts, admission and intake policies, and their hiring plans as levers to promote general non-discrimination policies. Indeed, the rabbinical and congregational leaders of reform Judaism urged the six hundred and fifty Reform congregations in the country to boycott banks, construction companies, or businesses that discriminate against Negroes. An entirely different approach was announced recently by the American Jewish Congress which reported a joint project with the Urban League (a Negro service organization) to provide business and credit counseling to the Negro small businessman.

The soul searching going on within both groups is bound to strengthen the ties between them. These two minorities, with their long history of persecution and discrimination, with their great stake in strengthening the American pledge of freedom and equality for all, will undoubtedly continue their joint efforts to realize the American dream of full equality in a free society.

48 : *The "New Negro" and the Protestant Churches*

Gayraud S. Wilmore, Jr.

. . . In the United States there is a white church and a Negro church—with very little communication between them. There are some twelve million Negro Protestants and over 600,000 Negro Roman Catholics in the nation. Of the Protestants, ten million hold membership in five denominations: the National Baptist Convention, U.S.A., Inc.; the National Baptist Convention of America; the African Methodist Episcopal Church; the African Methodist Episcopal Zion Church; and the Christian (formerly Colored) Methodist Episcopal Church. These, plus several smaller all-Negro denominations, pretty much constitute Negro Protestantism in the United States today. Less than 5 per cent of the nation's Negro Protestants are affiliated with predominantly white denominations.

Despite their similarity to the typical American religious body and despite class differences within the Negro community, Negro churches are of a kind. That is, all of them are institutions of the Negro ghetto. . . .

Mr. Wilmore is Associate Professor of Social Ethics at Pittsburgh Theological Seminary (Presbyterian).

Much more so than the typical white urban church, the proud and substantial Negro churches have preserved the relatively unsophisticated American Protestantism of the nineteenth and early twentieth centuries . . . the ethical revivalism of the latter part of the nineteenth century and the social gospel reformism which came later. The Negro churches have changed but little; what is different about them today is a new sense of power in the war against racial discrimination.

No man is more responsible for the Negro church's new spirit of resistance than Martin Luther King, Jr.; nevertheless King is in reality a symbol of an ethos that has been coming to maturity in the Negro Christian community since New Deal days. The Albany Movement, the unseating of Detroit's mayor in 1961, the boycotts led by the Negro clergy of Philadelphia against the oil companies, the community-organization movements spurred by Negro churches in Chicago and Los Angeles—all these are examples of what King has called the "new Negro" working for first-class citizenship through the church. . . .

The new Negro is not always a churchman, in the usual sense of that term. He may be, but he may also be a college student in Greensboro, Nashville, or Amherst who dislikes gospel songs and spirituals because they remind him of "jackleg" preachers and the degradation of the Negro. He may be a member of the Congress of Racial Equality or the Fellowship of Reconciliation who long ago wrote off the church as a reactionary, war-mongering anachronism. He may be an attorney on the staff of the National Association for the Advancement of Colored People who goes to church only because his pastor is an NAACP chapter president or because he needs names on a petition in a school-desegregation case. He may be an agnostic writer living in New York City, or a Pittsburgh laborer who works too hard during the week or spends too many hours in bars on Saturday night to get up on Sunday morning. The church-led desegregation movement has many fellow travelers. . . .

The close association of the new, self-respecting Negro with the church in the struggle for first-class citizenship does not mean that we are witnessing a wholesale reconversion to Christianity—at least not to Christianity as the white man understands it. It does mean that we are witnessing the emergence of a Negro church which is seeking alliances with thousands of "new" Negroes who have long wanted something from the church they have not heretofore been able to get—leadership and, in the broadest sense, political power. . . . They want a church which has divested itself of moralistic complacency about the *status quo* and become a revolutionary force revealing the true religious significance of human life in a world where naked power is rampant.

The "new Negro" movement includes not only the great mass of underprivileged Negroes but also the growing Negro middle class and intelligentsia. It is the latter two groups which are most alienated from organized Christianity, in large part because of the unsavory image of a racially segregated Protestant church—an image especially offensive to younger Negroes. Negro congregations in the predominantly white denominations—Methodist, Presbyterian, Episcopal, Disciples—have not been able to counteract the influence of that image by virtue of being a part of those denominations. . . .

But for many Negro intellectuals an even more serious indictment of the church than segregation in pew and pulpit is what seems to them to be white Christians' timid acquiescence to, if not active participation in, discriminatory patterns of social and economic life in America and elsewhere. This is not only the primary reason for the black intellectual's growing tendency to reject Christianity; it is also the cause of the increasing estrangement of the whole Negro Christian community from the white Christian community. If the white Protestant church does not more speedily enter the struggle in which the Negro is engaged, the psychological and ideological distance between the two communities may become so great as to prevent authentic integration for years after the merely spatial distance has been closed. . . .

The fact is that the white community's continued rejection of the Negro makes the most spirited Negro crusader feel like a displaced person. He is no less frustrated than those among the Negro masses who give way to apathy and resignation. "New" Negroes may not overtly support the pseudo-Muslim and black racist groups, but many are ready to take what they can of the material fruits of desegregation while spurning cultural and religious integration. In Negro middle-class circles one hears the cynical refrain: "The only thing we want from Mr. Charley is his money." . . .

The new Negro believes that desegregation of individual congregations will be of little consequence for the Negro and for the spiritual vitality of the society. To the extent that congregational life continues to revolve around platitudinous preaching, tired ritual, and bland fellowship, racial integration in American Protestant churches will be irrelevant. . . .

More important today than token desegregation of individual congregations is the kind of image that the Protestant church presents to the American Negro community and to the other colored peoples of the world. That image must of course communicate something about the openness, if not the *de facto* inclusiveness, of the church in regard to social integration and fellowship. But more than this, the church's image will have to challenge the new Negro's impression of the white Protestant as at best a condescending, paternalistic gradualist and at worst a vicious wielder of power who in the South opens White Citizens Council meetings with prayer and who in the North champions conservative Republicanism. In short, the image Protestantism must somehow convey to the new Negro is that of a revolutionary force committed to distinguishing and separating the Christian understanding of life from the idealizations and norms of middle-class white society. This is what the new Negro wants from the church.

I do not wish to imply that the new Negro does not hanker after material blessings and social prestige. The Negro migrants to Atlanta, Washington, D.C., New York, or Detroit, and even more certainly their children who will graduate from Morehouse, Howard, New York University, and Wayne, are just as eager for a split-level suburban home and a foreign-made car as the next American. . . . To want Mr. Charley's money is to want his real estate and automobiles, but more than that it is to covet the power, dignity, and self-determination which—or so our society has taught us—money buys. . . .

While the Negro's yearnings for material goods and the symbols of affluence will persist, they will not mitigate the growing sense of social and political solidarity with black people throughout the world. The real heroes of the American Negro in 1963 are not the

Ralph Bunches and the Willie Mayses—though they are justly admired still—but the Martin Luther Kings, the Tom Mboyas, and the Kwame Nkrumahs.

Whether the predominantly white Protestant churches can capture the imagination and loyalty of the new Negro may depend on whether a counterpart movement can arise within those churches —that is to say, whether that part of the white Protestant intelligentsia which has become disenchanted with middle-class complacency and moralism can marshal sufficient resistance to the old ways to change the image of white Christianity. In the student Christian movement, in lay academies and renewal groups, among missionaries, staff members of inner city churches, and some of the younger clergy, there are signs which suggest that a new kind of white Protestant is no more unthinkable than a new kind of Negro Protestant.

If a *rapprochement* develops between the revolutionary Negro laity and the white Protestant laity in the next few years, it will not be because the ranks have closed to protect America from Communism, or because "creeping desegregation" has finally caught up with both white and Negro churches, or because through sharing white neighborhoods, schools, and churches Negroes have become "acceptable" to whites. It will develop because Christian brotherhood in America has come to mean a relationship which seeks to build upon the rubble of an irrelevant spirituality a new barrier against the tragic disillusionments of a post-Christian age and because white Protestants have finally realized the truth of Richard Wright's affirmation that "the ties that bind us are deeper than those that separate us." ("Look at us and know us and you will know yourselves, for *we* are *you*, looking back at you from the dark mirror of our lives.") Christian brotherhood will then mean something profoundly human and incisively political; it will mean standing with and for one another in the exasperating and bewildering realities of secular life. This is what the new Negro— and many "new" white Christians—want from the church.

49 : *White and Negro "Extremism"*

Harry S. Ashmore

. . . Negroes have moved, in less than a generation, from the passive role of supplicants to active participation in a mass crusade against the form and substance of inequality. To this point, the tide of history has run with them, and they have been supported by the national conscience. Even in the South, the devotion of most whites to the *status quo* has been countered by a sense of personal guilt. At the ethical operating level, the United States Supreme Court has systematically translated the Constitution's libertarian spirit into the law of the land. Having won every critical test before the bar, Negroes can now carry their protest onto the sidewalks of the deep South with the full protection of the federal presence.

The parallel between Southern white resistance and the Negro crusade is striking and significant. One begot the other, and, substituting black for white, the language, the symbols, even the characteristics of the most conspicuous leaders and organizations are interchangeable.

At the far limits are the Ku Klux Klan and the Black Muslims

Mr. Ashmore, a Pulitzer Prize winner in journalism and former Editor of the *Arkansas Gazette*, is author of *The Other Side of Jordan* (1960), *An Epitaph for Dixie* (1958), and *The Negro and the Schools* (1954).

—both ostensibly committed to the same declared aim, absolute segregation of the races. Both are secret societies that indulge in mystical, quasi-religious activities and rig up the faithful in uniforms. Both are ardent dues collectors. Both have a great fondness for parades and rallies and unbounded faith in their ability to intimidate their enemies. Both preach unbridled racial hatred and covertly encourage violence. Many of the past national leaders of the Klan have wound up in prison, usually on fraud charges, and Malcolm X, [once] the most active of the Muslim apostles, is a former jailbird.

Or consider General Walker and James Baldwin. Both are men of education and attainment, fully endowed with the status symbols of their respective trades. Both came late to the racial battlefield, and have long been isolated from the rank and file for whom they now profess to speak—General Walker in the course of a distinguished military career, Baldwin in the years of literary exile that brought him deserved recognition as a writer. General Walker is unable to turn his back completely on his red-necked followers, or Baldwin on the Black Muslims, although both are obviously socially discomfited. Both deal with the race problem in stirring terms of personal, apocalyptic visions: General Walker sees the Visigoths of Communism already over the walls, and Baldwin thinks a dark-skinned host has assembled at Armageddon. These revelations give each an exclusive patent on the verities. General Walker finds even so stalwart an anti-Communist as Senator Thomas Dodd "blind" on home-grown subversion, and Baldwin believes Martin Luther King has reached the end of his rope.

The most notable political leaders also pair out neatly. Orval Faubus of Arkansas and Adam Clayton Powell of Harlem are wily old professionals who have found in the race issue the key to what appears to be permanent office. When he needs to be re-elected, Governor Faubus simply hollers, "Nigger!" When Congressman Powell faces similar necessities, he cries, "Discrimination!" If this tends to cut them off from their political colleagues, who can't afford to say so, but with reason consider each a liability to his cause, it has its compensations. Powell is able to travel at public expense, and Faubus has the pleasure of operating the most comprehensive state political machine since the late Huey Long's.

These and men like them have made most of the headlines that mark the steady progress of the Negro crusade. They are eternally ready to provide reporters with a harsh word and a dire prediction. They are in fact prime figures in the action and reaction, and the history of the period doubtless would have been different without them. Yet they are symbols, not leaders. They have been able to unleash powerful emotions, but the task of controlling the resulting force for coherent purpose has been left to others. For the white Southern leadership, the failure is clear and final; segregation cannot endure. For the Negro leadership, the test is only beginning.

It is at least possible that recovery from the emotional excesses of the recent past will serve to further reduce the incidence and virulence of Southern bigotry. In the period of convalescence ahead, white Southerners will be required to form new institutions and arrangements to replace those they can no longer doubt are unacceptable to their Negro neighbors. They have no real choice except to examine the possibility that they have nothing to lose and much to gain by seeing to it that Negroes reach their declared goals of increased economic opportunity and unlimited access to the facilities and amenities of the community. Not the least of the benefits could be the restoration of the bonds of genuine affection between whites and Negroes that enriched the older Southern tradition.

An increasing share of the burden of creating the necessary conditions for this development in the South, and for maintaining them in the North, is passing to the Negro leadership. The process that has contained the manifestations of white bigotry has encouraged the expression of Negro bigotry—and this has had inevitable response among a people whose grievances are real.

There has emerged a set of Negro myths as dangerous and as debilitating as their white Southern counterparts. The basic proposition here is that no white man can really understand how a Negro feels. This, in effect, accepts the argument of white racists that Negroes are inherently different. Since Negroes can hardly be expected to equate racial difference with inferiority, the result is the spurious doctrine of black supremacy long preached on the street corners of Harlem and now heard in more respectable precincts.

At its crudest, the Negro mythology has produced the Black Muslims and their effort to exploit the emotional response of American Negroes to the racial unrest that doomed colonialism in Africa and Asia. The identification of the Black Muslims with the true sons of Allah is about as valid as the Ku Klux Klan's claim to the traditions of the Scottish Highlands. Negroes have been in this country as long as any other Americans, and there has been no mass immigration since the slave trade was banned more than a century ago. The historic relationship of American Negroes to Africa is now devoid of cultural or religious significance. It is purely a matter of pigmentation, and this, as they discover at every point of contact with genuine African nationalists, is of minor consequence.

At a more sophisticated level, it is argued that the unique Negro experience under slavery and enforced segregation has had a purifying effect on those who suffered it. Baldwin, who occasionally seems to confuse himself with Job, gives the proposition a religious cast, contending that the black man represents a kind of original white sin, which, by means never made entirely clear, must be purged. Norman Mailer, Jack Kerouac, and other *avant-garde* white novelists have attempted to distill out of the jazz, marijuana, and uninhibited sex of the Negro Bohemian fringe the thesis that only alienation reveals ultimate truth.

These fantasies have led to public seizures of emotional segregation and have produced an outright attack on the older heroes of the Negro movement. Roy Wilkins of the NAACP is accused of selling his people down the river because there are white members on his board of directors. Adam Clayton Powell proclaims that Negroes cannot support any interracial organization that has white leadership. Attorney General Robert F. Kennedy, who with considerable effect has been devoting his time to service as advocate and negotiator for the Negro cause, is treated to derisive laughter simply because he is white. William Worthy, Jr., the controversial Negro journalist, has reached the remarkable conclusion that no white man can support the American Negro unless he also supports Fidel Castro. Here, as in the white South, passionate irrationality precludes effective discussion of the issue and of the practical means of resolving it. A leading Negro entertainer, shaken by the excesses of his peers, has privately confessed that he nevertheless has found it necessary to remain silent in order to avoid the dread epithet, "Uncle Tom."

The Negro mythology, like the white, constitutes a mirror image of reality. The degradation of the slums has crushed far more spirits than it has purified. Only the strongest members of any race emerge without crippling scars from a lifetime of deprivation, callous mistreatment, and scornful abuse. That such individuals have now appeared in significant number to lead the marching columns of protest is a tribute to the older generation of white and colored leaders they have impatiently shouldered aside. It was the lonely battlers of the Urban League, the NAACP, the New Deal, and the labor movement who brought about the reforms that freed many of the new generation from the ghetto and unshackled their militant spirit.

These dedicated young men and women, armed with pride and dignity, will find, if they look back, that they are still a minority among their own people. For most Negroes, the weight of oppression has eroded away the will and the capacity to seize the new opportunities and face the new risks. A high proportion have slipped irrevocably into the sloth and crime of slum life and constitute a social problem that is not affected by the argument that the fault is the community's, not theirs.

The Negro crusade, like any other, is fueled by emotion and does not welcome the dampening strictures of logic. As the only domestic social movement of current consequence, it has magnetic attraction for the sort of radicals and reformers who gave vent to their general protest against society by supporting the labor movement before the unions went flabby with success and affluence. For these, proud in their moral fervor, thrilled by vicarious martyrdom, and comfortably removed from the scene of battle, the outcome of a given engagement is of little consequence. The situation is somewhat different for the tacticians in the field.

The most successful of these by far is the Reverend Martin Luther King, Jr. Upon the solid base of the legal successes won by the now-eclipsed NAACP, he has promoted the mass demonstrations that have penetrated Southern resistance even in the final redoubts of Alabama and Mississippi. For the front-line leaders, it has been, and will continue to be, a delicate balancing act.

Dr. King needs the emotional voltage, and the financial support, generated by the firebrands at the great rallies in the North and West. But he also needs an open line, usually routed through the Department of Justice, to the white men who must issue the orders to desegregate. He can hardly file a public dissent when Professor Kenneth Clark of City College of New York takes issue with At-

torney General Kennedy and proclaims that the Negro people are
no longer going to beg favors from the white power structure. But
Dr. King is in Birmingham, and Professor Clark isn't, and it is Dr.
King who in the end will sit down and negotiate the compromise
settlement that will mark another step forward for the Negro
people.

Considerations of strategy as well as his Christian devotion to
nonviolence sent Dr. King into the pool halls of Birmingham to remind the boys in the back rooms that switch-blade knives provide
no answer to the dynamite of white hoodlums. So long as violence
is directed against Negro demonstrators, elemental standards of
justice and federal guns automatically are on their side. Let Negroes initiate the attack, or even reply in kind, and the balance will
shift—and without this essential support, Negroes again will be a
helpless minority in an aroused white community.

Martin Luther King not only subscribes to, but has given real
meaning to, the battle cry of the movement: No white man has a
right to ask a Negro to wait any longer for equality. But, as a practicing Christian, Dr. King also has to recognize that every white
man has a right to insist that the quest for equality not be marked
by a trail of blood.

It is on this critical point that Dr. King has had to part company
with a good many of those who have lately swung aboard the freedom train. He speaks for justice. They cry out for vengeance. There
was a moving, simple eloquence in the statement Dr. King's followers issued after a truce had been worked out in Birmingham:
"The city of Birmingham has reached an accord with its conscience." All his adult life, Dr. King has preached and practiced
in the service of a mission to unite a national community put
asunder by the inhumanity of slavery and segregation. He could no
more accept the mad design of the Muslims for a separate Negro
state, or the admonition of the intellectuals who urge that bitterness be nurtured in the ghettos of the mind, than he could join
forces with George Wallace, Ross Barnett, and Orval Faubus.

These are the surface elements of a racial crisis moving inexorably
toward a showdown. All are the product of the tragic American
failure to resolve the great moral issue that has tainted the nation's
free institutions and truncated its ideals—the failure that once
before led to fratricide.

It is, as Gunnar Myrdal has said, a peculiarly American dilemma. The Negro crusade has the sound of revolution, and many frightened whites and a few loquacious Negroes see it as such. Yet its goal is the opposite of that set by dark-skinned revolutionaries abroad, who seek to drive out their white rulers and shape their destiny on their own terms. Here, Negroes are demanding only admission to a closed white society that has imposed its standards while callously denying full access to its protections and benefits.

The demand is made as a matter of right, not as a device to create a new social order. It cannot be rejected, or further postponed, without still more damage to our diminished libertarian tradition and to our tarnished religious ethic. The high price the South has paid for intransigence is now being levied against the nation as a whole. The white community's effective abdication of moral purpose has produced a paralyzing failure of will on the part of the political leadership. Only now is there recognition that we can't get on with the nation's urgent business until we have begun, at least, to take care of the Negro's needs.

The Supreme Court, in splendid isolation, has discharged its responsibilities. The Court has defined the national policy forbidding racial discrimination and laid down the ground rules for its implementation. This should have brought Congress to the necessary business of fashioning new laws to replace those that have been swept off the statute books. Tangled in its antiquated rules, intimidated by the uncertain temper of its constituency, Congress has indulged instead in a fruitless decade of angry recrimination.

Eisenhower hoped until the end of his term that the race problem somehow would go away. Kennedy . . . understood that it will not, but he [gave] it low priority—and only [in 1963 did he bring] himself to use the full weight of his office to force the issue upon the lawmakers. . . .

It is true that the ultimate solution will not be found in laws, but in the dark places of men's minds and hearts. But it is also true that laws are the manifest of the national purpose, and when government is unwilling, or unable, to provide them, there is no standard to which the wise and just may repair.

It is argued that the moderates have failed, and this is so. But it does not follow that moderation as a policy has failed. The fact is that it has not yet been tried. White, and now Negro, extremists have successfully blocked the scattered efforts to bring the leader-less mass of Americans to the kind of accommodations that will achieve harmony as well as justice. Yet this, surely, is the minimum essential, since Negroes and whites somehow must fashion the future on terms acceptable to both.

History and the peculiarities of our political system provide explanations, and even excuses, for our failure to live up to the moral imperative we have never denied. And the realities of the depressed Negro community make it clear that there will be no neat and orderly solution to social problems compounded by racial prejudice on both sides. But we have run out of options. The restoration of domestic tranquillity demands nothing less than a renewed national commitment to the guarantees of life, liberty, and the pursuit of happiness, this time without reservations.

50 : *Middle-Class Negroes and the Negro Masses*

Whitney M. Young, Jr.

. . . Available figures on Negro income levels reflect the growth of a new and vital middle class. Some 20 per cent of the Negro family population are in the $7,000 a year or over income bracket, while some 60 per cent are in an income bracket of $3,000 or under. This means that the conventional way of looking at general social-class divisions does not hold true for Negroes because there is a distinct, drastic jump from the low-income level to the middle-class group with no upper-income class, and only a tiny lower middle class.

This poses serious problems for those who work in the field of race relations and who are concerned about what is happening in the Negro community. There is a grave danger of the possible alienation of the middle-class Negro from those of his race, who, due to automation or other factors, are in an almost dependent category of the lower class. This alienation works both ways. The middle-class Negro often (sometimes unconsciously) disassociates

Mr. Young is the Executive Director of the National Urban League.

himself from the lower-class Negro, not because of any personal dislike of him, but because he is symbolic of a phase in history that he wants to forget. To the middle-class Negro, the black ghetto often is symbolic of discrimination, embarrassment, humiliation, second-class citizenship, and inferiority. The alienation or withdrawal of the middle-class Negro, therefore, is not so much an expression of a desire to escape Negroes in the lower-class category as an unconscious desire to escape what has been associated with that status.

On the other hand the Negro in the lower-class group sees in the flight of the middle-class Negro from his neighborhood a desire to disassociate himself from the rest, and this causes a tension. This is of real concern to those of us involved in efforts to advance the Negro community because while the desire of the middle-class [Negro] is to escape a condition, his flight often results in a loss of leadership that is needed to inspire and uplift the group which cannot afford escape.

Another problem created by the withdrawal of the middle-class Negro is the development of different values and different goals by the two groups. Middle-class Negroes possess status or symbolic goals to which the lower class may be completely indifferent. Negroes in the low or poorer class are concerned with reality or welfare goals. For example, the opening to Negro use of rest-room facilities in a Southern airport terminal may mean a great deal to middle-class Negroes, but little or nothing to the lower class. Winning such a right would be of symbolic importance primarily to the middle class.

Today, almost without exception, the leadership of the Negro's civil-rights struggle is drawn from the middle-class group. The danger exists, therefore, that because of the widening alienation of the classes, each class may at times be working toward different goals. This is evidenced in support by working or lower-class Negroes for certain schools and public-housing projects near or in their ghetto districts, and a resultant clash with middle-class Negroes who may oppose erection of such buildings because they regard them as strengthening segregation instead of weakening it. The welfare values of the lower-class Negro can force him to see tangible benefits in such facilities wherever they may be built. . . .

For generations in the South an established middle-class leadership group existed which could identify with the lower-class masses they represented because they were subjected to the same pressures because of skin color. One of the chief differences between the status of the Negro in the South and the North is that in the South Negroes have experienced prejudice regardless of economic level. In the North the middle-class Negro is able to escape some of the pressure of racial prejudice by physically withdrawing from the ghetto.

Middle-class Americans are extremely concerned about conformity. Negroes who enter the middle class become even more rigid in their class values, more conscious of status than do white middle-class folk. The new Negro middle class clings more desperately to the status symbols, is more careful and correct in behavior.

. . . In the white community there are more stages in social advancement. The rise from low-income status to upper is marked by various class levels between the two extremes—lower middle class, upper middle class, etc. For the Negro there is no in-between status; he must jump directly from lower-class status to the higher with no way stops or intermediate steps.

The Negro in America today all too often faces a choice between being a highly skilled technician or professional, or being a waiter, porter, or domestic; between living in a fabulous house in the suburbs or in a tenement in the slums; between sending his kids to a fashionable prep school or to an overcrowded, ill-equipped public school in a deprived neighborhood; between acceptance by heads of government and barons of industry or daily rejection by callous and indifferent human beings; between caviar and steak or bread and water. . . .

Negro leadership is drawn mainly from the professionals, persons who in the white community would not enjoy such eminence, would in fact be largely ignored. In a typical Negro community schoolteachers and physicians are personages of real importance, as are the executive secretaries of the local Urban League and YMCA. In the white community such persons have very little rating.

The average Negro professional has leadership responsibilities imposed upon him because of his position in a disadvantaged and deprived group. The Negro doctor, in addition to being a good doctor, has to assume some responsibility for social leadership. Many are refusing to accept these responsibilities, preferring to concentrate on their professional careers and on the acquisition of wealth. . . .

Certain middle-class Negroes are now exhibiting an unfortunate tendency to be indifferent if not actually hostile to those black Americans less fortunate and privileged. A generation is coming of age that was born in the North of middle-class parents and spent all of their lives in an environment relatively free of prejudice and restrictions. Educated in predominantly white schools, they have never experienced real rejection owing to their color and have never been a part of the Negro struggle. This type feels that it is a mark of their emancipation not to identify with the Negro effort for freedom, that it is a measure of their sophistication that they do not belong to the NAACP or support the Urban League or engage in antidiscrimination activity. After having been taught all their lives that they could escape the indignities and penalties attached to being Negro, they often find themselves humiliated or blocked by racial barriers. Instead of joining with their fellow Negroes to oppose the enemy, they become bitter and disillusioned.

The middle class will continue to furnish the cadres for Negro leadership for years to come. Only a handful of the Negro leaders have come from labor—outstanding men like A. Philip Randolph and George L. P. Weaver, Assistant Secretary of Labor. The competition of the middle class for civil-rights leadership roles in the Negro community usually has overwhelmed the uneducated Negro candidates from the lower economic class. The latter was generally outclassed, outtalked, and outmaneuvered by his more highly trained middle-class rivals. The uneducated Negro thus seldom got a chance at Negro leadership, to try his wings and show what he could do. He never got the thrill of sacrifice or the satisfaction of victory. This is not true of leadership of churches, fraternal groups, and social clubs where middle-class Negroes are not as active in their participation. . . .

While the Negro middle class is growing in numbers and influence the large mass of unskilled, unemployable Negroes is growing at an even faster rate. Unless the rate of growth of the latter group is soon checked we will soon see in America a large class of dependent, permanently unemployed with Negroes contributing a disproportionate share. This holds alarming implications for the economic future of the Negro middle class because its income and wealth still derive preponderantly from the Negro community. Most Negro professionals earn their living from Negro clienteles.

The role of the Negro middle class will become increasingly vital and dynamic, especially in the struggle for human rights and first-class citizenship. Though the income and status gap between lower- and middle-class Negroes is widening, it must not be forgotten that the Negro middle-class person essentially cannot rise above the general condition of his entire people. He must rise along with the group or not at all. The social advantages or economic security enjoyed by an individual member of an oppressed minority will only be temporary until the least disadvantaged and the most impoverished of that group improves his status, and freedom is achieved for all. This was pointedly illustrated several years ago when the son of Nobel Prize winner and United Nations Under-Secretary Ralph Bunche was rejected by the West Side Tennis Club in Forest Hills, New York, when he sought to get tennis instruction there. Bunche himself, while visiting Atlanta, was denied accommodations at a major hotel while a white man wearing overalls was being registered.

The educationally privileged Negro middle class will share the horrors and hardships of his more handicapped working-class brother as long as racism exists in our society and color is still the determining factor in the treatment accorded the citizens of an imperfect democracy.

51 : *The White Liberal's Retreat*

Murray Friedman

. . . In the eight and a half years that have elapsed [since the Supreme Court's decision in 1954], a reaction to desegregation and to militant efforts by Negroes to achieve it has emerged among many of those who greeted the high Court decision so enthusiastically. These second thoughts have developed as a result of the pain and turmoil involved in making what proved to be difficult social adjustments. In some measure, too, historical anxieties about and antipathy to the Negro have reasserted themselves. Such a retreat or pullback on the part of liberal whites (including many conservatives who are liberal on race issues) has important consequences for civil-rights progress.

One of the indications of this retreat appeared following the wave of resistance that swept through the South after the 1954 decision. Northern liberals expected opposition, but when violence developed in Little Rock, Clinton, and other parts of the South and public schools were closed, they were startled by the extent of the upheaval. Gallup polls have shown, as Charles Stember has noted in his recent study, *Education and Attitude Change*, a shift in

---

Mr. Friedman, who holds a doctorate in American political and social history from Georgetown University, is Pennsylvania Area Director of the American Jewish Committee.

attitude in 1957 among better-educated whites. Increasingly, they have been willing to accept a slower and smaller amount of desegregation in the South. . . .

This new understanding of Southern adjustment problems on the part of white supporters of integration also results from certain changes that have taken place in the North. The heavy exodus of Negroes from the South since World War II has, to a large degree, shifted the center of the race problem to the metropolitan areas of the North and West. The Negro is no longer an abstraction to the white liberal but a concrete reality—in many instances, a potential or actual next-door neighbor, a classmate of his child's, a co-worker at office or workbench. This confrontation very often points up the gap between the worlds of the Negro and the liberal white.

The white lives in a middle-class society marked by an emphasis and overemphasis on education, aspiration, and advancement. The world of the Negro frequently is the urban slum. It is a world of slum housing and slum living, where violence, family dislocation, and blunted hopes are the norms. (There is, of course, a middle-class Negro community, and it is growing, but most whites have little or no experience with it.) Contact with it produces shock and disgust, as in the description by Marya Mannes of the West Seventies in New York, where she grew up. There are still some nice people there, she writes, but they are lost in a "brown sea of squalor."

Liberal whites are, consequently, caught in the dilemma of believing in equal rights for Negroes and even of working for them, while at the same time attempting to escape from the real and fancied disadvantages of desegregation. In recent years, they have helped put on the books of many cities and states laws banning discrimination in the sale or rental of housing, yet they themselves have been moving to the farthest reaches of the cities and to the suburbs. They have pushed up the enrollment at private and parochial schools, shut their eyes to the widespread practice of gerrymandering of school-district lines to avoid integration, and helped to create pressures for separating slow from rapid learners in the public schools, a process which often results in keeping middle-class white children apart from Negro and Puerto Rican youngsters.

I do not want to oversimplify this situation. The movement out of the older areas of cities has always been a form of advancement for Americans. And the pressure for separating slow from rapid learners represents in no small measure concern among middle-class whites that educational excellence be encouraged. Liberals are genuinely worried about what the introduction of unprepared slum children will do to their schools. They are fearful that physical commingling of middle-class children with culturally deprived youngsters will depress the level of the schools serving the former while the latter, unable to keep up because of inadequate preparation and background, will become even more embittered and hostile. The result is that many liberals, while opposed to color lines, are helping to make these lines stronger and tighter. . . .

To add to his dilemma, the liberal white is increasingly uneasy about the nature and consequences of the Negro revolt. Out of the bitterness and want that have been the lot of the Negro in our society has come a civil-rights revolution whose explosive power worries and even frightens those people who traditionally have been sympathetic to the Negro. The NAACP and the Urban League were fashioned early in the century by a coalition of whites and Negroes to change old and create new law on civil rights and help adapt the Negro to his new urban environment. These essentially middle-class techniques of social action are now labeled too slow by newer Negro (and some white) "direct actionists," who have turned to sit-in's and boycotts in the North as well as in the South, "buy black" campaigns, and strident demands by Negro leaders that Negroes be elected or appointed to office on a frankly racial basis. There has also been a growth in the Negro nationalist movement.

Liberals are increasingly resentful of these demands. In testimony before a congressional committee investigating alleged discrimination against Negroes and Puerto Ricans in unions recently, David Dubinsky cried, "I'll be damned if I will support the idea of the professional Negro, the professional Jew, the professional Italian that a man should be a union officer because of his race, color, or creed. He should be an officer on his merits, ability, character." Quite so. But ethnic and religious considerations have long been a factor in public life, partly for practical reasons but also as a means of providing upward mobility for minorities. It is rather late in the game for liberals to hold up this yardstick rigidly to the Negro.

White leaders who have not or who are thought not to have adjusted to the new tempo of racial change have come under bitter attack. (The Chicago *Daily Defender* recently called Dean McSwain of Northwestern University, chairman of the Chicago Mayor's Committee on School Board Nominations, "a well-known Negro hater" and charged his committee was "composed of men and women who are little removed from the Ku Klux Klan and White Citizens Council mentality" because they had proposed no Negroes for school-board vacancies.) These harsh criticisms, which many white liberals see as making little or no distinction between friends and enemies, have angered many of them.

Involved also in the disenchantment of some liberals with the new Negro is the realization that they are being thrust aside from positions of leadership in the civil-rights effort. Having controlled this fight for so long and dictated much of its strategy, the liberals resent being pushed out. Jewish civil-rights groups, for example, have always felt a special interest in the Negro. Jews were active in the creation of the NAACP; for many years it has had Jewish presidents. More and more, Negroes are going it alone. Newer, completely Negro-led groups, such as Martin Luther King's Southern Christian Leadership Conference, the Student Nonviolent Co-ordinating Committee, and A. Philip Randolph's Negro Labor Council have charged or indicated by their actions that white civil-rights groups and the more conservative Negro organizations have been moving too slowly or not moving at all. This has produced considerable friction within the civil-rights coalition, as evidenced in the bitter debates between Randolph and George Meany of the AFL-CIO. The NAACP has recently added to the tension by leveling charges of racial discrimination against the Jewish leadership of the International Ladies Garment Workers Union.

The attacks upon Jewish civil-rights leadership have been still another element in the growing estrangement of liberals from the Negro. A middle-class group with special-status fears growing out of their own experiences with discrimination, Jews are worried about Negroes moving into their neighborhoods, which are often the first to be broken in the Negro advance. They are caught between their belief in interracial justice and a desire to join the middle-class exodus to the suburbs, a desire which has been heightened by evidence of Negro anti-Semitism and the rise of the "black nationalist" movements. Jews, however, continue to remain in the forefront of the civil-rights fight; they are often found in the leadership of efforts to stabilize mixed neighborhoods and are usually the first to welcome newly moved-in Negro families.

In the final analysis, a liberal, white, middle-class society wants to have change, but without trouble. And this an aroused Negro community cannot provide, as was demonstrated in the freedom-rides crisis. When the first riders went into Anniston and Birmingham, Alabama, in May 1961, and were initially greeted by violence, there was strong sympathy for them. As the rides continued, however, the public mood shifted to apprehension.

Attorney General Robert Kennedy called for a cooling-off period. The head of the St. Louis Catholic Interracial Council, a veteran of more than twenty years in civil-rights work, announced his opposition to the efforts of outsiders to bring about racial change while supporting sit-in's. "Whatever is used that increases racial tension," he concluded, "is not good, per se." By June 21, the Gallup poll reported that 63 per cent of those aware of the rides disapproved of them.

In his concern about avoiding social turmoil in race relations, the liberal white stands in danger of trying to contain the civil-rights revolution. He cannot do this, nor would it be wise to do so if he could. It is a revolt well within the American tradition of social protest. Negro militancy, while it undoubtedly presents certain dangers, has accomplished the white liberal's goal of bringing about civil-rights advances. Within a year after the first rides, barriers to racially integrated travel in the South largely disappeared. Important social change is rarely accomplished without conflict; moreover, such change in the South has always required pressures from other parts of the country. If the pent-up bitterness of the Negro community is not relieved by the type of gains symbolized in the accomplishments of the freedom rides or the equally successful boycotts to obtain jobs organized by Negro ministers in many Northern cities, it might easily burst out in new and socially irresponsible directions, perhaps in the further growth of the racist, Negro nationalist movements.

Another area of difficulty lies in the rift that has been developed between the white intellectual and the Negro. To no group is the Negro more indebted. It was the sociologists, anthropologists, psychologists, and liberal thinkers and writers who, beginning in the thirties, attacked the myth of the inferiority of Negroes and helped gain wide acceptance for the belief that Negroes should be accorded equal rights and opportunities. One of the major grounds on which the United States Supreme Court rested its decision on desegregation was the evidence of social scientists that public-school segregation created in the minds of Negro children feelings of inferiority and denied them equal protection of the laws. It is significant that the Supreme Court has increasingly come under attack from critics outside the South for the reasoning used in its desegregation decision, although few challenge the end result of the decision. Lawyers have taken the high Court to task for basing itself "upon the quicksands of social psychology."

Since 1954, there have been indications of a change in the way in which the Negro and racial problems are viewed by intellectuals. There has even been an attempt to make racism scientifically respectable. One group has emerged which includes Carleton Putnam, a businessman and historian; Henry E. Garrett, former head of the Department of Psychology at Columbia and past president of the American Psychological Association; and Nathaniel Weyl, author of *The Negro in American Civilization*, who argue that Negroes are inferior biologically and in innate ability to whites. They cite various studies which show that the I.Q. of Negro children is below that of white youngsters, the discrepancy becoming greater with advancing years, and point to the high rate of Negro crime and social disorganization. They attribute this to differences in brain structure between African Negroes and whites rather than to environmental shortcomings, deprivation, and discrimination.

While theories on racial differences have been repudiated by most social scientists, the appearance of these ideas and the seriousness with which they have been treated by some scholars and liberal thinkers are significant. Commenting on an article by Professor Garrett comparing Negro and white I.Q.'s in the summer, 1961, issue of *Perspectives in Biology*, Professor D. J. Ingle, head of the Department of Physiology at the University of Chicago, writes, "There are reasons for thinking that racial differences in intelligence may be real." And in a review of Weyl's book, Nathan Glazer, who collaborated with David Riesman in *The Lonely*

Crowd, while critical of Weyl's reliance on African brain-size data and on other points, concludes that he "is clearly free of any prejudice and deserves credit for having raised for public discussion crucial aspects of the Negro question which receive little discussion in academic and liberal circles, and which are usually left in the hands of bigots and incompetents. . . . What are we to make of the high rates of [Negro] crime and delinquency, illegitimacy, family break-up and school dropout?"

That there are intelligence and behavioral differences between Negroes and whites, taken as groups, is of course true. Most social scientists attribute these differences to the special historical experience of the Negro. The important thing is that these differences are not fixed, as the racial-difference theorists believe. We know that in New York's Demonstration Guidance project and Higher Horizons programs, conducted in slum schools, dramatic successes have been achieved in raising I.Q.'s and improving the behavior of Negro and Puerto Rican children. These programs point to the importance of making up for cultural shortcomings and stimulating the motivation of children to learn and behave rather than investigating African brain size.

The question that Glazer poses has been a source of growing concern to liberal thinkers (and to some Negro leaders) since 1954. John Fischer, in a widely discussed article, several months ago called upon Negro leaders to look up from the civil-rights fight they are waging and give attention to remedying the behavioral and cultural shortcomings of the Negro. This emphasis has led to efforts such as Dr. Shepard's in St. Louis, to upgrade Negro slum children before they are thrown into the more difficult world of the middle-class white, and to the dramatic successes achieved by New York's Demonstration Guidance project and Higher Horizons programs. These efforts are a reflection of growth in the liberal's understanding of the full dimensions of the race problem.

There is some indication, however, that the effort, as Fischer puts it, to bring about "changes in the habits, character and ambitions of a lot of Negroes" is causing some liberals to accept postponement of pupil desegregation, especially in slum areas, although they continue to accept the goal of integration. In his important and well-received book *Slums and Suburbs,* James Conant, while sharply attacking discrimination against the Negro, nevertheless sees no need to try to eliminate public-school segregation that results from housing patterns and is not enforced by law. "I think it would be far better for those who are agitating for the deliberate mixing of children," he writes, "to accept *de facto* segregated schools as a consequence of a present housing situation and to work for the improvement of slum schools whether Negro or white." He would have the community turn its attention to pouring money and social services into these schools and into slum areas in order to bring its citizens up to the level of a middle-class society.

Few would deny that this needs to be done, and in massive proportions, but one can measure the distance the pendulum has swung when it is suggested that public-school desegregation be dropped out of the process of dealing with the race problem in Northern cities. It has always been a cardinal tenet of the liberal belief that segregation plays a major role in contributing to the social dynamite stored up in the Negro slum because of the second-class citizenship it automatically confers upon the Negro.

How desegregation should take place and with what safeguards, so as to protect educational excellence and maintain sound educational practice, are, of course, valid questions with which we must wrestle. But the public schools, which shape the thinking and attitudes of children and transmit our goals and values, should not be divorced from the effort to bring about an integrated society.

While the statement that there has been a pullback on the part of liberal whites will shock many of those who sincerely want to help Negroes obtain full citizenship, the phenomenon is nothing new in American history. It occurred following Civil War Reconstruction, when many of the Negro's stanchest allies retreated or withdrew completely from the civil-rights battle. It has been difficult to sustain the effort to bring the Negro into the main stream of American life in the face of the strains this creates—his cultural and economic shortcomings and the open and covert opposition to integration that exists in all parts of the country. For hostility to according the Negro social equality has been almost as powerful a force in American life as has been the effort to secure these rights for him. On a trip through the United States in 1831, de Tocqueville wrote, "The prejudice of race appears to be stronger in the states that have abolished slavery than in those where it still exists; and nowhere is it as intolerant as in those states where servitude has never been known."

One other historical parallel may help to illuminate the process I am describing and to account for, particularly, the appearance of racist theories. In the latter part of the nineteenth and early twentieth century, there emerged a racist philosophy among certain intellectuals that coincided with the influx into the country of large numbers of impoverished immigrants from Southern and Eastern Europe. The counterparts of Putnam, Weyl, and Garrett —who, incidentally, came to dominate intellectual thought on racial issues down to the 1930's—also felt there are innate mental and behavioral differences between these new and older racial groups, the inhabitants of Southern and Eastern Europe possessing characteristics that would make them a burden to the community. It is not hard to see that the appearance of many Negroes in the cities of the North and West, the immigrants of our own day, has produced a similar reaction among many, including sympathetic, whites.

I do not mean to imply that all the moral fervor has gone out of the white liberal's crusade on behalf of the Negro. Many whites have taken part in freedom rides and sit-in's. A pilot experiment has been completed in Philadelphia in which 175 college and graduate students from campuses around the country spent part of their summer vacation tutoring primarily Negro youngsters to overcome school difficulties.

Nevertheless, an issue or series of issues has developed between many liberals and the Negro, the heart of which seems to be this: many liberals are hinting to a restless Negro group that they postpone their most urgent demands because many Negroes are not yet ready to be integrated into a white middle-class society and the social costs, in terms of conflict, may be too high. One writer in the liberal *New Leader* suggests a new Negro strategy of disengagement to repair the damaged communication lines between whites and Negroes. In other words, to the Negro demand for "now," to which the deep South has replied "never," many liberal whites are increasingly responding "later." But the Negro will accept nothing short of first-class citizenship, now. It will call for a great deal of patience and understanding among those who make up the civil-rights coalition if racial progress is not to be seriously jeopardized.

A SELECTED BIBLIOGRAPHY OF THE CIVIL-RIGHTS STRUGGLE

 Alan F. Westin

This bibliography follows the main categories used in the readings. Its focus is on commentary about the civil-rights struggle of Negroes in the 1960's, especially 1961 to 1963. The selections used in this volume are not included in the bibliography unless they were part of a larger work or report; the complete references for the selections are given in the Credits section. For earlier publications and general aspects of civil rights, discrimination, and race, see Alexander D. Brooks, A *Bibliography of Civil Rights and Civil Liberties* (New York: Civil Liberties Educational Foundation, 1962).

GENERAL SURVEYS AND INTERPRETATIONS
OF THE CIVIL-RIGHTS STRUGGLE

ASHMORE, HARRY S., *The Other Side of Jordan* (New York: W. W. Norton, 1960).

BARRON, MILTON L., ed., *American Minorities* (New York: Alfred A. Knopf, 1957).

BASTIDE, ROGER, *et al.*, "The Negro in the United States of America," *International Social Science Bulletin*, IX (1957), No. 4.

——, "A Century of Struggle: Emancipation Proclamation, 1863–1963," *The Progressive*, Special Issue (December 1962).

——, *Civil Rights in the United States* (Washington: Congressional Quarterly Service, 1963).

DUTSCHER, ALAN, "Progress and the American Negro," *Contemporary Issues* (January 1963).

GREENBERG, JACK, *Race Relations and American Law* (New York: Columbia U. Press, 1959).

HARRIS, ROBERT J., *The Quest for Equality* (Baton Rouge, La.: Louisiana State U. Press, 1960).

HARTMAN, PAUL, *Civil Rights and Minorities* (5th rev. ed.; New York: Anti-Defamation League, 1962).

JAVITS, JACOB KOPPELL, *Discrimination U.S.A.* (New York: Harcourt, Brace, & World, 1960).

KONVITZ, MILTON RIDVAS, *A Century of Civil Rights* (New York: Columbia U. Press, 1961).

LUSTIG, N. K., *et al.*, "Five Articles on Race and Race Relations," *Social Forces* (March 1962).

MACK, RAYMOND W., *Race, Class, and Power* (New York: American Book Co., 1963).

MARROW, ALFRED J., *Changing Patterns of Prejudice* (Philadelphia: Chilton Co., 1962).

MENDELSON, WALLACE, *Discrimination* (Englewood Cliffs, N.J.: Prentice-Hall, 1962).

MYERS, GUSTAVUS, *History of Bigotry in the United States* (New York: Capricorn Books, 1960).

MYRDAL, GUNNAR, *An American Dilemma* (2nd ed.; New York: Harper and Row, 1962).

OHIO CIVIL RIGHTS COMMISSION, *Legal Trends in De Facto Segregation* (Columbus, Ohio, December 1962).

O'NEILL, JOSEPH E., ed., *The Breaking of the Walls: Aspects of Segregation* (New York: Macmillan, 1961).

RAAB, EARL, ed., *American Race Relations Today* (Garden City, N.Y.: Doubleday, 1962).

TUMIN, MELVIN M., *et al.*, *Desegregation: Resistance and Readiness* (Princeton, N.J.: Princeton U. Press, 1958).

UNITED STATES COMMISSION ON CIVIL RIGHTS, *The 50 States Report, Submitted to the Commission on Civil Rights by the State Advisory Committees, 1961* (Washington, 1961).

——, *Freedom to the Free; A Century of Emancipation, 1863–1963* (Washington, 1963).

——, *The National Conference and the Reports of the State Advisory Committees to the U.S. Commission on Civil Rights, 1959* (Washington, 1960).

——, *Report, 1959* (Washington, 1959).

——, *Report, 1961*, Five Vols.: I. *Voting*, II. *Education*, III. *Employment*, IV. *Housing*, V. *Justice* (Washington, 1961).

——, *With Liberty and Justice for All* (Washington, 1959).

VANDER ZANDEN, JAMES W., *American Minority Relations* (New York: Ronald Press, 1963).

WESTIN, ALAN F., "John Marshall Harlan and the Constitutional Rights of Negroes: The Transformation of a Southerner," 66 *Yale L. J.* 637 (1957).

WEYL, NATHANIEL, *The Negro in American Civilization* (Washington: Public Affairs Press, 1960).

WOODWARD, COMER VANN, *The Strange Career of Jim Crow* (New York: Oxford U. Press, 1955).

NEGRO PERSPECTIVES

BALDWIN, JAMES, "The Dangerous Road before Martin Luther King," *Harper's Magazine* (February 1961).

——, *The Fire Next Time* (New York: Dial Press, 1963).

——, "The Hard Kind of Courage," *Harper's Magazine* (October 1958).

——, "Letter from the South," *Partisan Review* (Winter 1959).

BATES, DAISY, *The Long Shadow of Little Rock* (New York: David McKay, 1962).

BENNETT, LERONE, JR., "The Mood of the Negro," *Ebony* (July 1963).

BERRY, BREWTON, *Almost White* (New York: Macmillan, 1963).

COTHRAN, TILMAN C., AND PHILLIPS, WILLIAM, JR., "Negro Leadership in a Crisis Situation," *Phylon* (Summer 1961).

DORSEY, EMMETT E., "The American Negro and His Government—1961," *The Crisis* (October 1961).

JEFFERSON, ANNETTA G., "The Negro as the Conscience of America," *The Crisis* (February 1961).

KING, MARTIN LUTHER, JR., "Equality Now," *The Nation* (February 4, 1961).

——, *Letter from Birmingham City Jail* (Philadelphia: American Friends Service Committee, 1963).

——, *Stride toward Freedom: The Montgomery Story* (New York: Harper & Row, 1958).

LINCOLN, CHARLES ERIC, "Anxiety, Fear, and Integration," *Phylon* (Fall 1960).

LOMAX, LOUIS E., *The Negro Revolt* (New York: Harper & Row, 1962).

——, "What Mass Protests Can't Do," *Saturday Review* (July 6, 1963).

THOMPSON, DANIEL C., *The Negro Leadership Class* (Englewood Cliffs, N.J.: Prentice-Hall, 1963).

THORNE, RICHARD, "Integration or Black Nationalism: Which Route Will Negroes Choose?" *Negro Digest* (August 1963).

WALKER, GERALD, "Is the White Southerner Really Inferior?" *Negro Digest* (June 1963).

WORTHY, WILLIAM, "The Angriest Negroes," *Esquire* (February 1961).

NEGRO CIVIL-RIGHTS MOVEMENTS

BABCHUK, NICHOLAS, AND THOMPSON, RALPH B., "The Voluntary Associations of Negroes," *American Sociological Review* (October 1962).

EDWARDS, G. FRANKLIN, "The Changing Status and Self-Image of Negroes in the District of Columbia," *The Journal of Intergroup Relations* (Winter 1962–1963).

FISCHER, JOHN, "What the Negro Needs Most: A First Class Citizens' Council," *Harper's Magazine* (July 1962).

GARFINKEL, HERBERT, *When Negroes March* (Glencoe, Ill.: The Free Press, 1959).

HATCHETT, JOHN F., "The Moslem Influence among American Negroes," *Journal of Human Relations* (Summer 1962).

HUGHES, LANGSTON, *Fight for Freedom: The Story of the NAACP* (New York: Berkley, 1962).

ISAACS, HAROLD R., *The New World of Negro Americans* (New York: John Day, 1963).

KILLIAN, LEWIS M., AND SMITH, C. U., "Negro Protest Leaders in a Southern Community," *Social Forces* (March 1960).

KREN, G. M., "Race and Ideology," *Phylon* (Summer 1962).

KROSNEY, HERBERT, "America's Black Supremacists," *The Nation* (May 6, 1961).

LINCOLN, CHARLES ERIC, *The Black Muslims in America* (Boston: Beacon Press, 1961).

LONG, HERMAN H., "Marginal Man and New Negro Identity," *New South* (April 1962).

MONAHAN, THOMAS P., AND MONAHAN, ELIZABETH H., "Some Characteristics of American Negro Leaders," *American Sociological Review* (October 1956).

MORSELL, JOHN A., "The Meaning of Black Nationalism," *The Crisis* (February 1962).

NIEBUHR, REINHOLD, "The Rising Tide of Color," *The New Leader* (January 23, 1961).

PFAUTZ, HAROLD W., "The Power Structure of the Negro Sub-Community: A Case Study," *Phylon* (Summer 1962).

SAMUELS, GERTRUDE, "Two Ways: Black Muslim and NAACP," *The New York Times Magazine* (May 12, 1963).

STREET, DAVID, AND LEGGETT, JOHN C., "Economic Deprivation and Extremism: A Study of Unemployed Negroes," *The American Journal of Sociology* (July 1961).

TILLMAN, J. A. JR., "The Quest for Identity and Status: Facets of the Desegregation Process in the Upper Midwest," *Phylon* (Winter 1961).

WILSON, JAMES Q., *Negro Politics: The Search for Leadership.* (Glencoe, Ill.: The Free Press, 1960).

SOCIOLOGICAL ANALYSES OF ANTI-NEGRO PREJUDICE AND CIVIL-RIGHTS PROTEST SOURCES

ALLPORT, GORDON W., "Prejudice: Is It Societal or Personal?" *The Journal of Social Issues*, XVIII (1962), No. 2.

BANKS, WALDO R., "Changing Attitudes towards the Negro in the United States: The Primary Causes," *The Journal of Negro Education* (Spring 1961).

BERKOWITZ, LEONARD, AND GREEN, JAMES A., "The Stimulus Qualities of the Scapegoat," *Journal of Abnormal and Social Psychology* (May 1962).

BOGARDUS, EMORY S., "Stages in White–Negro Relations in the United States: An Outline," *Society and Social Research* (October 1960).

GREENFIELD, ROBERT W., "Factors Associated with Attitudes toward Desegregation in a Florida Residential Suburb," *Social Forces* (October 1961).

HAMBLIN, ROBERT L., "The Dynamics of Racial Discrimination," *Social Problems* (Fall 1962).

JAHODA, MARIE, *Race Relations and Mental Health* (New York: Columbia U. Press, 1960).

KATZ, IRWIN, AND BENJAMIN, LAWRENCE, "Effects of White Authoritarianism in Biracial Work Groups," *Journal of Abnormal and Social Psychology* (November 1960).

McKAY, ROBERT B., "Social Science, Segregation, and the Law," *School and Society* (April 8, 1961).

MARNEY, CARLYLE, *Structures of Prejudice* (New York: Abingdon Press, 1961).

RAAB, EARL, AND LIPSET, SEYMOUR, *Prejudice and Society* (New York: Anti-Defamation League, 1959).

RHYNE, EDWIN H., "Racial Prejudice and Personality Scales: An Alternative Approach," *Social Forces* (October 1962).

SINGER, LESTER, "Ethnogenesis and Negro-Americans Today," *Social Research* (Winter 1962).

THOMPSON, DANIEL C., AND LIEF, HAROLD I., "Development of Attitudes in Respect to Discrimination," *American Journal of Orthopsychiatry* (January 1962).

WASHBURN, SHERWOOD L., "The Study of Race," *American Anthropologist* (June 1963).

WHITAM, FREDERICK L., "Subdimensions of Religiosity and Race Prejudice," *Review of Religious Research* (Spring 1962).

EQUALITY OF RIGHTS

Voting and Political Issues

"Abolition of Poll Tax in Federal Elections," *Hearings before Subcommittee No. 5 of the Committee on the Judiciary, March 12–May 14, 1962* (House of Representatives, 87th Congress, 2d Session, 1962).

BACOTE, C. A., "The Negro in Atlanta Politics," *Phylon* (Fourth Quarter 1955).

BERMAN, DANIEL, *A Bill Becomes a Law: The Civil Rights Act of 1960* (New York: Macmillan, 1962).

CARTER, BARBARA, "The Fifteenth Amendment Comes to Mississippi," *The Reporter* (January 17, 1963).

"Congressional Authority to Restrict the Use of Literacy Tests," 50 *Calif. L. Rev.* 265 (1962).

GLANTZ, OSCAR, "The Negro Voter in Northern Industrial Cities," *Western Political Quarterly* (December 1960).

HEYMAN, IRA MICHAEL, "Federal Remedies for Voteless Negroes," 48 *Calif L. Rev.* 190 (1960).

HOLLOWAY, HARRY A., "The Negro and the Vote: The Case of Texas," *Journal of Politics* (August 1961).

"Literacy Tests and Voter Requirements in Federal and State Elections," *Hearings before the Subcommittee on Constitutional Rights of the Committee on the Judiciary, March 27–April 12, 1962* (Senate, 87th Congress, 2d Session, 1962).

McCONAUGHY, JOHN B., AND GAUNTLETT, J. E., "Survey of Urban Negro Voting Behavior in South Carolina," 13 *S. C. L. Q.* 365 (1962).

MATHEWS, DONALD R., AND PROTHRO, JAMES W., "Social and Economic Factors and Negro Voter Registration in the South," *The American Political Science Review* (March 1963).

PRICE, HUGH D., *The Negro and Southern Politics* (New York: New York U. Press, 1957).

STEINBERG, C., "The Southern Negro's Right to Vote," *American Federationist* (July 1962).

TAPER, BERNARD, *Gomillion v. Lightfoot: The Tuskegee Gerrymander Case* (New York: McGraw-Hill, 1962).

"Voting Rights," *Hearings before the Committee on the Judiciary, February 9 and 16, 1960* (House of Representatives, 86th Congress, 2d Session, 1960).

WERDEGAR, KATHRYN MICKLE, "The Constitutionality of Federal Legislation to Abolish Literacy Tests," 30 *Geo. Wash. L. Rev.* 723 (1962).

WILSON, JAMES Q., "How the Northern Negro Uses His Vote," *The Reporter* (March 31, 1960).

WORSNOP, RICHARD L., "Protection of Voting Rights," *Editorial Research Reports* (April 18, 1962).

Employment; Corporate and Union Policies; Professional Groups

BIRNBAUM, OWEN, "Equal Employment Opportunity and Executive Order 10925," 11 *U. of Kan. L. Rev.* 17 (1962)

BLOCH, HERMAN D., "Craft Unions, a Link in the Circle of Negro Discrimination," *Phylon* (January 1958).

——, "Negroes and Organized Labor," *Journal of Human Relations* (Summer 1962).

BROOKS, TOM, "Negro Militants, Jewish Liberals, and the Unions," *Commentary* (September 1961).

——, "The Negro's Place at Labor's Table," *The Reporter* (December 6, 1962).

BUCKLEY, LOUIS F., "Discriminatory Aspects of the Labor Market of the 60's," *Interracial Review* (March 1961).

BULLOCK, PAUL, *Merit Employment* (Los Angeles: Institute of Industrial Relations, U.C.L.A., 1960).

DEWEY, DONALD, "Southern Poverty and the Racial Division of Labor," *New South* (May 1962).

EDWARDS, G. FRANKLIN, *The Negro Professional Class* (Glencoe, Ill.: The Free Press, 1959).

ELLIS, GEORGE H., JR., "The Constitutional Right to Membership in a Labor Union—Fifth and Fourteenth Amendments," 8 *J. of Public Law* 580 (1959).

"Equal Employment Opportunity," *Hearings before the Special Subcommittee on Labor of the Committee on Education and Labor, October 23, 1961– January 24, 1962* (House of Representatives, 87th Congress, 1st and 2[d] Sessions, 1961, 1962).

"Equal Opportunity in Apprenticeship Programs," *Hearings before the Special Subcommittee on Labor of the Committee on Education and Labor, August 21–23, 1961* (House of Representatives, 87th Congress, 1st Session, 1961).

FITZHUGH, H. NAYLOR, ed., *Problems and Opportunities Confronting Negroes in the Field of Business* (Washington: U.S. Department of Commerce, 1962).

FLEISCHMAN, HARRY, "Is Labor Color Blind?" *The Progressive* (November 1959).

FLEISCHMAN, HARRY, AND RORTY, JAMES, *We Open the Gates: Labor's Fight for Equality* (New York: National Labor Service, 1958).

GREER, SCOTT, *Last Man In: Racial Access to Union Power* (Glencoe, Ill.: The Free Press, 1959).

——, "The Place of the Negro in the American Labor Movement," *American Review* (Winter 1961).

GROVES, H. E., "States as 'Fair' Employers," 7 *Howard L. J.* 1 (1961).

HARTMAN, PAUL, *Comparative Analysis of State Fair Employment Practices Laws* (New York: Anti-Defamation League, 1962).

HAYES, MARION, "A Century of Change: Negroes in the U.S. Economy, 1860– 1960," *Monthly Labor Review* (December 1962).

HILL, HERBERT, "Organized Labor and the Negro Wage Earner: Ritual and Reality," *New Politics* (Winter 1962).

——, "Patterns of Employment Discrimination," *The Crisis* (March 1962).

——, "Racism within Organized Labor: A Report of Five Years of the AFL– CIO, 1955–1960," *The Journal of Negro Education* (Spring 1961).

HOPE, JOHN, II., "Central Role of Intergroup Agencies in the Labor Market: Changing Research and Personnel Requirements," *The Journal of Intergroup Relations* (Spring 1961).

——, "Equal Employment Opportunity: Changing Problems, Changing Techniques," *The Journal of Intergroup Relations* (Winter 1962–1963).

MALONEY, W. H., JR., "Racial and Religious Discrimination in Employment and the Role of the NLRB," 21 *Md. L. Rev.* 219 (1961).

MICHIGAN F.E.P.C., *Four Years on the Job in Michigan* (Lansing, Mich., January 1960).

MORROW, JOSEPH J., "Integrating the Negro into the Office," *The Office* (March 1955).

NORGREN, PAUL H., comp., *Racial Discrimination in Employment: Bibliography* (Princeton, N.J.: Princeton U. Press, 1962).

NORGREN, PAUL H., et al., *Employing the Negro in American Industry* (Princeton, N.J.: Princeton U. Press, 1959).

RICH, J. C., "The NAACP versus Labor," *The New Leader* (November 26, 1962).

SAWYER, DAVID A., "Fair Employment in the Nation's Capital: A Study of Progress and Dilemma," *The Journal of Intergroup Relations* (Winter 1962–1963).

SOVERN, M. I., "The National Labor Relations Act and Racial Discrimination," 62 *Columbia L. Rev.* 563 (1962).

STRUTT, JOSEPH W., *Survey of Non-White Employees in State Government* (Harrisburg, Pa.: Human Relations Commission, March 1963).

UNITED STATES BUREAU OF LABOR STATISTICS, *The Economic Situation of Negroes in the United States* (Washington: U.S. Department of Labor, 1962).

WEISS, LEO, "Federal Remedies for Racial Discrimination by Labor Unions," 50 *Georgetown L. J.* 457 (1962)

Education

ANASTASI, ANNE, "Psychological Research and Educational Desegregation," *Thought* (Autumn 1960).

ANDERSON, MARGARET, "After Integration—'Higher Horizons,'" *The New York Times Magazine* (April 21, 1963).

BLOSSOM, VIRGIL T., *It Happened Here* (New York: Harper, 1959).

BUCKLEY, WILLIAM F., JR., "Footnote to *Brown* v. *Board of Education*," *National Review* (March 11, 1962).

CAMPBELL, ERNEST Q., *When a City Closes Its Schools* (Chapel Hill, N.C.: U. of North Carolina Press, 1960).

CARMACK, WILLIAM R., AND FREEDMAN, THEODORE, *Factors Affecting School Desegregation* (New York: Anti-Defamation League, 1962).

CLARK, KENNETH B., "The Desegregation Cases: Criticism of the Social Scientist's Role," 5 *Villanova L. Rev.* 224 (1959–1960).

CRAMER, M. RICHARD, "School Desegregation and New Industry: The Southern Community Leaders' Viewpoint," *Social Forces* (May 1963).

"Federal Courts and Integration of Southern Schools: Troubled Status of the Pupil Placement Acts," 62 *Columbia L. Rev.* 1448 (1962).

GLAZER, NATHAN, "Is 'Integration' Possible in the New York Schools?" *Commentary* (September 1960).

GREGORY, FRANCIS A., *et al.*, "From Desegregation to Integration in Education," *The Journal of Intergroup Relations* (Winter 1962–1963).

"Integration in Public Education Programs," *Hearings before the Subcommittee on Integration in Federally Assisted Public Education of the Committee on Education and Labor, March 1, 1962–June 15, 1962* (House of Representatives, 87th Congress, 2d Session, 1962).

MASLOW, WILL, "*De Facto* Public School Segregation," 6 *Villanova L. Rev.* 353 (1961).

MASLOW, WILL, AND COHEN, RICHARD, *School Segregation, Northern Style* (New York: Public Affairs Committee, 1961).

POINSETT, ALEX, "School Segregation up North," *Ebony* (June 1962).

ROBISON, JOSEPH B., "*De Facto* Segregation in the Northern Public Schools: Its Anatomy and Treatment," *Journal of Jewish Communal Service* (Fall 1962).

SAMUELS, GERTRUDE, "Little Rock Revisited—Tokenism Plus," *The New York Times Magazine* (June 2, 1963).

SEDLER, R. A., "School Segregation in the North and West: Legal Aspects," 7 *St. Louis U. L. J.* 228 (1963).

SHAGALOFF, JUNE, "Public School Desegregation—North and West," *The Crisis* (February, 1963).

SOUTHERN REGIONAL COUNCIL, *Desegregation in Higher Education* (Atlanta, April 1, 1963).

TAYLOR, W. L., "Actions in Equity by the U.S. to Enforce School Desegregation," 29 *Geo. Wash. L. Rev.* 539 (1961).

TRILLIN, CALVIN, "An Education in Georgia," *The New Yorker* (July 13, 1963).

UNITED STATES COMMISSION ON CIVIL RIGHTS, *Civil Rights U.S.A./Public Schools North and West 1962* (Washington, 1962).

——, *Civil Rights U.S.A./Public Schools Southern States 1962* (Washington, 1962).

——, *Equal Protection of the Laws in Public Higher Education, 1960* (Washington, 1961).

——, *Third Annual Conference on Problems of Schools in Transition from the Educators' Viewpoint* (Washington, 1961).

WALKER, GERALD, "Englewood and the Northern Dilemma," *The Nation* (July 6, 1963).

WOLFF, MAX, ed., "Toward Integration of Northern Schools," *Journal of Educational Sociology* (Special Issue, February 1963).

Public Accommodations

BABOW, IRVING, "Discrimination in Places of Public Accommodation: Findings of the San Francisco Civil Rights Inventory," *The Journal of Intergroup Relations* (Autumn 1961).

DIXON, R. G., JR., "Civil Rights in Air Transportation and Government Initiative," 49 *Va. L. Rev.* 205 (1963).

——, "Civil Rights in Transportation and the I.C.C.," 31 *Geo. Wash. L. Rev.* 198 (1962).

GREMLEY, WILLIAM H., "A Survey of Eating Places," *Journal of Intergroup Relations* (Autumn 1960).

McKINNEY, THEOPHILUS E., JR., "United States Transportation Segregation, 1865–1954," *Quarterly Review of Higher Education among Negroes* (July 1954).

MORLAND, KENNETH, *Lunch-Counter Desegregation in Corpus Christi, Galveston, and San Antonio, Texas* (Atlanta: Southern Regional Council, May 1960).

"Racial Discrimination by Restaurant Serving Interstate Travelers," 46 *Va. L. Rev.* 123 (1960).

Van Alstyne, W. W., "Civil Rights: A New Public Accommodations Law for Ohio," 22 *Ohio State L. J.* 683 (1961).

Housing

Abrams, Charles, *Forbidden Neighbors* (New York: Harper, 1955).

——, "The Housing Order and Its Limits," *Commentary* (January 1963).

Branscomb, A. W., "Analysis of Attempts to Prohibit Racial Discrimination in the Sale and Rental of Publicly Assisted Private Housing," 28 *Geo. Wash. L. Rev.* 758 (1960).

Clark, Dennis, *The Ghetto Game* (New York: Sheed and Ward, 1962).

Cohen, Oscar, "The Benign Quota in Housing: The Case For and Against," *The Anti-Defamation League Bulletin* (January 1959).

Colley, N. S., and McGhee, M. L., "California and Washington Fair Housing Cases," 22 *Law in Trans.* 79 (1962).

Frazier, Edward Franklin, "The Urban Ordeal of Negroes," *Negro Digest* (December 1962).

Glazer, Nathan, and McEntire, Davis, eds., *Studies in Housing and Minority Groups* (Berkeley: U. of Calif. Press, 1960).

Grier, Eunice, and Grier, George, *In Search of Housing: A Study of Experiences of Negro Professional and Technical Personnel in New York State* (New York: State Commission Against Discrimination, 1960).

Grodzins, Morton, *The Metropolitan Area as a Racial Problem* (Pittsburgh: U. of Pitt. Press, 1958).

Handlin, Oscar, *The Newcomers: Negroes and Puerto Ricans in a Changing Metropolis* (Cambridge: Harvard U. Press, 1959).

Iskander, Michel G., "The Neighborhood Approach in Intergroup Relations," *The Journal of Intergroup Relations* (Winter 1961–1962).

Jacobs, Arthur P., "Benign Quotas: A Plan for Integrated Private Housing," 70 *Yale L. J.* 126 (1960).

Jennett, Richard P., "Do Negroes Lack Courage to Move to the Suburbs?" *Negro Digest* (June 1962).

Johnson, Reginald A., *Racial Bias and Housing* (New York: National Urban League, 1963).

Kozol, L. H., "Massachusetts Fair Housing Practices Law," 47 *Mass. L. Q.* 295 (1962).

Ladd, W. M., "The Effect of Integration on Property Values," *American Economic Review* (September 1962).

Lieberson, Stanley, "The Impact of Residential Segregation on Ethnic Assimilation," *Social Forces* (October 1961).

McGhee, Milton L., and Ginger, Ann Fagan, "The House I Live In: A Study of Housing for Minorities," 46 *Cornell L. Q.* 194 (1961).

McGraw, B. T., "Potentials for Equal Opportunity in Housing and Community Development," *The Journal of Intergroup Relations* (Spring 1962).

McKee, James B., "Changing Patterns of Race and Housing: A Toledo Study," *Social Forces* (March 1963).

MERCER, NORMAN A., "Discrimination in Rental Housing: A Study of Resistance of Landlords to Non-White Tenants," *Phylon* (Spring 1962).

MILLER, LOREN, "Government's Role in Housing Equality," *The Journal of Intergroup Relations* (Winter 1959–1960).

NESBITT, GEORGE B., AND YANKAUER, MARIAN P., "The Potential for Equalizing Housing Opportunity in the Nation's Capital," *The Journal of Intergroup Relations* (Winter 1962–1963).

NORTHWOOD, L. K., "The Threat and Potential of Urban Renewal: A 'Workable Program' for Better Race Relations," *The Journal of Intergroup Relations* (Spring 1961).

PALMORE, ERDMAN, AND HOWE, JOHN, "Residential Integration and Property Values," *Social Problems* (Summer 1962).

PFARRER, DONALD, "The Tipping Point in Village Creek," *The Reporter* (February 1, 1962).

RICHEY, ELINOR, "Kenwood Foils the Block-Busters," *Harper's Magazine* (August 1963).

——, "Splitsville, U.S.A.: An Ironic Tale of Urban Renewal and Racial Segregation," *The Reporter* (May 23, 1963).

ROBERTS, RICHARD J., "Fair Housing Laws: A Tool for Racial Equality," *Social Order* (January 1962).

ROTHMAN, JACK, "The Ghetto Makers," *The Nation* (October 7, 1961).

SCOTT, BARBARA W., *The Status of Housing of Negroes in Pittsburgh* (Pittsburgh: Pittsburgh Commission on Human Relations, May 1962).

SHAFFER, HELEN B., "Interracial Housing," *Editorial Research Reports* (February 6, 1963).

UNITED STATES COMMISSION ON CIVIL RIGHTS, *Civil Rights U.S.A./Housing in Washington, D.C., 1962* (Washington, 1962).

UNITED STATES HOUSING AND HOME FINANCE AGENCY, *State Statutes and Local Ordinances and Resolutions Prohibiting Discrimination in Housing and Urban Renewal Operations* (Washington, 1962).

Law Enforcement

ALFANGE, DEAN, JR., " 'Under Color of Law': *Classic* and *Screws* Revisited," 47 *Cornell L. Q.* 395 (1962).

GRIMSHAW, ALLEN D., "Urban Racial Violence in the United States: Changing Ecological Considerations," *The American Journal of Sociology* (September 1960).

JENKINS, HERBERT T., "Police, Progress, and Desegregation in Atlanta," *New South* (June 1962).

KEPHART, WILLIAM M., *Racial Factors and Urban Law Enforcement* (Philadelphia: U. of Pa. Press, 1957).

MCMILLAN, GEORGE, "Racial Violence and Law Enforcement," *New South* (November 1960).

"Negro Defendants and Southern Lawyers: Review in Federal Habeas Corpus of Systematic Exclusion of Negroes from Juries," 72 *Yale L. J.* 559 (1963).

SHAPIRO, HARRY H., "Limitations in Prosecuting Civil Rights Violations," 46
    Cornell L. Q. 532 (1961).
SITTON, CLAUDE, "When a Southern Negro Goes to Court," *The New York
    Times Magazine* (January 7, 1962).
VONTRESS, CLEMMONT E., "Patterns of Segregation and Discrimination: Con-
    tributing Factors to Crime among Negroes," *The Journal of Negro Edu-
    cation* (Spring 1962).

TECHNIQUES IN THE CIVIL-RIGHTS STRUGGLE

APPLE, R. W., JR., "The Ivy-League Integrationists," *The Reporter* (Febru-
    ary 14, 1963).
"A Time of Demonstrations," *The Nation* (November 9, 1963).
CARL, EARL LAWRENCE, "Reflections on the Sit-ins," 46 *Cornell L. Q.* 444
    (1961).
CLEGHORN, REESE, "Epilogue in Albany: Were the Mass Marches Worth-
    while?" *The New Republic* (July 29, 1963).
DELAVAN, V., *et al.*, "Why They Sat In," *Social Progress* (February 1961).
ERVIN, RICHARD W., "Freedom of Assembly and Racial Demonstrations," 10
    Clev. Marsh. L. Rev. 88 (1961).
FLEMING, HAROLD C., "The Changing South and the Sit-ins," *The Journal of
    Intergroup Relations* (Winter 1960–1961).
KARST, K. L., AND VAN ALSTYNE, W. W., "Comment: Sit-ins and State Action
    —Mr. Justice Douglas Concurring," 14 *Stanford L. Rev.* 762 (1962).
LEWIS, O. C., "The Sit-in Movement: Progress Report and Prognosis," 9
    Wayne L. Rev. 445 (Spring 1963).
MABEE, CARLETON, "Evolution of Non-Violence: Two Decades of Sit-ins,"
    The Nation (August 12, 1961).
"March on Washington," *The Crisis* (October 1963).
PECK, JAMES, *Cracking the Color Line: Non-Violent Direct Action Methods
    of Eliminating Racial Discrimination* (New York: CORE, 1960).
PHILLIPS, W. M., JR., "Boycott: A Negro Community in Conflict," *Phylon*
    (Spring 1961).
POLLITT, DANIEL H., "Dime Store Demonstrations: Events and Legal Prob-
    lems of the First Sixty Days," 1960 *Duke L. J.* 315 (1960).
PROUDFOOT, MERRILL, Diary of a Sit-in (Chapel Hill, N.C.: U. of North Caro-
    lina Press, 1962).
"Registration in Alabama," *The New Republic* (October 26, 1963).
ROSTOW, EUGENE V., "The Freedom Riders and the Future," *The Reporter*
    (June 22, 1961).
RUDMAN, N. G., "Sitting-in on the Omnibus—the 1961 Segregation Cases,"
    22 *Law in Trans.* 206 (1963).
SCHWELB, FRANK E., "The Sit-in Demonstration: Criminal Trespass or Con-
    stitutional Right?" 36 *N.Y.U. L. Rev.* 779 (1961).
"Sit-ins and State Action," 14 *Stanford L. Rev.* 762 (July 1962).

SOUTHERN REGIONAL COUNCIL, *The Freedom Rides, May 1961* (Atlanta, 1961).

"The Common-Law and Constitutional Status of Anti-Discrimination Boycotts," 66 *Yale L. J.* 397 (1957).

VANDER ZANDEN, JAMES W., "The Non-Violent Resistance Movement against Segregation," *The American Journal of Sociology* (March 1963).

WOFFORD, JOHN G., "The Ballot Box, the Grocery List," *The Reporter* (October 31, 1957).

RELATIONS WITHIN THE CIVIL-RIGHTS CAMP

BALFOUR, BRICKNER, *New Jewish Initiatives in the Field of Race* (New York: Union of American Hebrew Congregations, 1963).

FIEDLER, LESLIE A., "Negro and Jew—Encounter in America," *Midstream* (Summer 1956).

GREENBERG, J., "Race Relations and Group Interests in the Law," 13 *Rutgers L. Rev.* 503 (1959).

GRIMSHAW, ALLEN D., "Negro–White Relations in the Urban North: Two Areas of High Conflict Potential," *The Journal of Intergroup Relations* (Spring 1962).

LA FARGE, JOHN, *The Catholic Viewpoint on Race Relations* (2nd ed.; Garden City, N.Y.: Hanover House, 1960).

LONG, HERMAN H., "Some Major Issues of Intergroup Relations for the Sixties," *The Journal of Intergroup Relations* (Autumn 1960).

MALEV, WILLIAM S., "The Jew of the South in the Conflict on Segregation," *Conservative Judaism* (Fall 1958).

MANTINBAND, CHARLES, "From the Diary of a Mississippi Rabbi," *American Judaism* (Winter 1962–1963).

MARCINIAK, EDWARD, "Interracial Councils in Chicago," *America* (September 20, 1958).

MARTIN, JAMES G., "Intergroup Tolerance-Prejudice," *Journal of Human Relations* (Winter–Spring 1962).

MORSELL, JOHN A., "Legal Opposition to Desegregation: Its Significance for Intergroup Agencies in the Years Ahead," *The Journal of Intergroup Relations* (Winter 1959–1960).

PODHORETZ, NORMAN, "My Negro Problem—and Ours," *Commentary* (February 1963).

RECORD, WILSON, *Minority Groups and Intergroup Relations in the San Francisco Bay Region* (Berkeley: Institute of Governmental Studies, U. of Calif. Press, 1963).

ROBINSON, JAMES H., AND CLARK, KENNETH B., "What Negroes Think about Jews," *The Anti-Defamation League Bulletin* (December 1957).

WILKINS, ROY, "Jewish–Negro Relations: An Evaluation," *American Judaism* (Spring 1963).

Credits

CHAPTER 1, "Color and American Civilization," is reprinted from James Baldwin, *The Fire Next Time* (New York: Dial Press, 1963), pages 108 to 120. Copyright © 1963 by James Baldwin, and used with the permission of the publishers, The Dial Press, Inc.

CHAPTER 2, "Letter from Birmingham Jail," is reprinted from Martin Luther King, Jr., "Letter from Birmingham Jail," *New Leader*, June 24, 1963, pages 3 to 11.

CHAPTER 3, "The Unpredictable Negro," is reprinted from Louis Lomax, "The Unpredictable Negro," *New Leader*, June 5, 1961, pages 3 to 4.

CHAPTER 4, "Outgrowing the Ghetto Mind," is reprinted from "Outgrowing the Ghetto Mind," *Ebony*, August 1963, page 98.

CHAPTER 5, "The Management of the Civil-Rights Struggle," is reprinted from a WGBH Symposium on Civil Rights, WGBH-TV, Boston, Massachusetts, July 23, 1963.

CHAPTER 6, "Freedom Now—but What Then," is reprinted from "Loren Miller, "Freedom Now—but What Then," *The Nation*, June 29, 1963, pages 539 to 542.

CHAPTER 7, "A Marshall Plan for the American Negro," is reprinted from a statement by the Board of Trustees, National Urban League, June 9, 1963.

CHAPTER 8, "Black Muslims and Civil Rights," is reprinted from Malcolm X, "Playboy Interview: Malcolm X," *Playboy*, May 1963, pages 53 to 63. Copyright © 1963 by H.M.H. Publishing Co., Inc.

CHAPTER 9, "Ending Jim Crow Schools in Boston, 1855," is reprinted from Louis Ruchames, "Race and Education in Massachusetts," *The Negro History Bulletin*, December 1949, pages 53 to 71, by permission of the Association for the Study of Negro Life and History, Inc.

CHAPTER 10, "Ride-in's and Sit-in's of the 1870's," is reprinted from Alan F. Westin, "Ride-in," *American Heritage*, August 1962, pages 57 to 64. Copyright © by the American Heritage Publishing Company, Inc.

CHAPTER 11, "The March on Washington Movement during World War II," is reprinted from A. Philip Randolph, "Why Should We March," *Survey Graphic*, November 1942, pages 488 to 489.

CHAPTER 12, "A Chronology of the New Civil-Rights Protest, 1960–1963," is reprinted from Claude Sitton, "Three-and-One-Half-Year-Old Protest Movement Comes of Age in Capital March," *The New York Times*, August 29, 1963, page 20, columns 6 to 7. Copyright © by the New York Times Company, and reprinted by permission.

CHAPTER 13, "Bullets and Ballots in Greenwood, Mississippi," is reprinted from Claude Sitton, "Tension Builds Up after Gun Attack," *The New York Times*, April 6, 1963, page 20, columns 1 to 8. Copyright © by the New York Times Company, and reprinted by permission.

CHAPTER 14, "The Pattern of Southern Disenfranchisement of Negroes," is reprinted from a symposium, *The Electoral Process*, Part II, Vol. 27, No. 3, Summer 1962, pages 455 to 467. Copyright © 1962 by Duke University, and reprinted by permission from *Law and Contemporary Problems*, published by the Duke University School of Law, Durham, North Carolina.

CHAPTER 15, "Jobs for Negroes—the Unfinished Revolution," is reprinted from A. Philip Randolph, "The Unfinished Revolution," *The Progressive*, December 1962, pages 20 to 25.

CHAPTER 16, "The Waste of Negro Talent in a Southern State," is reprinted from Gene Roberts, Jr., "Waste of Manpower: Race and Employment in a Southern State," *South Atlantic Quarterly*, Spring 1962, pages 141 to 150. Copyright © 1962 by Duke University Press.

CHAPTER 17, "Racial Barriers in Union Apprentice Programs," is reprinted from Herbert Hill, "Racial Discrimination in the Nation's Apprenticeship Training Programs," *Phylon*, Fall 1962, pages 215 to 225.

CHAPTER 18, "Corporate Hiring Policies and Negroes," is reprinted from "Jobs for Negroes: How Much Progress in Sight?" *Newsweek*, July 15, 1963, pages 68 to 72.

CHAPTER 19, "School Segregation Statistics in the South—the Crawling Revolution," was written by Alan F. Westin for this book.

CHAPTER 20, "The Techniques of Southern 'Tokenism,'" is reprinted from J. Kenneth Morland, "Token Desegregation and Beyond," a report sponsored by the Southern Regional Council and the Anti-Defamation League of B'nai B'rith, pages vi, 1 to 6, and 13 to 14.

CHAPTER 21, "Englewood, New Jersey—a Case Study in *De Facto* Segregation," is reprinted from Paul Hope, "Englewood is a Symbol in Integration Drive," *Washington Evening Star*, June 3, 1963, as reprinted in the *Congressional Record*, July 10, 1963, pages A-4311–A-4312.

CHAPTER 22, "The Facts of *De Facto*," is reprinted from "The Facts of *De Facto*," *Time*, The Weekly Newsmagazine, August 2, 1963, pages 30 to 31. Copyright © 1963 by Time, Inc.

CHAPTER 23, "The Struggle for Equal Service at Public Facilities," is reprinted from *Freedom to the Free, Sentry of Emancipation: 1863–1963*, pages 175 to 184. Copyright © 1963 by the US Commission on Civil Rights.

CHAPTER 24, "Humiliation Stalks Them," is reprinted from Roy Wilkins, testimony before the Senate Commerce Committee, July 22, 1963, on the public accommodations provisions of the late President Kennedy's proposed 1963 Civil-Rights Bill (S1732), pages 655 to 661 of the Committee Record.

CHAPTER 25, "Cambridge Demonstration Resumed," is reprinted from Charles Rabb, "Cambridge Demonstration Resumed," *Washington Post and Times Herald*, July 9, 1963.

CHAPTER 26, "Breaking the Color Line in Memphis, Tennessee," is reprinted from Russell Sugarmon, Jr., testimony, Hearings before the US Commission on Civil Rights, Memphis, Tennessee, June 25–26, 1962, pages 111 to 114.

CHAPTER 27, "The Realities of Discrimination in San Francisco," is reprinted from Irving Babow, "Restrictive Practices in Public Accommodations in a Northern Community," *Phylon*, Spring 1963, pages 5 to 12.

CHAPTER 28, "The Color Line in Northern Suburbia," is reprinted from James H. Kirk and Elaine D. Johnson, report, Hearings before the US Commission on Civil Rights, San Francisco, California, January 27–28, 1960, pages 713 to 718.

CHAPTER 29, "The Struggle for Open Housing," is reprinted from Frances Levenson and Margaret Fisher, "The Unfinished Revolution," *The Progressive*, December 1962, pages 25 to 29.

CHAPTER 30, "Color Blind or Color Conscious?—Benign Quotas in Housing," is reprinted from Peter Marcuse, "Benign Quotas Re-examined," *Journal of Intergroup Relations*, Spring 1962, pages 101 to 106.

CHAPTER 31, "Keeping Negroes 'in Their Place' in Georgia," is reprinted from the 1961 report of the US Commission on Civil Rights, vol. 5, *Justice*, pages 9 to 12.

CHAPTER 32, "Police Tactics in Mississippi," is reprinted from a report by the Mississippi Advisory Committee, US Commission on Civil Rights, January 1963, *Congressional Record*, February 21, 1963, pages 2653 to 2656.

CHAPTER 33, "Segregated Justice in Birmingham," is reprinted from Charles Morgan, Jr., "Integration in the Yellow Chair," *New South*, February 1963, pages 11 to 16.

CHAPTER 34, "Police Inaction and Anti-Negro Violence," is reprinted from the 1961 report of the US Commission on Civil Rights, vol. 5, *Justice*, pages 29 and 37 to 41.

CHAPTER 35, "Keeping Negroes 'in Their Place' in Detroit," is reprinted from a 1961 statement by the US Commission on Civil Rights, pages 18 to 20.

CHAPTER 36, "Negroes and the Police in Los Angeles," is reprinted from Loren Miller, testimony, Hearings of the US Commission on Civil Rights, Los Angeles, California, January 25–26, 1960, pages 289 to 292.

CHAPTER 37, "Boycott in Philadelphia," is reprinted from Hannah Lees, "The Not-Buying Power of Philadelphia's Negroes," *The Reporter*, May 11,

171 D